# SOCIETAL IMPACT ON AGING

**K. Warner Schaie, Ph.D.,** is the Evan Pugh Professor of Human Development and Psychology and Director of the Gerontology Center at the Pennsylvania State University. He has previously held professorial appointments at the University of Nebraska, West Virginia University, and the University of Southern California. Dr. Schaie received the B.A. from the University of California-Berkeley, and the M.S. and Ph.D. degrees from the University of Washington, all in psychology. He is the author or editor of 22 books and of over 150 journal articles and chapters related to the study of human aging. Dr. Schaie is the recepient of the Distinguished Scientific Contributions Award of the American Psychological Association and of the Robert W. Kleemeier Award for Distinguished Research Contributions from the Gerontological Society of America.

**W. Andrew Achenbaum, Ph.D.,** is Deputy Director of the Institute for Gerontology and Professor in the Department of History at the University of Michigan. His books include *Old Age in the New Land* (Johns Hopkins, 1978), *Shades of Gray* (Little, Brown, 1983), *Social Security: Visions and Revisions* (Cambridge, 1986) and *Voices and Visions of Aging* (Springer Publishing Company, 1993).

# SOCIETAL IMPACT ON AGING

## HISTORICAL PERSPECTIVES

**K. WARNER SCHAIE,** PhD
**W. ANDREW ACHENBAUM,** PhD
**EDITORS**

SPRINGER PUBLISHING COMPANY
NEW YORK

*Cover and interior design by Holly Block*

Springer Publishing Company, Inc.
536 Broadway
New York, NY 10012-3955


93 94 95 96 97 / 5 4 3 2 1

---

**Library of Congress Cataloging-in-Publication Data**

Societal impact on aging : historical perspectives / K. Warner Schaie,
W. Andrew Achenbaum, editors.
    p. cm.
   Includes bibliographical references and index.
   ISBN 0-8261-8200-3
   1. Aged—United States—Social conditions—Congresses.
2. Retirement—United States—History—Congresses. 3. Aged—
Institutional care—United States—History—Congresses.
4. Creative ability in old age—Congresses. I. Schaie, K. Warner
(Klaus Warner), 1928–    II. Achenbaum, W. Andrew.
HQ1064.U5S5983   1993
305.26'0973—dc20                            93-4292
                                                 CIP

---

Printed in the United States of America

# Contents

# Contributors

**W. Andrew Achenbaum, Ph.D.**
University of Michigan
Institute of Gerontology
300 North Ingalls
Ann Arbor, Ml 48109-2007

**Emily S. Andrews, Ph. D.**
Mathmatica Policy Research
600 Marilyn Avenue, S.W.
Suite 550
Washington, DC 20224

**Edward Berkowitz, Ph.D.**
The George Washington University
Department of History
Washington, DC 20052

**Thomas R. Cole, Ph.D.**
The University of Texas Medical Branch
Institute for the Medical Humanities
Room 2.208, Ashbel Smith Building
Galveston, TX 77550

**Michel Dahlin, Ph.D.**
University of Colorado-Colorado Springs
History Department
Colorado Springs, CO 80933-7150

**Nancy Folbre, Ph.D.**
University of Massachusetts, Amherst
Department of Economics
Amherst, MA 01003

**Brian Gratton, Ph.D.**
Arizona State University
Department of History
Tempe, AZ 85287-2501

**Carole Haber, Ph.D**
University of North Carolina-Charlotte
Department of History
Charlotte, NC 28223

**Anna G. Maciel, Ph.D.**
Max Planck Inistitute for Human
   Development and Education
Lentzeallee 94
D-1000 Berlin 33
Germany

**Jon R. Moen, Ph.D.**
The University of Mississippi
Department of Economics & Finance
University, MS 38677

CONTRIBUTORS

**Jill Quadgno, Ph.D.**
Florida State University
Department of Sociology
Tallahassee, FL 32306-2011

**Roger L. Ransom, Ph.D.**
University of California, Riverside
Department of History
Riverside, CA 92521-0204

**Debra Street, Ph.D.**
Florida State University
Department of Sociology
Tallahassee, FL 32306-2011

**Dennis Shea, Ph.D.**
The Pennsylvania State University
Department of Health Policy and
    Administration
114 C Henderson Building
University Park, PA 16802

**Ursula M. Staudinger, Ph.D.**
Max Planck Inistitute for Human
    Development and Education
Lentzeallee 94
D-1000 Berlin 33
Germany

**Richard Sutch, Ph.D.**
University of California
Institute of Business and Economic
    Research
Berkeley, CA 94720

**David G. Troyansky, Ph.D.**
Texas Tech University
Department of History
Box 4529
Lubbock, TX 79409-1013

**David D. Van Tassel, Ph.D**
Case Western Reserve University
Department of History
Cleveland, OH 44108

**Maris A. Vinovskis, Ph.D.**
University of Michigan
Department of History
Ann Arbor, MI 48109-1045

**Samuel H. Williamson, Ph.D.**
Miami University
Department of Economics
Oxford, OH 45056

# Preface

This is the sixth volume in a series on the broad topic of "Societal Impact On Aging." The first five volumes were published by Erlbaum Associates under the series title "Social Structure and Aging." The present volume is the first published under the Springer Publishing Company imprint. It comprises the edited proceedings of a conference held at Pennsylvania State University, October 16–18, 1991.

The conference series originated from the deliberations of a subcommittee of the Committee on Life Course Perspectives of the Social Science Research Council chaired by Matilda White Riley in the early 1980s. That subcommittee was charged with developing an agenda and mechanisms that would serve to encourage communication between scientists who study societal structures that might affect the aging of individuals and those scientists who are concerned with the possible effects of contextual influences on individual aging. The committee proposed a series of conferences that would systematically explore the interface between social structures and behavior, and in particular to identify mechanisms through which society influences adult development. when the senior editor was named director of the Penn State Gerontology Center, he was able to identify the implementation of this conference program as one of the Center's major activities.

The five previous volumes in this series have dealt with the societal impact on aging in psychological processes (Schaie & Schooler, 1989); age structuring in comparative perspective (Kertzer & Schaie, 1989); self-directedness and efficacy over the life span (Rodin, Schooler, & Schaie, 1991); aging, health behaviors, and health outcomes (Schaie, Blazer, & House, 1992); and caregiving in families (Zarit, Pearlin, & Schaie, 1993). The present volume was designed to provide a historical account of how changes in major social institutions and structures have impacted the elderly in the 19th and 20th centuries.

The strategy for each of these volumes has been to commission six review chapters on three major topics by established subject matter specialists who have credibility in aging research. We then invite two formal discussants for each chapter; usually one drawn from the writer's discipline and one from a neighboring discipline. This format seems to provide a suitable antidote against the perpetuation of parochial orthodoxies as well as to make certain that questions are raised with respect to the validity of iconoclastic departures in new directions.

The field of historical gerontology is still emerging and much of the work conducted thus far has been concerned with identifying chronologies rather than providing detailed descriptions and interpretation of historical processes. Hence, as elaborated in the afterword, we identified two major needs to be addressed in this volume. First we wished to provide a set of detailed case studies. And second, we wanted to engage historians in the generation of gerontological theory-building so that this task is not left exclusively to behavioral and social scientists, who generally have little interest in historical perspectives. We believe that this volume will serve to facilitate the creation and dissemination of historical scholarship that will advance gerontology as it speaks in a timely manner to researchers in the social, behavioral, and biomedical sciences.

To focus the conference, the editors chose three topics of broad interest to gerontologists. Historians with a demonstrated track record were then selected and asked to move into closer interaction with those interested in theory-building in a multidisciplinary setting.

The volume begins by a close examination of the *invention of retirement,* an institution of relatively recent vintage. The history of the labor force participation rates of older men has been controversial. Contemporary research suggests that partial retirement, early retirement, "normal" retirement, and returning to employment from retirement, are all fluid concepts. These concepts depend as much on changing conceptions of older workers as the state of the economy and the age of the industry under investigation. Historians suggest that it is quite difficult to date *when* and *how much* decline took place in the male labor force participation in the United States and other industrialized societies in the period from 1800 to 1945. Two case studies were therefore commissioned that examine the historical "facts" and patterns surrounding the development of the concept of retirement from the labor force. One of the case studies comes from the leading proponents of economic history and the second from the perspective of a historian of aging.

The second topic in this volume deals with the issue of *institutionalizing the elderly*. This topic invites revisionist historical efforts in two important directions. Ever since the first generation settlers in Williamsburg, Virginia built an almshouse on the outskirts of town to house those incapable of caring for themselves, institutionalization has been an enduring strategy for dealing with dependency, regardless of a person's age. Many reformers now propose to minimize its use, given the cost of long-term care, both in financial and psychological terms . To put the history of old-age institutionalization into context, we moved in two ways. First we commissioned a case study on the "invisible elders" in lunatic asylums in antebellum Massachusetts. Next we commissioned an analysis in depth that examines the role of the state in developing and supporting institutional care for the elderly.

The third topic ties together two strands of literature that have been neglected by gerontologists, *late-life creativity* and *gerontocracies*. Unlike our first two topics, in which gerontological historians take cues from behavioral and social scientists, it is the historians who now take a proactive stance, perhaps anticipating where gerontologists might soon be found. Again two case studies were commissioned. The first is a close examination of the late life contributions of the eclectic developmental psychologist G. Stanley Hall, focusing on Hall's "prophetic" view of senescence, the forces that shaped these contributions, as well as their impact on gerontological thought. The second case study focuses on the papacy as a classic test case of how gerontocratic institutions emerge and survive. The question is asked whether the papacy actually does represent a gerontocracy. The effects of late entry into a position of authority are examined and the impact of longevity of incumbents on church and society is scrutinized.

We are grateful for the financial support of the conference that led to this volume provided by conference grant AG 09787 from the National Institute on Aging, and by additional support from the College of Health and Human Development of the Pennsylvania State University. We are also grateful to Barbara Impellitteri and Barbara Labinski for handling the conference logistics, and to Anna Shuey for coordinating the manuscript preparation.

K. Warner Schaie
W. Andrew Achenbaum

## REFERENCES

Kertzer, D., & Schaie, K. W. (1989). *Age structuring in comparative perspective*. Hillsdale, NJ: Erlbaum.

Rodin, J., Schooler, C., & Schaie, K. W. (1991). *Self-directedness and efficacy: Causes and effects throughout the life course*. Hillsdale, NJ: Erlbaum.

Schaie, K. W., Blazer D., & House, J. (1992). *Aging, health behaviors, and health outcomes.* Hillsdale, NJ: Erlbaum.

Schaie, K. W., & Schooler, C. (1989). *Social structure and aging: Psychological processes.* Hillsdale, NJ: Erlbaum.

Zarit, S. H., Pearlin, L., & Schaie, K. W. (1993). *Social structure and caregiving: Family and cross-national perspectives.* Hillsdale, NJ: Erlbaum.

# CHAPTER 1

# Inventing Pensions
## The Origins of the Company-Provided Pension in the United States, 1900–1940

Roger L. Ransom
Richard Sutch
Samuel H. Williamson

> When it was the rule for a man to pass his life in his native village, and to
> see his children and grandchildren grow up around him, he might reason-
> ably rely in his declining years upon the willing aid of kindred and neighbors.
> But what was once the rule is now the exception.
>
> **Industrial Commission of Wisconsin, "Report on Old Age Relief,"**
> **March 1915 [p. 4]**

Industrial pensions, which are commonplace in the industrial economy of
the late-twentieth century United States, are a relatively recent economic
institution. Indeed, they were almost unknown at the beginning of the century. The first formal industrial pension in the United States was apparently
established in 1875 by the American Express Company, then a relatively
small freight expediting firm (Hatch 1950, p. 89). The plan provided for
retirement of employees 60 years or older with 20 years of service upon
the recommendation of the general manager. The annual allowance was one-
half the average pay during the last 10 years of employment, with a maxi-

1

mum of $500. As a noncontributory plan, the entire cost of the pension was borne by the employer (Latimer, 1932, p. 21). The second American pension plan was put into place in 1882 by a felt manufacturer, however, the company failed in 1898 (Latimer, 1932, pp. 39–40). The next formal pension plan to be established was in 1884 by the Baltimore & Ohio Railroad, which set up a scheme similar to that adopted by American Express (Licht, 1983, pp. 212–213). The Baltimore & Ohio Plan, although widely discussed, was not emulated until the Pennsylvania Railroad introduced its model plan 16 years later in 1900.[1]

The Pennsylvania Railroad plan required 30 years of service to be eligible for benefits; retirement was compulsory at age 70; and the benefits received by employees upon retirement were defined on the basis of years of service and salary. The employer paid the entire cost. The Pennsylvania plan was widely imitated by other railroads over the next seven years. By the end of 1905, 18 American railroads had adopted formal pension plans covering 35% of railroad employees in the country. In the first years of the new century, few manufacturing companies had followed the lead of the railroads. Notable exceptions were Carnegie Steel in 1901, Standard Oil of New Jersey in 1903 and E.I. du Pont in 1904.[2] Within a few years, however, pension plans offered by American companies began to proliferate rapidly. Seven new plans were established in 1907 and 1908, six in 1909, thirteen in 1910, and beginning in 1911 substantial growth is evident in Figure 1.1.[3] Although only a fraction of industrial workers were employed by a company with a pension plan by 1930, it is clear that the majority of large firms in the country had adopted plans and that pension schemes were widely regarded as part of the package of pay and benefits that a "progressive" employer would offer.[4]

What accounts for the rapid implementation of pensions in the early decades of the twentieth century? Many commentators on pensions have noted that the United States lagged far behind the developed countries of Europe in establishing publicly-supported social insurance for old age. While the reasons for this tardiness are no doubt complex, we would emphasize two features rarely mentioned in previous treatments.

First, it seems likely that the government pensions established for Civil War veterans provided sufficient support for enough older individuals shortly after the turn of the century to damp the magnitude of the old-age dependency problem and perhaps to check the public's willingness to create another pension scheme supported by the general taxpayer. The existence of the military pensions apparently had a perceptible effect on retirement decisions in 1910. Civil War veterans were tempted to leave the labor

Number

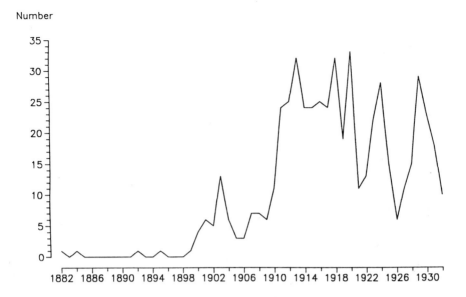

Figure 1.1. The number of industrial pension plans established each year, 1882–1932.

force at an earlier age than non veterans for at least two reasons. First, many of these men had suffered war-related disabilities that would make work difficult and less remunerative. With even a modest stipend as an encouragement, they chose to retire rather than continue work. Second the military pension itself had became a significant supplement so that it encouraged earlier retirement, even in the absence of a physical disability.[5] Evidence from the 1910 Census suggests that the labor force participation of veterans was about 10 percentage points below that for nonveterans of comparable age.[6]

While there seems little doubt that the military pensions and the effects of wartime disabilities had a significant effect on the aggregate labor force participation of older men around 1910, it is important to point out that the Civil War pensions did not represent a retirement plan that younger workers could count on when making their plans for old age. The military pensions were a one-time event. Even Civil War veterans could not have anticipated federal pensions at the time they were discharged and reentered the labor force. It was not until 1907 that the pension eligibility was liberalized so that any veteran could receive a pension simply by virtue of his advanced age. By that time, most would have already reached retirement age after a lifetime of work and asset accumulation. By 1920, when almost all of the Civil War veterans were in their seventies, the impact of that war on the aggregate labor force participation was probably negligible. The legacy of the Civil War pension system on the saving and labor force participation of the generation of Americans growing up in the twentieth century was therefore minimal. By delaying the social impact of the old age dependency problem, Civil War pensions may have delayed the introduction of a more comprehensive government provided social insurance. Indeed, if anything, the fact that the next generation could not count on government help when they reached old age, as had many before them, only heightened the demand for private solutions.

A second and far more profound factor affecting the introduction of pensions in the United States was a remarkably advanced "life-cycle savings" system that drew upon two uniquely American virtues: self-reliance and thriftiness as a means for self-advancement. Propelled by the rapid expansion of the industrial sector and supported by the development of life insurance and improvements in mortgage finance, this system worked sufficiently well that it probably retarded alternative approaches to the problem of old age security. By the end of the nineteenth century industrialization of the American economy had proceeded to the point where over one-third of the labor force were engaged in urban occupations that paid them a wage or salary and put their continued employment at the discretion of an employer.[7] A sufficiently large number of men had been working for wages long enough that the problem of old-age security had become a major preoccupation of workers, their families, and society at large.[8] As the workers perceived it, they could not depend upon the industrial system to provide employment at high wages throughout their entire life. As they aged, workers faced the prospect of declining capacity, downward occupational mobility, reduced wages, and perhaps even forced retirement.[9] If workers were to avoid dependency upon family or charity when they reached old age, they would have to prepare for these contingencies by saving and accumulating assets while still at the peak of their earning capacity.[10] Substantial numbers of workers reported saving more than 12% of their prime-year incomes. Overall, the national saving rate was close to 20% in the last decades of the nineteenth century.[11] These savings were invested in bank accounts, but more often were used to finance home ownership and a special form of life insurance that amounted to a rudimentary individual "pension plan" (Haines and Goodman, 1991 and 1992, Rotella and Alter, 1991, and Ransom and Sutch, 1987).

The insurance policies that gained particular favor were called "Tontine Insurance." With such a policy the premium payments made by the worker to the insurance company were split into two streams. One portion of the premium covered the cost of simple term insurance on the worker's life that afforded protection to his family in the event of his premature death. The remaining portion of the premium was invested by the company in a "savings" fund that grew and accumulated interest over the life of the policy. The policy was referred to as a "Tontine" because of the feature that divided this pool of accumulated assets and distributed them only to the policy holders who had survived to the end of the policy term (typically 20 years). Because the survivors shared in the contributions of those who had died or allowed their policies to lapse, the realized rate of return on the savings exceeded the return on other investments (Ransom & Sutch, 1987, Table 2, p. 387). The substantial cash payment to each policy holder at maturity provided an additional cushion against the contingencies of old age. So popular were these tontine policies that almost two-thirds of all insurance in force in 1905 was of this form and 9 million polices had been sold to a nation with only 18 million households (Ransom & Sutch, 1987, pp. 384–385).

This individualistic old-age support system based on life-cycle saving seemed to function reasonably well, but by no means perfectly, for those who chose to pursue the strategy. It worked so well, in fact, that retirement rates in this era were surprisingly high. In a series of articles, we have argued that the national rate of labor force participation for men 60 and over was a near constant, stable at about 65%, from 1870 to 1940.[12] Figure 1.2 plots our current estimates for the census years of 1870, 1880, 1900, 1910, 1930, and 1937, together with the Bureau of Census figures for 1950 and subsequent years.[13] Throughout this 67-year period, 35% of men 60 and over were retired.

While these life-cycle saving practices of industrial workers at the turn of the century proved satisfactory for many, the weaknesses of the system were becoming increasingly evident. The difficulties were several. First, there was a minority of individuals who, for whatever reason, did not save and consequently became dependent upon younger family members or became wards of public or private charity when old age dictated a decline or cessation of income. A second difficulty with the system of self-reliant provisioning for old age was that some of those who tried to save failed to save enough. When they reached retirement age, their resources appeared inadequate. These were the victims of miscalculation or bad luck. As they aged, these people attempted to postpone their planned retirement until their resources became sufficient to the task. This tactic posed a problem for employers who were confronted with older (and often less productive) workers reluctant to leave their jobs. Employers, not uncommonly, were willing to assist

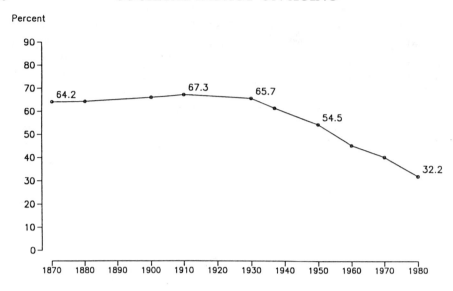

**Figure 1.2. The labor force participation rate of men 60 and over, 1870–1980.**

in such cases by assigning a less demanding, but also less well-paying, task to the older worker, but this was a less-than-satisfactory solution from either perspective. The worker was discouraged not only by his failed expectations but by the demotion and loss of income as well. The employer came to see many of these older workers as liabilities, despite their reduced payroll cost, because the demotion of older workers, unless handled very delicately, produced resentment and lowered morale generally on the shop floor. Furthermore, extended employment at reduced pay simply deferred the problem indefinitely. As the working population gradually aged and an increasing fraction of workers probably reached retirement age with inadequate reserves, employers became concerned that a system based on paternalistic charity and informality could not remain profitable.[14]

## THE ABOLITION OF TONTINE INSURANCE AND THE "CRISIS OF 1906"

Despite these weaknesses of the life-cycle support system and the anxieties of society about "old-age dependency," the system might have continued to muddle along with only slow evolution, had not a sudden and unexpected legal change removed one of the pillars upon which it was based. In 1906, after a public scandal of alleged mismanagement and impropriety in the insurance industry and an extensive investigation which exposed abuses in the handling of tontine insurance funds, the State of New York prohibited any further issue of tontine insurance. Other states quickly followed suit and the individually purchased pension disappeared.[15] Because existing policies were permitted to remain in force, the immediate impact on older workers was not substantial. However, the change left younger workers without access to the life-cycle asset that had previously formed the centerpiece of most individual financial plans.

Our argument is that these developments in the insurance industry—which we refer to as the "Crisis of 1906"—set in motion a reorganization of the old age security system in industrial America. Among the direct consequences of this crisis are four changes that we will discuss in this paper:

• The introduction and spread of group insurance
• The introduction of career-oriented personnel policies by large industrial firms
• The introduction and spread of private pension systems
• The imposition of age bars, seniority preference, and mandatory retirement

## GROUP INSURANCE

The abolition of tontine insurance posed a direct and immediate challenge to the insurance industry, which lost the right to sell its best-selling consumer product. The impact of eliminating the tontine policy on the four largest tontine companies which were the focus of the investigation—New York Life, Mutual of New York, Equitable of New York and Prudential—was dramatic. Figure 1.3 presents data on the new issue of policies by these four companies, and Table 1-1 details the immediate impact of the Crisis of 1906 on the insurance business. The four tontine companies experienced a decline in sales from a level of just under $1 billion in 1904 to barely one-third that level at the end of 1907, and their share of the market dropped from 58% to only 28%. Annual issuance of new policies by these firms did not again reach the 1904 level until the end of World War I. The rest of the insurance industry was not rocked as severely as the tontine leaders, however the industry experienced a painful period of readjustment in the decade that followed the abolition of the tontine.

Once the excitement surrounding the New York insurance investigation had settled down, insurers expected to go back to selling ordinary life insurance. However, they soon discovered that without either the annuity

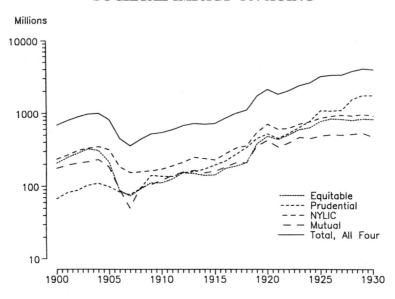

Figure 1.3. New issues of ordinary insurance by the four major tontine companies, 1900–1930.

feature or the extra-high returns produced by the tontine effect, ordinary insurance had restricted appeal—particularly to the working class. It was not long before a financial innovation appeared which would address the problem.[16] In 1911 Equitable Life Assurance Society of New York (the same innovative company that had introduced tontine insurance in 1868) wrote the first group insurance policy covering 125 employees of the Pantasote Leather Company. The following year Equitable established a department specializing in group insurance and issued its first major policy to Montgomery Ward (Stalson, 1942, pp. 641–42; Buley, 1967, pp. 775–79; Graham, 1924, p. 129). Group life insurance is purchased by the employer to provide blanket insurance for employees. All workers are protected, despite their age or medical history. By 1917, guidelines governing the terms of this new form of insurance had emerged. A group policy must cover at least 50 persons and coverage must be offered to employees as a group. Premiums must be paid by the employer, though the employee may contribute towards the cost of insurance. The major advantage of industrial insurance over ordinary insurance lay with the lower premiums possible through the spreading of risks and the lower costs of collection of premiums.

Once introduced, the concept caught on quickly. Within two years of

**Table 1.1 Sales of Ordinary Insurance Four largest Tontine Companies; 1904 and 1907 (Millions of Dollars)**

| Company | Peak (1904) | Trough (1907) | Percent decline |
|---|---|---|---|
| Mutual | 232 | 50 | −78.4 |
| Equitable | 307 | 73 | −76.2 |
| NYLIC | 346 | 155 | −55.2 |
| Prudential | 109 | 76 | −30.3 |
| All Four | 994 | 354 | −61.4 |
| Total New Insurance, All Firms | 1,729 | 1,272 | −26.4 |
| Market Share of Tontine Finns | 57.5% | 27.8% | |

Source: The Spectator Company (1930). *The Insurance Yearbook,* 1874–1911.

Equitable's pioneering action, two of the larger marketers of industrial insurance—Travellers and Aetna—also entered the group insurance business.[17] The Prudential and Metropolitan of New York—both firms that had specialized in tontine insurance before 1906—were marketing group life insurance by 1917. In 1921, which is the first date for which there is reasonably complete data on market shares by firm, *The Spectator Insurance Yearbook* reported data for 35 companies that collectively issued $151 million of group

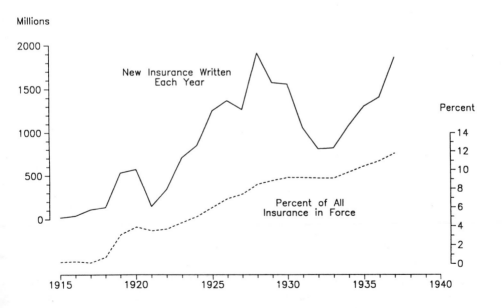

Figure 1.4. The growth of group insurance, 1915–1937.

insurance. From there the growth was steady. Figure 1.4 presents data on the dollar value of group insurance written each year, together with the fraction of all insurance in force that was accounted for by group insurance.[18] By the end of the 1920s, after only 15 years of experience, group insurance accounted for 10% of all new ordinary life insurance policies sold in the United States. In 1930, the value of all outstanding group insurance totaled just under $10 billion, or about 10% of all insurance in force. The number of workers covered by group insurance reached 5.6 million workers in 1930.[19]

Our expectation is that the adoption of this new instrument would be spearheaded by those firms which were most affected by the demise of the tontine. This was in fact the case. Throughout the 1920s the growth in group insurance business was dominated by the five firms that set the early pace—Equitable, Travelers, Aetna, Metropolitan Life, and Prudential. For all these firms the growth of group life insurance was a major factor in their recovery from the depths of the slump produced by the Crisis of 1906. By 1921, when group insurance was still something of a novelty, group policies represented almost 15% of the outstanding insurance written by these firms. By the end of the decade group policies accounted for nearly one-fourth of their outstanding insurance.[20] In addition to these large firms, there was a growing number of smaller firms who specialized in group insurance.[21] This burst of activity prompted William Graham, vice president of the Equitable, to boast in 1924 that:

> *When we consider that Group Insurance is available only where there are fifty or more eligible for the group, and that, therefore, it does not cover the employees of small concerns, agricultural workers, individual workers and others not permanently engaged in mass production, it is seen that Group Insurance has made considerable headway in reaching the available number of groups to be covered."*
> *(Graham, 1924, p. 130)*

Edward Foster, of the National Bank of Commerce in New York, was equally enthusiastic about the impact of the new form of insurance. "Without a doubt," he claimed in 1928, "the inauguration of group life insurance in 1911 marked one of the most progressive steps taken in the life insurance field during the last two decades" (1928, p. 3).

While the invention and intensive marketing of group insurance in the 1910s and 1920s is a testimony to the previous importance of tontine insurance as well as to the viability of the life insurance industry, group insurance did not, at least at first, provide an efficient life-cycle asset for industrial workers seeking to manage their savings. Most early group life policies were simple straight life insurance, providing only renewal term insurance. Late in the 1920s, group annuity policies were created that provided pension-like benefits to workers financed by employers. It is our impression, however, that these instruments were not a significant business feature until after 1932. The significance, for the history of industrial pensions, of the early rise of group insurance is that their acceptance helped to set the precedence of employer involvement in the life-cycle planning of the workers. We shall discuss the employer motivation for accepting this intermediary role in the next section.

## THE INTRODUCTION OF INCENTIVE WAGES AND INTERNAL LABOR MARKETS

The abolition of tontine insurance came at a time when the American Industrial labor market was poised to make a major structural shift away from short-term contracting and toward implicit long-term contracts and career development within the firm. We shall argue that the abolition of the tontine increased the worker's willingness to accept the new system.

The desire by workers for some form of substitute for the tontine insurance policy was not the only change that was occurring at this time to make pensions attractive to companies. As mass production techniques raised the throughput speed and increased the interdependency of the various stages of production in American industry, as the development of transportation and communication networks and the discovery of the effectiveness of advertising and merchandising expanded markets to national and even international scale, and as new technology and the merging of competitors increased both plant and firm size, the American corporation developed more structured and more bureaucratized management systems (Nelson, 1975; Chandler, 1977). This was no less true in labor management than in inventory, marketing, or production management. One manifestation of these changes was the Personnel Departments that began to appear in some of the larger firms after 1908 and spread rapidly during and after World War I (Jacoby, 1985). Established to help bring about organizational changes and, at least in part, as a response to the labor union movement, personnel departments were intended to stabilize labor relations. This required reducing the responsibility and power of the foreman to set wages, improving employee morale, and above all increasing efficiency by reducing shirking, moderating labor turnover, and facilitating the introduction of new production technology.

There were many aspects to the new approach to labor management, but perhaps the centerpiece of the strategy was the introduction of the "internal labor market." At the turn of the century, before the new system had been adopted, the labor contract was of short duration and labor turnover was high. Consequently, workers tended to be paid a wage that closely matched their current productivity. As a worker aged, therefore, his wage at first rose as he gained experience and skill, but then it reached a peak around age 40, after which it began to decline as productivity declined. Cross-section samples of industrial workers collected around the turn of the century all display humped-shaped wage profiles with peak earnings usually coming well before age 45 (Ransom & Sutch, 1991). As one example, we display in Figure *1.5 a* typical cross-section age-earning profile. This one is based on a sample of more than 6000 industrial workers, collected by the U.S. Department of Labor in 1890.[22] There are two distinct reasons for the hump shape evident in the diagram. First, the age-earning profile for workers in the same occupation would show a decline for older workers, presumably because productivity on the job declined as the worker aged. Second, in the late-nineteenth century, industrial workers frequently changed jobs late in life, moving to less demanding but also less remunerative employment; a machine operator might take a job (or be forced to take a job) as a floor sweeper or doorman.

The internal labor market replaced short-term contracts with implicit long-

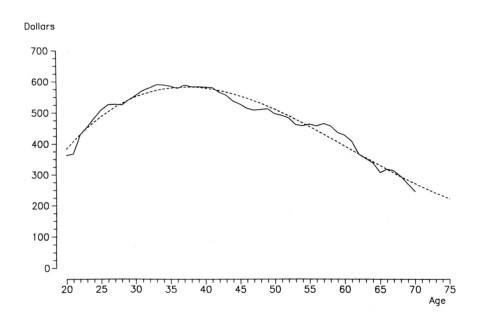

Figure 1.5. Age-earnings profile of male wage earners, 1890.

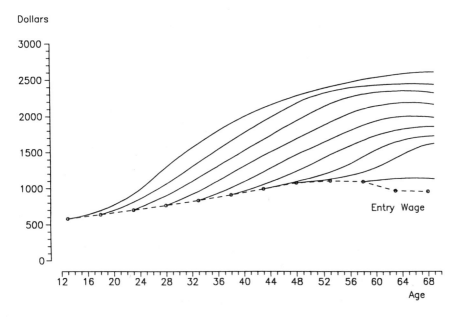

Figure 1.6. Age-earnings profile of male railroad workers by cohorts defined by age of entry, 1933.

term ones. A structured hierarchy of jobs arranged with standard wage rates attached to each job replaced a system where each man was paid a wage that reflected his personal productivity. Firms attempted to concentrate their hiring at the entry level jobs and then to promote from within, moving men up the job ladder to higher and higher pay steps. Workers with seniority were protected from discharge during periods of business decline and younger workers, who were discharged during such periods, were often promised their old jobs back when times improved. With this system the worker could expect his wage to increase steadily as he aged.

In Figure 1.6 we present earnings profiles for railroad workers based on cross sectional data. The data was collected from 82,611 full-time employees that were on the payroll of 13 railroads in December of 1933.[23] The dashed line across the bottom of the diagram represents the average entry wage at each age. Each rising curve on the diagram represents the cross-section profile for a different cohort of workers. The cohorts are defined by the age they began working for the railroad. What is clearly evident is that workers' incomes rose as they aged and that this gradient was more the return to seniority than a portable return to physical age.

The ever higher job classifications into which he was promoted gave the successful worker higher pay and, initially, his maturing experience and growing skills actually produced a higher productivity. But beyond some point the higher job classifications rewarded the worker with a rate of pay higher than his short-term productivity would seem to warrant. This "overpayment" of older workers was made possible because of a corresponding "underpayment" of younger workers. The relationship between the wage profile and productivity is illustrated by a diagram in Figure 1.7.

Because of the underpayment of workers with low seniority, it might seem that the new system would have met with resistance by younger workers. We suggest, however, two reasons why protest was minimal and workers for the most part were willing to work at a firm with a rising wage profile like that we have diagramed.

First, for any worker who intended to make a career at a single firm, the underpayment of wages when he was young would be repaid (with interest) when he was older. The "forced saving" implicit in the new pay schedule mimicked the saving patterns that a worker attempting to follow a life-cycle savings scheme would voluntarily wish to adopt. Thus deferred wages provided a sort of protection against a lack of discipline. More importantly,

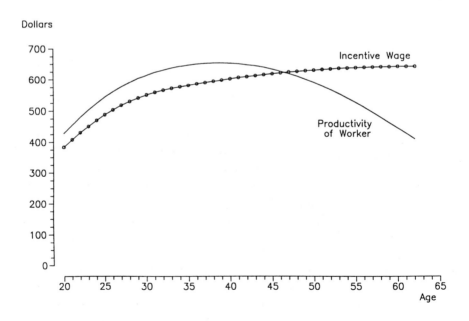

**Figure 1.7. A hypothetical wage structure for a firm with an internal labor market.**

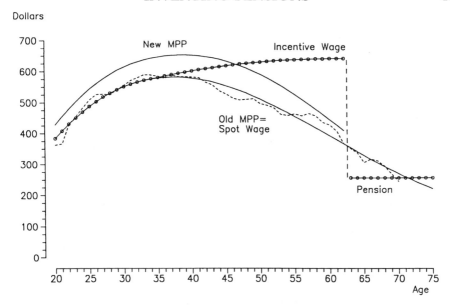

Figure 1.8. The effect of introducing pensions to a firm with an internal labor market.

we think, is that the implicit rate of return on these forced savings could be higher than the market alternative. The firm could "invest" them at its own internal rate of return which we expect would be higher than any bank rate the worker was likely to find. Moreover, because the forced savings of young workers who would not remain with the firm long enough to collect the "overpayments" were forfeit, the return to the survivors would be augmented by a tontine effect.

The second reason that the new system could be introduced without worker objection is that it was designed to increase productivity. It was believed that the internal labor market would reduce turnover and improve morale and thus increase overall productivity. The productivity for each worker would be raised above that which had prevailed under the old system. In addition, the practice of paying the older workers more than their productivity may have produced an "efficiency wage" effect, that reduced shirking and produced a willingness to repay the employer with extra effort.[24] Figure 1.8 illustrates the point. The old productivity profile is shifted up to a new position. The rising wage schedule is then introduced in such a way that no worker has his wage reduced and yet forced saving for young workers is instituted. Despite the fact that young workers would not receive a share in the productivity gain resulting from the new plan, they could not find a more remunerative job working for a competitor who still used the old labor contract system. So the firm can capture those gains and use them to pay older workers more than their productivity.

## THE GROWTH OF PENSIONS AFTER THE CRISIS OF 1906

One implication of the shift from a humped-shaped age-earnings profile to a rising profile was an increase in the relative wage paid older workers. Internal labor markets could, therefore, be expected to have induced a longer attachment to the labor force and have been part of the reason for a decline in retirement during the period between 1908 and 1930.[25] As a consequence, firms adopting the new employment policies would have to find a way to control the timing of retirement. It was quite often the case that rising wage profiles were accompanied by a prescribed retirement age. Compulsory retirement appealed to employers for several reasons. Among those mentioned in the literature on retirement from this period are (1) that rules governing retirement would make it easier to remove older workers who had become unproductive or dangerous on the job, (2) that expensive older workers could be replaced at a lower cost by younger ones, and (3) that the removal of older workers from high positions on the promotion ladder would enable the firm to offer promotion to younger workers on a predictable schedule. Worker acceptance of mandatory retirement was facilitated by the introduction of company-provided pensions for the retired workers.

Most of the early plans were established as non-contributory; all of the costs were borne by the employer. There seemed to be two reasons for the preference for non-contributory plans. First, employers wished to make clear that the employee had no contractual right to the pension funds and that with dismissal or voluntary departure the worker would forfeit all claim to retirement benefits.[26] The second reason to favor non-contributory plans was that initially most states prohibited any compulsory deductions from wages by statute. Thus, contributory plans would have to be voluntary, and that would have lessened their appeal from the employer's standpoint. In the mid-1920s states began to repeal or amend the prohibition on wage deductions and there was an increasing use of contributory plans with mandatory participation.[27]

The cost of employer provided pensions was, of course, paid by workers in reduced wages—they were simply another form of forced saving. Employees would find the forced saving implicit in a company pension plan attractive in the wake of the abolition of tontine insurance. Given the poorly developed capital markets of the time, it was difficult for an individual worker to find a practical, efficient way to pursue a life-cycle saving scheme on his own and private pensions provided the tontine feature, which promised higher-than-market rates of return. Also, pension plans appeared to offer more certainty regarding the prospective date of retirement. Thus they removed much of the risk that planned retirement would have to be postponed due to miscalculation or bad luck.

It would be a mistake, however, to conclude that pensions were forced upon unwilling or indifferent employers. As we have already hinted, pensions made it easier to adopt the internal labor market pay scale and to impose rules that regulated the age of retirement. Company managers also pushed the idea that pensions would improve efficiency. They would:

- help reduce labor turnover and thus reduce training costs and permit the firm to capture more of the productivity associated with experience and tenure
- improve morale of the work force and thus reduce shirking and the likelihood of work stoppages associated with worker grievances
- create a pay and benefits package that exceeded the going wage and thus elicit an extra effort from the worker in exchange.[28]

A fourth source of apparent efficiency gains was sometimes mentioned, but it seems to us to be based on a confusion. When an employer adopted a pension system, the change required a pay schedule that under paid workers relative to their productivity while obviously over paying the pensioners. While no worker would be exploited over the course of his or her lifetime by such a structured pay schedule, there nevertheless would be a transitory cash-flow gain to the firm associated with the switch from the old to the new system. This windfall arose because the underpayment of the workers exceeded the sum required to pay the pensioners. This was so as a consequence both of the demography of the workplace and of the initial income-age profiles adopted in early internal labor market plans. Since the young workers would eventually age, the cash flow enhancement would eventually disappear.[29]

The real efficiency gains associated with pensions could be shared between the workers and the company and thus pensions could boost profits while preserving labor peace. Pensions are, of course, a system of deferred wages (or forced saving) and require that the worker be underpaid when he is young in order to permit the payment of a pension when he is retired. This is true independently of the forced saving required by internal labor markets. Had there been no efficiency gain, young workers might have resisted the introduction of pensions, since their wages would have to have been lowered. The history of early pensions suggests, however, that firms were sufficiently confident of efficiency improvements that they held the nominal wages of young workers constant while increasing the wages with seniority and, of course, providing pensions for those who retired. (See Figure 1.8.) Whether or not the introduction of pensions and the spread of internal labor markets were the cause, we do know that turnover in manufacturing declined substantially between 1910 and 1930 and that the decline was almost entirely produced by a decline in the voluntary quit rate (Owen 1991). Figure 1.9 plots the best-known time series on quits for the period from 1910 (when the data begin) to 1940 as a solid line graph (Ross, 1958, pp. 903–920). Even if we recognize in hindsight that some of the decline in the quit rate evident in the chart, particularly after 1929, can be attributed to deteriorating labor market opportunities for workers seeking new jobs, the decline in the 1920s is real.[30] In the chart a dashed line indicates the quit rate after we have adjusted it to remove the effects of changes in the unemployment rate.[31] A substantial decline in quits is still evident.

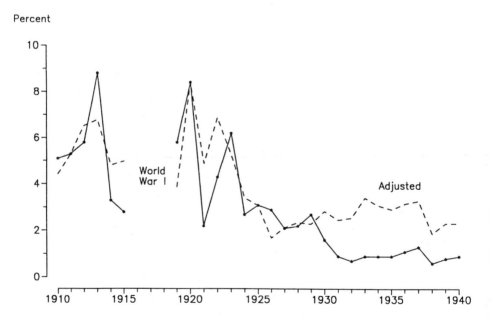

Figure 1.9. Quit rates in manufacturing before and after adjustment for the impact of unemployment, 1910–1940.

Beyond the efficiency gains, managers frequently emphasized another advantage of pensions. With a retirement system in place, they could set a definite date for retirement for each employee. Whether this was couched in the form of a mandatory retirement date or was achieved by structuring the rules in such as way as to make it highly advantageous for workers to retire at a certain target age, existence of such targets meant that an employer could discharge an older worker without the necessity of finding physical or mental infirmity or otherwise demeaning the worker's self-respect. In any internal labor market system in which wages are deferred and older workers overpaid, it is important that time of retirement be established by rules rather than worker preference (Lazear, 1979). Often personnel managers who enumerated the advantages of pensions stated this point in a way that may confuse modern observers. They tended to emphasize the fact that older workers were paid more than they were worth, and that pensions provided a mechanism for discharging such "burdens" from the payroll. Two points should be made. First, it is no doubt correct that under the pay system that existed before pensions, employers frequently felt compelled to carry older workers on the payroll at rates of pay that exceeded their productivity. As we stated earlier, this was an act of charity. A formal pension system removed the need for such charity and thus benefitted the firm.[32] Second, the evidence in the reports of managers claiming that older workers were overpaid suggests to us that adoption of internal labor markets was widespread by the mid-1920s. Indeed, some contemporary observers said as much (Dooley & Washburn, 1929, p. 5).

## THE AGING OF THE POPULATION

Underlying these dynamic changes in the labor markets and helping to both propel and shape them, were largely invisible but nevertheless powerful demographic forces that increased the fraction of the population considered "old." The aging of the population was the consequence of the declining birth rate, a phenomenon that had marked American development from 1800 and would continue until 1933.[33] However, before 1911, new immigrants continually added young workers to the population and tended to stabilize the age distribution despite the declining native birth rate. After 1911, a slow-down of immigration and, after 1921, the sharp restriction on immigration, ended this offsetting effect. The working population began to noticeably age. Table 1-2 presents the data while Figure 1.10 plots the proportion of the male working-age population that was 60 and over.[34]

The gradual aging of the working population in the 1920s probably had its own influence on the move to adopt pensions and to impose manda-

**Table 1.2 Proportions of the Total and Male Working-Age Populations That Were "Old" by Several Definitions, 1870–1940**

| Year | Proportion of male working-age population that is | | | Proportion of male working-age population that is | | |
|---|---|---|---|---|---|---|
| | 55 and Over | 60 and Over | 65 and Over | 55 and Over | 60 and Over | 65 and Over |
| 1870 | 14.5 | 10.0 | 6.0 | 14.8 | 10.0 | 5.9 |
| 1880 | 15.7 | 10.9 | 6.6 | 15.9 | 10.9 | 6.5 |
| 1890 | 16.5 | 11.5 | 7.2 | 16.4 | 11.4 | 7.1 |
| 1900 | 16.8 | 11.6 | 7.3 | 16.6 | 11.4 | 7.2 |
| 1910 | 16.9 | 11.7 | 7.4 | 16.8 | 11.4 | 7.2 |
| 1920 | 18.3 | 12.7 | 7.9 | 18.5 | 12.6 | 7.7 |
| 1930 | 20.0 | 13.8 | 8.8 | 20.2 | 13.8 | 8.7 |
| 1940 | 22.6 | 15.9 | 10.4 | 22.7 | 15.8 | 10.2 |

Note: "Working-Age" is defined as 20 years old and over.
Source U.S. Bureau of the Census. *Historical Statistics of the United States, Colonial Times to 1970*, U.S. Government Printing Office, 1975, Volume 1, Series A119–134, p. 15.

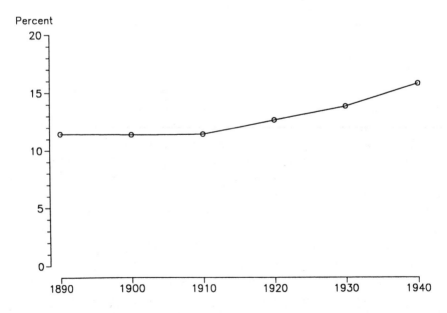

Figure 1.10. The proportion of the male working-age population that was 60-years old and over, 1890–1940.

tory retirement rules. For employers who had not yet installed pension plans, the increasing number of older workers who were ill-prepared and thus reluctant to retire would have placed an increasing strain on the charity of the employer. For them, pensions probably seemed an increasingly attractive way to deal with the growing problem. On the other hand, the aging of the work force posed new dilemmas for employers who had established job hierarchies and pensions. They began to experience an increasing scarcity of young entry-level workers, which drove up hiring costs. The growing number of "overpaid" workers above 60 also created problems. The change in the age mix reduced the cash flow advantages of the pension system and some employers complained of an inadequate number of tasks suited to the capacities of the older worker. Moreover, the rising average age of the work force would increase the cost of group insurance, because the premium was based on the age structure of the group insured.

## AGE BARS IN INDUSTRY DURING THE INTERWAR PERIOD

The solution to these difficulties, from the firm's point of view, was to attempt to reduce the average age of its own workers through specific age management policies. Chief among these were the introduction of age bars, which prohibited or restricted the hiring of a new worker who was older than some arbitrary limit. Typically, 40 or 45 was set as the maximum age for newly hired workers. Of course, while each firm might try to manage its own age distribution in this way, the age distribution of the work force as a whole would be unaffected. The result of this type of "beggar-thy-neighbor" solution was to increase the job search problem for any unemployed older worker, to sharply reduce quits by older workers, and to increase public resentment over age discrimination that seemed to relegate men over 40 to an "industrial scrapheap."

In the late 1920s a concern was expressed in the popular press and various other forums of public opinion that older workers were being barred from industrial employment. On the eve of the Great Depression, October 15, 1929, the National Association of Manufactures (NAM) met in New York City to discuss the problem of "The Older Worker in Industry." Attesting to the interest in the topic, the session attracted the largest attendance of the sessions. Roderic Olzendam, Director of Industrial Relations at the Metropolitan Life Insurance Company, gave the keynote address. He asserted that:

> During 1927, 1928, and 1929, there were approximately one hundred magazine articles devoted exclusively to this newcomer on our industrial stage. Fifty writers have prepared extensive articles on him for the press. Sixty authors have devoted a

*chapter or more of their books to him. Speeches have filled the air . . . A dozen investigations have been made . . . There seems to be rather a formidable problem traveling along under the title "The Older Man in Industry" (Olzendam, 1929, p. 4; also see National Association of Manufactures, 1929, p. 111).*

According to NAM's Employment Relations Committee, the "formidable problem" was that employers were establishing arbitrary maximum hiring-age limits.

*The result of an investigation of several hundred manufacturing firms shows that . . . twenty-eight percent of the manufacturing plants do have a maximum hiring age limit, refusing to hire new employees beyond certain fixed ages, but many of them make exceptions in the case of former employees . . . The most frequent limits are 45 for the unskilled and semi-skilled and 50 for the skilled.[35]*

The American Management Association had conducted a similar survey the year before. Only 9 of 64 firms surveyed reported explicit age bars, but a "large majority" had "a tacit understanding that the employment office should not take on older men and women" (Dooley and Washburn, 1929, p. 4).

Other surveys confirmed these charges. Equitable Life canvassed its group insurance patrons in 1929 and obtained 516 responses from 1,600 inquiries. Sixteen percent reported "definite rigid maximum age hiring limits." Twenty-four percent had no fixed age limit, but reported that past experience had taught them that "the vast majority of their employees" should range in age from 25 to 65. Sixty percent reported no age limits (Graham, 1929, p. 16). A 1930 investigation in Maryland received 858 replies covering 173,724 employees. Only 86 firms, about 10%, reported a policy mandating a maximum hiring age. However, these firms employed 34.7% of the workers covered. Another 32 firms reported a preference for younger workers, although they had no written rule (Murphy, 1930, pp. 7–9.) A study undertaken in 1932 by the U.S. Department of Labor covered 224 establishments in a range of manufacturing industries. Seventy-one firms (31.7%) reported age bars. The percentage was as low as 9% for the industry labeled "automobiles and parts" and as high as 78% for "petroleum refining" (U.S. Bureau of Labor Statistics, 1932, Table 5, p. 1010).

Large firms were more likely to have formal rules prohibiting the employment of older workers than small firms. A survey returned by 2,808 establishments of all sizes in California (out of 5,269 questionnaires mailed) discovered age limitations for hiring new workers at plants employing 39% of the reported employment (California Department of Industrial Relations,

Table 1.3 Age Bars in California, March 1930

| | Number of firms surveyed | Total employees March 1930 | Percentage of firms with age limits | Percentage of employees covered |
|---|---|---|---|---|
| TOTAL | 2,808 | 534,608 | 10.9 | 39.1 |
| Manufacturing | 2,098 | 289,510 | 8.9 | 17.7 |
| Rubber Products | 15 | 5,437 | 20.0 | 47.7 |
| Chemicals | 104 | 41,133 | 15.4 | 38.2 |
| Lumber | 276 | 33,603 | 6.9 | 17.9 |
| Machinery | 204 | 18,182 | 7.8 | 15.1 |
| Tobacco Products | 6 | 1,523 | 16.7 | 14.8 |
| Food | 394 | 69,202 | 10.4 | 14.1 |
| Stone, Clay, Glass | 116 | 13,066 | 7.8 | 13.6 |
| Transport Equipment | 75 | 11,772 | 12.0 | 11.8 |
| Textiles | 215 | 15,508 | 7.0 | 11.0 |
| Musical Instruments | 16 | 1,408 | 6.3 | 9.6 |
| Iron, Steel | 103 | 15,361 | 11.7 | 6.6 |
| Metal Products | 66 | 3,461 | 4.5 | 2.7 |
| Leather | 24 | 1,553 | 0.0 | 0.0 |
| Miscellaneous | 284 | 37,215 | 11.3 | 14.5 |
| Non Manufacturing | 710 | 245,098 | 16.8 | 64.4 |
| Public Utilities | 71 | 136,548 | 39.4 | 94.4 |
| Transportation | 37 | 14,263 | 29.7 | 73.4 |
| Agriculture | 6 | 1,214 | 16.7 | 41.2 |
| Service | 23 | 7,861 | 26.1 | 38.1 |
| Trade | 58 | 9,400 | 24.1 | 25.6 |
| Mercantile | 337 | 58,810 | 12.8 | 18.5 |
| Construction | 156 | 14,693 | 9.0 | 10.3 |
| Mining | 3 | 906 | 0.0 | 0.0 |
| Miscellaneous | 19 | 1,403 | 10.5 | 7.8 |

Source: California Department of Industrial Relations, "Middle-Aged and Older Workers in California," *Special Bulletin,* Number 2 (August, 1930), Tables 1 and 2, pp. 19–24.

1930). More complete results are presented in Table 1-3. Its companion, Table 1-4, presents the California data arranged by firm size. In San Francisco, a privately supported placement bureau, the Employment Aid of San Francisco, was established in 1929 to provide a placement service for unemployed older men and women. "So many of the larger industries are refusing to employ workers over 40 or 50 that commercial agencies naturally give them only a minimum of attention." None of the placements by the Employment Aid made in the first eight months of operation were with large employers. "Some of the large employers at first proposed to help, but found it impracticable to do so" (U.S. Bureau of Labor Statistics 1930a, pp. 583–586).

Firms that had established pensions were probably more likely than firms that had not to impose age bars. In the question and answer period that

Table 1.4 Percentage of Establishments with Age Bars
Effect of Firm Size, California, March 1930

| Firm size | All firms | Manufacturing firms | Nonmanufacturing firms |
|---|---|---|---|
| Total | 10.9 | 8.9 | 16.8 |
| 500 or more | 29.8 | 17.3 | 49.3 |
| 450–499 | 29.4 | 30.8 | 25.0 |
| 400–499 | 23.5 | 15.4 | 50.0 |
| 350–399 | 18.8 | 10.0 | 33.3 |
| 300–349 | 10.9 | 11.1 | 10.5 |
| 250–299 | 12.1 | 13.5 | 7.1 |
| 200–249 | 13.2 | 16.0 | 7.7 |
| 150–199 | 12.3 | 7.2 | 25.0 |
| 100–149 | 13.6 | 13.0 | 15.2 |
| 50–99 | 8.9 | 7.2 | 15.1 |
| 25–49 | 7.9 | 7.9 | 7.9 |
| 6–24 | 7.2 | 6.3 | 10.1 |

Source: California Department of Industrial Relations, "Middle-Aged and Older Workers in California," *Special Bulletin*, Number 2 (August, 1930), Table 7, p. 33.

followed the presentation of the American Manufactures Association report, its author was asked: "Is it not true that the companies which have no age limits are, in most cases, companies which have no pension plan?" The report's co-author responded: "I neglected to ask specifically whether companies had pension plans or not, but I feel pretty sure from the letters received that this is the case" (Dooley & Washburn, 1929, p. 39). Murray Latimer's 1929 survey of industrial pension plans found that 41.9% of companies with pensions, employing 53.6% of the more than 3 million workers covered, imposed an explicit hiring age limit. Another 19%, with 10.5% of the workers, had no restriction but excluded new workers over a stated age from participating in the company pension plan.[36] An earlier study of pension plans taken in 1925 by the National Industrial Conference Board reported that "nearly one-half of all the plans studied expressly fix an age limit for persons entering into the employ of a concern for the first time" (National Industrial Conferenee Board 1925, p. 72). Because these proportions from surveys of firms with pensions (around 50%) are higher than those reported from surveys that canvassed firms with and without pension plans (ranging from 10 to 32%), it suggests an association between pensions and age bars.

Most of the contemporary observers treated the problem of age discrimination, particularly the existence of a "definite rigid maximum age" as a new problem which they associated with the introduction of pensions, group insurance, and internal labor markets. For example, one respondent to the 1928 American Management Association survey wrote that a "tacit understanding in the Employment Office [not to hire older workers] has existed for the last 5 years or more" (Dooley & Washburn, 1929, p. 4). Solomon Barkin believed that age bars first became a problem in 1926 (Barkin, 1933, p. 45). However, William Graebner in his *History of Retirement* suggests that these contemporaries were wrong about the recent appearance of age discrimination. He claimed it had been a problem for more than two decades. Speaking of the investigations undertaken in the early 1930s, he suggested:

> *These inquiries, lacking in historical insight, pointed to the technological environment of the 1920s and to a variety of short-term factors, particularly pensions, group insurance, and workmen s compensation, which as explanations of age discrimination conveniently ignored the historical needs of a capitalist economy for efficiency and control (Graebner 1980, p. 51).*

Graebner, however, presents no convincing evidence that formal age bars were in place in any widespread sense before 1925 and in any case, pensions, group insurance, and workmen's compensation do not seem to us to be "short-term factors."

Murray Latimer was concerned to defend pension plans against the charge that they were the cause of age discrimination. He attempted to bolster his case by assembling evidence on the timing of the introduction of age bars. However, what he found was far from compelling. He found no evidence of age discrimination in the United States before 1900 (Latimer, 1932, p. 793). He quoted from pre-World War I Bureau of Labor Statistics publications on steam railroads and street railways about age restrictions in those industries.[37] However, railroads were among the first corporations to create pensions so their earlier start with formal age bars would be expected.[38] Another study, undertaken in 1907 and 1908 by the U.S. Commissioner of Labor, of firms with relief or benefit funds found 41 non-rail companies out of 432 surveyed (9.5%) had a maximum hiring age (U.S. Commissioner of Labor, 1909, p. 395; also see Latimer, 1932, p. 795). Yet, only firms with benefit plans were surveyed in this report, so all were providing insurance and a disproportionate fraction also had "superannuation benefits." Thus the existence of maximum hiring ages in these 41 firms hardly establishes that age bars predated company provided life insurance, disability insurance, or pension plans. Indeed, the opposite conclusion might as easily be reached: 232 firms of a total of 461 firms with benefit associations (just over one-half) had established a maximum age for admission to membership in the benefit organization.

Whatever the truth about the trend in age bar practices before 1926, the problem became of much greater concern after the start of the Depression. As firm failure rates and unemployment rose, older workers lost jobs along with younger workers. It was widely believed that age discrimination and age bars made the prospects for reemployment much more difficult for the older worker.[39] In 1930 the Rochester Office of the Division of Employment of the New York Department of Labor, struggling with rising unemployment in the wake of the stock market crash, reported:

> *One of our greatest problems is the man or woman past 50 years of age out of a job who is mentally and physically fit, . . . Even with an intensive and persistent appeal for these people we are able to place only a small percentage of them.*

Often only temporary employment could be found and then it was often "out of consideration for the employment bureau appeal rather than the merits of the applicant" (U.S. Bureau of Labor Statistics, 1930c, p. 545).

The Depression, however, did not seem to increase the use of age bars.[40] A 1937 survey, by the National Industrial Conference Board, of 451 establishments employing 370 thousand wage workers found that 24.4% of the companies had maximum hiring ages.[41] In 1938 the National Association of Manufacturers collected 2,485 responses from its members. Only 7.5% reported explicit age bars, 89.1% reported no such limits, and 3.4% did not answer the question. However, an additional 38% of the companies reported that while they had no set age limit they gave preference to workers under forty in hiring new employees (National Association of Manufactures, 1938, pp. 7, 11, 52). The NAM figures may be low, however, since the Association had earlier (in February, 1938) taken a policy stand against age discrimination.[42] Also it should be noted that by this date the Fair Labor Standards Act and the Social Security Act had both been passed by Congress. Federal action had by then made many company policies moot.

## CONCLUSIONS

The results reported in this paper are preliminary. Much work remains to be done. Yet we can, on the basis of the work completed, state the following list of propositions that we believe are supported by the work accomplished to date:

1. The abolition of tontine insurance in 1906 created a demand for life-cycle efficient assets by workers and a willingness on their part to submit to forced saving to fund them.

2. Group insurance arose as a substitute for tontine insurance in the product mix of American insurance companies.

3. Industrial pensions also became popular after the first decade of the twentieth century. Workers were responding to the demands for greater economic security and the threat posed by the abolition of tontine insurance in 1906. Management was attempting to establish a more efficient labor market and pension plans provided a mechanism to help introduce both incentive wages and mandatory retirement.

4. The appearance of age discrimination in employment dated from the mid-1920s and was probably a consequence of internal labor markets, pensions, and group insurance.

## NOTES

[1]For a description of the Pennsylvania Railroad plan, see Latimer (1932, pp. 24-25), Riebenack (1909, p. 259), and Henderson (1909, pp. 220-24 and 233-238). It is not literally true that there were only three nineteenth century pensions established. According to Latimer there were three others. Two were established in 1892. The Consolidated Gas Company of New York set up a discretionary plan, but it was too informal to meet Latimer's criteria as a formal pension (Latimer, 1932, p. 35). The Solvay Process Company, a chemical manufacturer, initiated a plan also in 1892. However this plan was discontinued in 1899 because "the president believes that the class of workmen employed at Solvay are not yet ready to appreciate a scheme of this character" (Latimer, 1932, pp. 39-40).

[2]When Carnegie Steel was consolidated into the United States Steel Corporation in 1911, its pension plan was maintained and extended to all employees of the new company. When Standard Oil was dissolved in 1911, the several units formed after the breakup each continued the parent plan in force (Latimer, 1932, p. 40-41).

[3]The data plotted in Figure 1.1 was extracted from four studies of pensions carried out from 1915 to 1932. Each tried to find every private pension plan in operation at the time of compilation by using a variety of survey techniques. The first study was published in 1915 by the Carnegie Foundation and reported on 58 companies. The second was published ten years later by the National Industrial Conference Board which obtained data on 248 different formal plans. The third study was prepared by Abraham Epstein and was published by the Pennsylvania Old Age Pension Commission in 1926. Epstein reports that the commission received over 1,600 replies to their questionnaire and found that 594 firms were providing pensions, but he presents data only on the 370 that were operating "formal" plans (Epstein 1926, pp. 115-26). The final study was by Murray W. Latimer and was published in 1932 by the Industrial Relations Counselors. Latimer reported on 397 plans. We have collated the three studies, eliminating duplication and report data on 563 plans. We emphasize that this number of plans is surely a conservative estimate since the four sources held to strict definitions of what

constituted a formal pension plan and thus deliberately excluded many informal or transitory plans. Nevertheless, we have no reason to suspect that these biases would distort the overall picture of the timing of pension plan introduction in the United States. An appendix detailing our procedures is available from the authors on request. Also see Williamson (1992).

[4]We calculate that by 1930 over 3.6 million workers were covered by formal industrial pensions. [This number is computed in the appendix available from the authors.] This figure excludes a sizable number of additional workers covered by informal pensions and group annuity plans. There were approximately 26 million nonfarm employees in that year (Lebergott, 1964, Table A-4, p. 513).

[5]Between 1890 and 1910 the average amount paid as pensions ranged from about $140 per year to $175. The 1907 law had a rising schedule that offered $10 per month at age 62; $15 per month at 70; and $20 per month at age 75. At a time when an industrial worker's income would have been between $500 and $700, these orders of magnitude were significant.

[6]This estimate is based on the occupation given by the 1,610 men 60 years or older who were identified as Union veterans in the 1910 Public Use Sample.

[7]Hansen put the number of industrial wage earners in 1900 at 10,264 thousand, or 33.4% of the total number of gainfully occupied (Hansen, 1922, p. 504). Spurgeon Bell estimated the same percentage as 32.4% (Bell, 1940, p. 11). Lebergott's figures put non-farm employees (excluding domestic service employees) at 10,086 thousand or 37.4% of the employed Labor Force (Lebergott, 1964, Tables A-3 and A-4, pp. 512–513).

[8]Recent scholarship on turn-of-the-century perspectives on old age can be found in Achenbaum (1978), Graebner (1980), and Haber (1983).

[9]While physical impairment and reduced productivity can be expected to accompany aging no matter what the economic organization of society, it was widely believed that the industrial occupations of late-nineteenth century America were particularly wearing. A series of studies on the "Effect of Occupation on the Health and Duration of the Trade-Life of Workmen," was conducted in New Jersey between 1888 and 1891 and seem to support the conclusion that workers in typical New Jersey industries reached their peak productivity in their mid-fifties (New Jersey, 1890, 1891, and 1892; Ransom & Sutch, 1992). Also see Atack and Bateman (1991).

[10]Over the course of the nineteenth century, the traditional strategy of relying upon the support of grown children had fallen from favor (Ransom & Sutch, 1986b and 1986c).

[11]The national saving rate is based on the work of Gallman (1966) and Davis and Gallman (1973, 1991). Also see Ransom and Sutch (1984a, 1984b). Our own earlier work and that of other researchers with household budget data has documented the impressive saving rates that characterized late-nineteenth century industrial communities (Haines 1985, Ransom & Sutch, 1986b, 1986d, 1989b).

[12]Ransom and Sutch (1986a, 1989a, and with Williamson, 1991). Soon after 1937, labor

force participation of older men began a long downward trend reflecting a growing propensity to retire that has continued to this day.

[13]Our estimates for 1870 and 1880 are based on the census reports of "productive" occupations (Ransom and Sutch, 1986a). Although Achenbaum (1978) and Moen (1987) have questioned the reliability of these early census data (on very different grounds and with divergent opinions about the direction of enumeration bias), we have concluded that the data as reported are an acceptable basis for an estimate of the labor force participation rate of men 60 and over (Ransom and Sutch, 1989a). Our estimates for 1900 and 1910 are based on an analysis of samples drawn from the enumerators' manuscripts of the censuses of population taken in those years (Ransom and Sutch 1988 and with Williamson 1991). While our estimation methods have been criticized (Moen, 1987) and are admittedly imprecise, further examination by others suggests that they are reliable (Margo, 1991). The estimate for 1937 is based on the Enumerative Check Census of 1937 (U.S. Administrator of the Census of Partial Employment, Unemployment, and Occupations, 1937). Our estimate for 1930 is based on a revision of the published census data for that year. An appendix describing the 1930 data is available from the authors on request. The manuscripts of the 1890 census were destroyed some years ago and the manuscripts for 1920 have not yet been released for public use. The published Census returns for 1940 are suspect and are not presented here (Ransom & Sutch, 1986a).

[14]We suspect that the life-cycle savings plans of workers increasingly fell short of what was required in the late 1890s and early 1900s for several reasons. First, the industrial depression of the 1890s put many workers out of employment and forced them to reduce saving or even dissave for an unexpectedly long period of time (Carter & Sutch, 1991). Second, the tontine insurance funds paid a smaller final distribution (called a "deferred dividend") than had been advertised despite their high *rates* of return. This was the consequence both of inflated promises used to advertise the policies and the unanticipated general decline in interest rates during the last three decades of the nineteenth century (Ransom & Sutch, 1987). Finally, some workers found their stock of savings had been lost when a bank or insurance company failed in this era before financial regulation and deposit insurance (Bremer, 1935, pp. 25–28, and Grossman, 1989).

[15]Most of the tontine-issuing insurance companies were located in New York City. For a discussion of the tontine business, the insurance investigation, and the abolition of tontine insurance see Ransom and Sutch (1987).

[16]There was, to be sure, another form of life insurance that was aimed at working-class families. Beginning in the late 1880s, several major companies began to vigorously market industrial insurance. These policies were written for a relatively small face amount and the premiums were collected by the agent on a weekly or monthly basis. While the small scale and convenient premium payments made these policies popular among workers, the industrial policy lacked both the large terminal payments and the high rates of return associated with the tontine feature and were therefore an imperfect substitute when the tontine policies were discontinued. The largest companies specializing in industrial insurance were Prudential, John Hancock, and Aetna. At the time of the Crisis of 1906, industrial insurance accounted for $2.4 billion, or roughly 20% of all insurance in force. The average size of these policies at that time

was about $135, compared to an average of just over $2,000 for the ordinary life policy (Institute of Life Insurance, 1950, pp. 8, 14). William Graham gives a further reason why industrial insurance was not an effective substitute for tontine insurance among workers in large establishments. These workers, according to Graham, are "largely left out of the life insurance agent's field of activities" because workers at these plants "could not be solicited during working hours" (Graham, 1924, p. 1296).

[17]Although Aetna did not issue the standard 10- or 20-year contracts commonly associated with the tontine insurance of the major firms, the company aggressively marketed five-year policies with deferred dividends that represented a major share of their "ordinary insurance".

[18]The basic sources for data on group insurance before 1940 are the annual editions of *The Spectator Insurance Year Book*. However, that source includes data only for firms reporting to the New York State insurance commission, and presents no comprehensive data for group insurance before 1921–22. Stalson (1942) developed the first comprehensive series on group insurance. His figures form the foundation for the series developed by the Institute for Life Insurance and published in *The Historical Statistics of Life Insurance in the United States, 1759 to 1958*. Many of these data, which represent the most comprehensive compilation of data on insurance covering a long period of time in the United States, are reproduced in *Historical Statistics of the United States, Colonial Times to 1970*. These series do not, however, contain any firm level data. Whenever possible, we have chosen to rely on the Institute of Life Insurance series for aggregate evidence, and on *Spectator Insurance Yearbook* for firm-level data.

[19]The statistics on insurance in force are from Institute of Life Insurance (1960b, p. 7). The number of certificates is taken from Institute of Life Insurance (1960a, pp 23, 24).

[20]By 1930, group insurance as a fraction of total new business represented 40.3% for Aetna, 30.4% for Travelers, 22.8% for Metropolitan, and 20.1% for Equitable. (Spectator Company, 1930)

[21]The 1922 *Spectator Insurance Yearbook* identified six other firms whose outstanding group insurance represented at 15% or more of their total insurance in force; by 1930 there were 14 smaller firms with more than 20% of their insurance in force represented by group policies. While we do not have data on the number of persons covered by group policies with these firms, the average amount of insurance per policy written by these firms is substantially less than that of the big five. It is clear that the small firms were catering to smaller manufacturing establishments.

[22]The original survey results are reported by the U.S. Commissioner of Labor (1890, 1891). See Michael Haines (1985) and Ransom and Sutch (1988) for more details. It is not always wise to interpret a cross section arranged by age as if it represented the longitudinal experience of an individual growing older. We defend the practice in this context with two arguments. First, these data come from a period when both wages and the age distribution of the working class were stable. Second, young workers in the 1890s were likely to have made plans for their old age based on their impression of the working and living conditions of older men and women who were their contemporaries. Thus the data displayed in the figure may be a more accurate

representation of the expectations of turn-of-the-century workers than would the actual ex post data. This point is particularly true since it is unlikely that many workers accurately forecast the many changes that were to come to American labor markets after 1906.

[23]U.S. Federal Coordinator of Transportation (1944, Tables 1 and 48, np). The 13 railroads collectively employed about 22% of the total number of railway employees in the country. The data plotted are based on the employment histories and annual earnings between 1924 and 1933. They were smoothed using standard topological mapping procedures. The original source is an unpublished background paper found in the library of the Railroad Retirement Board in Chicago.

[24]See the papers by Lazear (1979, 1981) and those collected in the book by Akerlof and Yellen (1986).

[25]Mervyn King (1983) has shown that a change in the shape of the earnings profile can induce a strong effect on the desired age of retirement.

[26]This was an explicit part of most written pension rules. For example, see the plan of the International Harvester Company quoted in Downey (1915, pp. 9-10). The point that contributory pensions would establish employee rights the management was unwilling to grant was also emphasized by Robert Ball in his history of pensions (1952, p. 11).

[27]For a discussion of state restrictions on mandatory employee contributions, see Latimer (1932, pp. 672-674).

[28]All three sources of efficiency gains were emphasized in the literature on pensions, but the reduction of turnover was universally regarded as the most important. The second gain from pensions has been particularly stressed by those labor historians who have interpreted pensions as a strategy against labor unions. The third source of efficiency gains can be thought of as related to efficiency wage effects and "gift exchanges" (Akerlof & Yellen, 1986).

[29]In the early days of pensions we observe many managers speaking enthusiastically of the "payroll savings" achieved shortly after adoption of a new pension system. However, since this was a transitory phenomenon, these "savings" disappeared over the course of a generation. Thus some firms reported unexpectedly large pension costs 15 to 20 years after the plans were introduced (Edwards 1925a, 1925b). The imperfect knowledge of actuarial arithmetic that prevailed in this period undoubtedly led to a great deal of confusion and in some cases real embarrassment on the part of firms that financed their pension schemes out of current revenues rather than by accumulating an actuarially sound reserve fund.

[30]A log-linear regression of the quit rate against the unemployment rate (Lebergott's estimates) achieved an R-squared of 0.58. The relationship between quits and unemployment was strongly negative with an elasticity of −0.73 (with a standard error of only 0.09) when estimated using the data from 1910 through 1956 (omitting 1916 where no data on quits is available) published by Ross (1958, Table 1, p. 906).

[31]Arthur Ross [1958] argued that a better measure of labor market opportunities than the unemployment rate would be the percentage of the non-agricultural labor force

that was accounted for by the manufacturing sector. However, the implicit theory behind Ross's specification (that manufacturing workers were not able to search for jobs in the non-manufacturing or agricultural sectors) is no longer in favor with labor economists (Owen, 1991).

[32]Indeed, we suggest that the social and moral pressure that could be brought against the firm without a pension system to carry older workers who were unprepared for retirement was the primary channel through which the workers' desires for forced saving to finance deferred annuities was made known to the employer.

[33]For data on the birth rate see Yasuba (1961), Thompson and Whelpton (1933), and Ransom and Sutch (1989b). The declining birth rate itself was an important part of the explanation of why workers found pensions and the rising pay schedules of the modern labor market attractive. As Americans increasingly adopted the life cycle system of providing for old age security, they were able to discard the older strategy of relying upon their grown children to provide for them. Thus the decline in fertility and the rise of life-cycle security motives are simply two aspects of the "Life Cycle Transition" (Ransom and Sutch, 1986b, 1986c, and 1989b). In the first two decades of the twentieth century the decline in family size continued, leaving older workers either unable or unwilling to become dependents of their children.

[34]Life expectancy trends were upward but this factor was not strong enough to be relevant. See Ransom and Sutch 1988 for a discussion of the trends in mortality and life expectancy.

[35]Seymour (1929, p. 12). Elsewhere, in an earlier report, the percentage of firms covered in the NAM survey that had instituted age bars was reported as 30% (rather than 28%; U.S. Bureau of Labor Statistics (1929, p. 1024).

[36]Latimer (1932, Table 84, p. 798). Also see U.S. Bureau of Labor Statistics (1930b, p. 542). The figures cited are influenced by the inclusion of railroads and public utilities along with manufacturing firms. In Latimer's survey, 37% of the workers in manufacturing were employed by firms with explicit age bars (Table 85, p. 800).

[37]Lindsay (1901, p. 1032) and Weyl (1905, pp. 565–566; 604–608).

[38]An oft-stated view was that the formal age restrictions had first been introduced by the railroads. For example see the comments of the Commissioner of Labor of Louisiana, Frank E. Wood (1929, p. 63).

[39]Even before the Depression, a study reported in the *Bulletin of the Taylor Society* (1929, p. 222) indicated that the Massachusetts Public Employment Offices had a much lower success rate in placing unemployed men 55 and over than those below that age.

[40]This finding contrasts with the increasing discrimination against women and blacks during the 1930s. Claudia Goldin reports that employment bars directed at married women increased during the Great Depression (Goldin 1990, pp. 161–166). She explains this change as "a socially acceptable means of rationing employment during the 1930's" (p. 174). Presumably, scarce jobs should be preferentially given to men. Society would then expect husbands to "support" their wives. This same logic of job rationing did not apply to older males.

[41]Brower (1937; Table 16, p. 29). Only 405 firms responded to this question, 99 reported a maximum hiring age. The most common age cutoff reported was 50 years (33 firms), the second most common was 45 years (22 firms). The lowest was 30 years.

[42]The Board of Directors, at its February 1938 meeting, adopted the following resolution and sent it to all member firms:

> *The National Association of Manufacturers 1938 is opposed to the employment in industry of children under 16 years of age, and to the establishment of arbitrary upper age limits in the hiring or employment of workers below any which might be fixed for permanent retirement. It urges its members to carefully review their employment practices to see that no such arbitrary age limits are practiced in their companies, and instruct their respective employment officers to employ persons according to their qualifications without regard to any maximum age.*

The survey was apparently taken after the policy statement was distributed.

## REFERENCES

Achenbaum, W. A. (Fall, 1974). The Obsolescence of Old Age in America, 1865–1914. *Journal of Social History, 8,* 48–62.

Achenbaum, W. A. (1978). *Old age in the new land: The American experience since 1790.* Baltimore: Johns Hopkins University Press.

Akerlof, G. A., & Yellen, J. L. (Eds.). (1986). *Efficiency wage models of the labor market.* New York: Cambridge University Press.

Atack, J., & Bateman, F. (1991). *Louis Brandeis, work and fatigue at the start of the twentieth century: Prelude to Oregon's hours limitation law.* Department of Economics, University of Illinois, Champaign-Urbana.

Ball, R. M. (1952). *Pensions in the United States.* Washington, DC: U.S. Government Printing Office.

Barkin, S. (Feb. 1933). *The older worker in industry: A study of New York state manufacturing industries.* A Report to the Joint Legislative Committee on Unemployment Prepared Under the Auspices of the Continuation Committee of the New York State Commission on Old Age Security. New York Legislative Document Number 66.

Bell, S. (1940). *Productivity, wages, and national income.* Washington, DC: Brookings Institution.

Bremer, C. D. (1935). *American bank failures.* New York: Columbia University Press.

Brower, F. B. (1937). *Personnel practices governing factory and office administration.* New York: National Industrial Conference Board Study Number 233.

Buley, R. C. (1967). *The Equitable Life Assurance Society of the United States, 1859-1964.* New York: Appleton-Century-Crofts.

*Bulletin of the Taylor Society.* (1929). Employment age limitations. Author.

California Department of Industrial Relations. (Aug. 1930). *Middle-aged and older workers in California.* Special Bulletin, Number 2.

Carter, S. B., & Sutch, R. (1991). *The Great (or not-so-great) Depression of the 1890s.* Riverside, CA: Department of Economics, University of California.

Chandler, Jr., A. duP. (1977). *The visible hand: The managerial revolution in American business.* Cambridge, MA: Harvard University Press.

Davis, J. L. (1928, May). Old age at fifty. *North American Review*. (May). Reprinted in U.S. Bureau of Labor Statistics. *Monthly Labor Review*, 26 (1928, June), 1906–1097.

Davis, L. E., & Gallman, R. E. (1973). *The share of savings and investment in gross national product during the 19th century in the U.S.A.* Fourth International Conference of Economic History, Bloomington, 1968. pp. 437–466. Mouton La Haye.

Davis, L. E., & Gallman, R. E. (1991). *Savings, investment and economic growth: The United States in the nineteenth century.* Preliminary draft, Department of Economics, University of North Carolina, Chapel Hill.

Dooley, C. R., & Washburn, H. L. (1929). The Employment and Adjustment of the Older Worker, American Management Association. *General Management Series, Number 86.*

Downey, E. H. (March, 1915). *Report on old age relief.* Madison, WI: Industrial Commission of Wisconsin.

Edwards, G. (1925a, Nov. 20). Industrial pension plans collapsing. *The Annalist*, 637–638, 658.

Edwards, G. (1925b, Nov. 27). The way out of the industrial pension crisis. *The Annalist*, 667–668, 681.

Epstein, A. (1926). *The problem of old age pensions in industry: An up-to-date summary of the facts and figures developed in the further study of old age pensions.* Harrisburg, PA: Pennsylvania Old Age Pension Commission.

Epstein, A. (1928). *Challenge of the aged.* New York: Vanguard Press.

Foster, E. T. (1928, April–May). Development of insurance. *Commerce Monthly*, 3–10.

Gallman, R. E. (1966). Gross national product in the United States, 1834–1909. National Bureau of Economic Research *Output, Employment, and Productivity in the United States After 1800.* Studies in Income and Wealth, Volume 30, pp. 3–90. Princeton, NJ: Princeton University Press.

Goldin, C. (1990). *Understanding the gender gap: An economic history of American women.* New York: Oxford University Press.

Graebner, W. (1980). *A history of retirement: The meaning and function of an American institution: 1885–1978.* New Haven, CT: Yale University Press.

Graham, W. J. (1924, January 26). A dozen years of group insurance. *The Economic World*, 129–131.

Graham, W. J. (1929). Group insurance and plant pension plans as a cause of old age hiring limits. In *The Older Worker in Industry: Addresses at a Session of the (1929) Annual Meeting (of the) National Association of Manufacturers*, National Association of Manufacturers.

Grossman, R. S. (1989). *The macroeconomic consequences of bank failures under the national banking system.* U.S. Department of State, Washington, DC.

Haber, C. (1983). *Beyond sixty-five: the dilemma of old age in America's past.* New York: Cambridge University Press.

Haines, M. R. (1985). The life cycle, savings, and demographic adaptation: Some historical evidence for the United States and Europe (pp. 43–63). Alice S. Rosse (Ed.) *Gender and the life course.* New York: Aldine.

Haines, M. R., & Goodman, A. C. (1991). *Homeownership and housing demand in late nineteenth century America: Evidence from state labor reports.* Department of Economics, Colgate University, Hamilton, New York.

Haines, M. R., & Goodman, A. C. (1992). A home of one's own: Aging and homeownership in the United States in the late nineteenth and early twentieth centuries. Chapter 8 in D. I. Kertzer & P. Laslett (Eds.) *Aging in the past: Demography, society, and old age.* Berkeley, University of California Press.

Hansen, A. H. (1922, Dec.). Industrial classes in the United States in 1920. *Journal of the American Statistical Association.*

Hatch, A. (1950). *American Express: A century of service.* New York: Doubleday.

Henderson, C. R. (1909). *Industrial insurance in the United States.* Chicago: University of Chicago Press.

Institute of Life Insurance. (1950). *1950 life insurance fact book.* Author.

Institute of Life Insurance. (1960a). *1960 life insurance fact book.* Author.

Institute of Life Insurance. (1960b). *The Historical Statistics of Life Insurance in the United States 1759 to 1958.* Institute of Life Insurance, Division of Statistics and Research.

Jacoby, S. M. (1985). *Employing bureaucracy: Managers, unions, and the transformation of work in American industry, 1900-1945.* New York: Columbia University Press.

King, M. (1983, Dec..). The economics of saving. New York: *National Bureau of Economic Research Working Paper Series* Number 1247.

Latimer, M. W. (1932). *Industrial pension systems in the United States and Canada (2 vols.).* New York: Industrial Relations Counselors, Incorporated.

Lazear, E. P. (1979, Dec.) Why is there mandatory retirement? *Journal of Political Economy, 87,* 1261-1264.

Lazear, E. P. (1981, Sept.). Agency, earnings profiles, productivity, and hours restrictions. *American Economic Review, 71,* 606-620.

Lebergott, S. (1964). *Manpower in economic growth: The American record since 1800.* New York: McGraw-Hill.

Licht, W. (1983). *Working for the railroad: The organization of work in the nineteenth century.* Princeton, NJ: Princeton University Press.

Lindsay, S. M. (1901, Nov.). Railway employees in the United States. *Bulletin of the Bureau of Labor,* Number 37.

Margo, R. A. (1991, July). The labor force participation of older Americans in 1900: Further results. *Working Papers on Historical Factors in Long Run Growth.* Number 27. Cambridge, MA: National Bureau of Economic Research.

Moen, J. (1987, Sept.). The labor of older Americans: A comment. *Journal of Economic History, 47.* 761-67.

Murphy, A. L. (1930, Dec.). *The older worker in Maryland.* Maryland Commissioner of Labor and Statistics.

National Association of Manufacturers. (1929). Proceedings of the thirty-fourth annual meeting of the National Association of Manufacturers of the United States of America held at New York City, October 14-16. *American Industries, 30.*

National Association of Manufacturers (1938). *Workers over 40: A survey by the National Association of Manufacturers of its member companies to determine the status of "Workers 40 and Over."* Author.

National Industrial Conference Board. (1925). *Industrial pensions in the United States.* New York: Author.

Nelson, D. (1975). *Workers and managers: Origins of the new factory system in the United States, 1880-1920.* University of Wisconsin Press.

New Jersey, Bureau of Statistics of Labor and Industries. (1890). *Twelfth annual report of the Bureau of Statistics of Labor and Industries of New Jersey for the year ending October 31, 1889.* Trenton, NJ: F. F. Paterson.

New Jersey, Bureau of Statistics of Labor and Industries (1891). *Thirteenth annual report of the Bureau of Statistics of Labor and Industries of New Jersey, for the year ending October 31, 1890.* Trenton, NJ: Trenton Electric Printing Company.

New Jersey, Bureau of Statistics of Labor and Industries. (1892). *Fourteenth annual report of the Bureau of Statistics of Labor and Industries of New Jersey for the year ending October 31st, 1891.* Trenton, NJ: John L. Murphy.

Owen, L. (1991). *The decline in turnover of manufacturing workers: Case study evidence from the 1920s.* PhD Dissertation, Department of Economics, Yale University.

Ransom, R. L., & Sutch, R. (1984a, Dec.). Domestic saving as an active constraint on capital formation in the American economy, 1839–1928: A provisional theory. *Working Papers on the History of Saving,* Number 1. Institute for Business and Economic Research, University of California, Berkeley.

Ransom, R. L., & Sutch, R. (1984b, Dec.). A system of life-cycle national accounts: Provisional estimates, 1839–1938. *Working Papers on the History of Saving,* Number 2. Institute for Business and Economic Research, University of California, Berkeley.

Ransom, R. L., & Sutch, R. (1986a, March). The labor of older Americans: Retirement of men on and off the job, 1870–1937. *Journal of Economic History, 46.*

Ransom, R. L., & Sutch, R. (1986b). The life-cycle transition: A preliminary report on wealth holding in America. Chapter 10 in *Income and wealth distribution in historical perspective.* University of Utrecht.

Ransom, R. L., & Sutch, R. (1986c, April). Did rising out-migration cause fertility to decline in antebellum New England? A life-cycle perspective on old-age security motives, child default, and farm-family fertility. California Institute of Technology Social Science Working Papers, Number 610. California Institute of Technology, Pasadena.

Ransom, R. L., & Sutch, R. (1986d). Unequalled thrift: An inquiry into the saving behavior of Americans at the turn of the century. Paper presented at the Ninety-Ninth Annual Meeting of the American Economic Association, New Orleans, Louisiana, December 27–30.

Ransom, R. L., & Sutch, R. (1987, June). Tontine insurance and the Armstrong Commission: A Case of stifled innovation in the American life insurance industry. *Journal of Economic History,* 379–390.

Ransom, R. L., & Sutch, R. (1988). The decline of retirement in the years before Social Security: U.S. retirement patterns, 1870–1940. In R. Ricardo-Campbell & E. P. Lazear (Eds.) *Issues in contemporary retirement* (pp. 3–37). Hoover Institute.

Ransom, R. L., & Sutch, R. (1989a, March). The trend in the rate of labor-force participation of older men, 1870–1930: A reply to Moen. *Journal of Economic History, 49,* 170–183.

Ransom, R. L., & Sutch, R. (1989b). Two strategies for a more secure old age: Life cycle saving by late-nineteenth century American workers. *Working Paper Series on Long Run Growth,* Number 2. National Bureau for Economic Research, Cambridge, Massachusetts.

Ransom, R. L., & Sutch, R. (forthcoming, 1993). The impact of aging on the employment of men in working class communities at the end of the nineteenth century: A cross-section analysis of surveys from Maine, New Jersey, California, Michigan and Kansas. In I. Kertzer & P. Laslett (Eds.) *Aging in the past: Demography, society, and old age.* University of California Press.

Ransom, R. L., Sutch, R., & Williamson, S. H. (1991). Retirement, past and present. In (Ed.) H. Munnell, *Retirement and public policy: Proceedings of the second conference of the National Academy of Social Insurance* (pp. 23–50). Washington, DC: National Academy of Social Insurance.

Riebenack, M. (1909, March). Penn Railroad pension departments: Systems east and west of Pittsburgh and Erie, PA: Status to and including 1907. *The Annals of the American Academy of Political and Social Science, 32.*

Ross, A. (1958, Dec.). Do we have a new industrial feudalism? *American Economic Review, 48,* 903–920.

Rotella, E., & Alter, G. (1991, May). Buying homes with borrowed money: Workers use of credit in the late 19th century. Department of Economics, Indiana University.

Seymour, C. K. (1929). Maximum age hiring limits in industry, extent of such limits: Extract from 1919 report of Employment Relations Committee. In *The older worker in industry: Addresses at a session of the (1929) annual meeting (of the) National Association of Manufacturers.* National Association of Manufacturers.

The Spectator Company. (1930). *The Insurance Yearbook,* 1874–1911. Author.

Stalson, J. O. (1942). *Marketing life insurance: Its history in America.* Harvard University Press.

Thompson, W. S. & Whelpton, P. K. (1933). *Population trends in the United States.* New York.

U.S. Administrator of the Census. (1937). *The census of partial employment, unemployment, and occupations in 1937.* Washington, DC: U.S. Government Printing Office.

U.S. Bureau of Labor Statistics. (May 1929). Age limits on employment by American manufacturers. *Monthly Labor Review, 28.*

U.S. Bureau of Labor Statistics. (Sept. 1930a). Finding work for the middle-aged. *Monthly Labor Review, 31.*

U.S. Bureau of Labor Statistics. (Jan. 1930b). Age of applicants for work in relation to ease of placement. *Monthly Labor Review, 31.*

U.S. Bureau of Labor Statistics. (March, 1930c). Difficulty of Rochester employment office in placing older workers. *Monthly Labor Review, 31.*

U.S. Bureau of Labor Statistics. (Nov. 1932). Hiring and separation methods in American factories. *Monthly Labor Review, 13.*

U.S. Bureau of the Census. (1975). *Historical statistics of the United States, Colonial times to 1970* (2 Vols.) Washington, DC: U.S. Government Printing Office.

U.S. Commissioner of Labor. (1909). Workman's insurance and benefit funds in the United States. Twenty *Third Annual Report of the Commissioner of Labor, 1908.* Washington, DC: U.S. Government Printing Office.

U.S. Federal Coordinator of Transportation, Section of Labor Relations. (1944, Nov.). Acturial data and basic tables for valuation of retirement benefits to railroad employees. Unpublished background paper used in the preparation of *Annual earnings of railroad employees, 1924–1933, Employment attrition in the railroad industry, unemployment compensation for railroad employees.*

Weyl, W. E. (March 1905). Street railway employment in the United States. *Bulletin of the Bureau of Labor,* Number 57.

Williamson, S. H. (1992). U.S. and Canada pensions before 1930: A historical perspective. In J. A. Tumer & D. J. Beller (Eds.) *Trends in Pensions 1992.* U.S. Department of Labor, Washington, D.C.

Wood, F. E. (March 1929). What effect has so-called age limit on employment. Association of Governmental Officials in Industry of the United States and Canada: Fifteenth Annual Convention, New Orleans, Louisiana, May 21–24, 1928; *Bulletin of United States Bureau of Labor Statistics* Miscellaneous, Series Number 480.

Yasuba, Y. (1961). *Birth rates of the white population in the United States, 1800–1860: An economic study.* Baltimore: Johns Hopkins University Press.

# Pensions and Poverty: Comments on "Declining Pensions"

## Nancy Folbre

The preceding is a bold and beautiful chapter that links many interesting details regarding the evolution of financial instruments to the larger sweep of economic change in the U.S. between 1900 and 1940. I am persuaded by the central argument that innovations such as tontines and pensions had a significant impact on savings and retirement. But I remain a bit skeptical of the starring role assigned to the banning of tontines. Also, much of my curiosity about the causes and effects of company-provided pensions remains unsatisfied.

The three large questions I raise here pertain less to the specific claims made in the paper than to the larger project of understanding the history of retirement, savings, poverty, and public policy. (1) How successful, overall, were financial strategies for providing income security in old age? (2) How did changes in the labor force, other than the emergence of internal labor markets, affect the economic welfare of the elderly? (3) How did internal labor markets and associated pension plans vary in their implications for men and women?

Although tontines were an interesting and important phenomenon, their relative contribution to old age security remains unclear. By 1905, 9 million policies had been sold to a nation with only 18 million households. This is an impressive number, but how many households purchased more than one policy, and, more importantly, what was the approximate sum of money involved? Was it sufficient to allow workers to retire in their old age?

Both tontines and pensions offered a higher rate of return than savings. But they both had significant disadvantages as well: in the case of tontines, limited benefits for survivors and the risk of fraud (the reason given for outlawing them); and in the case of pensions, lack of portability, and threats associated with bankruptcy. Even with a lower rate of return, individual savings might have remained more important, and, as Ransom, Sutch and Williamson emphasize, savings rates were quite high in industrial communities.

The relative importance of all financial instruments in providing for old age requires more detailed scrutiny. A complex set of "implicit contracts" governing the responsibilities of children and other kin represented a form of old age insurance. The authors seem to assume that the family ethic had entirely disappeared by the early twentieth century, but a substantial body of historical research suggests that investments in children offered a positive, albeit declining rate of return for elderly parents. In 1910, for instance, women over 44 who were childless were nearly seven times more likely to be in poorhouses than those who had become mothers (Smith, 1979, p. 292). A study of the aged poor who were not dependent on public assistance, conducted by the Massachusetts Commission on Old Age Pensions in 1910, found that the percentage of single and widowed individuals receiving income from relatives was higher than the percentage receiving income from savings.

Household budget surveys did not encompass the most impoverished individuals, those dependent on other family members or relegated to the almshouse. They did, however, reveal a striking pattern among families headed by male wage-earners. In 1889–1890, children in households headed by men ages 40–44 contributed about 18% of all family income. By 1917–1919, their contributions in comparable households had declined to 5%. In older households, however, headed by men 60 years and older, children contributed about the same percentage of family income (30%–33%) in both periods. Sons and daughters clearly remained an important part of the old-age security portfolio (Haber & Gratton, 1993).

Savings and pensions were probably a supplement, rather than a substitute, for reliance on children and other kin. While savings, life insurance, and pensions served the needs of individuals as well as families, they were not necessarily more "individualistic," because they provided parents with an important source of leverage in the form of contingent bequests. Elderly people with considerable wealth could enjoy the best of both worlds–a steady and reliable flow of income combined with solicitous attention from their heirs (Parsons, 1984).

If savings gradually became more important to the retirement portfolio than children, income inequality among the elderly probably increased, for the simple reason that children are generally distributed more equally than money. Ransom, Sutch, and Williamson suggest that the Civil War pensions probably helped alleviate this problem in the United States. But it is worth noting that these pensions, available only to Union veterans, were distributed quite unevenly. While some Southern states offered state-financed benefits for Confederate veterans, they were less generous. Needless to say, few black men were eligible for either type of pension.

Concern with the plight of the elderly poor was a powerful theme in turn-of-the-century politics, particularly in industrialized states like Massachusetts. According to Abraham Epstein, the percentage of people in almshouses who were 65 or over increased from 25% in 1880 to 42.7% in 1910 (Epstein, 1922, p. 25). In Massachusetts, one of the more urbanized, industrialized states, 92% of those in state pauper institutions were 65 years of age and over (Epstein, 1922, p. 30). This trend reflected the tendency to expel the non-elderly from almshouses during the period. Still, we need to know more about the incidence of poverty among the elderly before we can assess the success of selfreliance, thrift, and pensions in addressing the life-cycle "problem."

The minority of individuals who failed to save was fairly substantial. A Commonwealth of Massachusetts study conducted in the 1920s covered 19,000 aged, while a National Civic Federation study investigated 14,000 aged, in 11 cities and two towns in four states—New York, New Jersey, Pennsylvania, and Connecticut. Both found that 55% of individuals over 65 either owned property worth $5000 a year or more or had incomes of $1000 a year. But about 17% of the elderly had no income or property of their own (Lubove, 1968, p. 134). Many of these were widows, a group that Ransom, Sutch, and Williamson never single out for attention, despite this group's particular economic vulnerability in old age.

These issues of poverty and inequality are important because they are relevant to the political movement for public pensions. In the early twentieth century a number of states established special State Commissions to collect information on the indigent elderly and to consider the option of public assistance. The State of Arizona abolished almshouses and established new provisions for old age assistance in 1915. This first law was declared unconstitutional, but Montana established a similar law in 1923, and other states began to follow suit. By 1930, New York, Massachusetts, California, and nine other states were involved.

The new state legislation recognized the inadequacy of family-based support while upholding it in principle. Virtually all the state laws passed (the exceptions were Arizona and the territory of Hawaii) excluded from assistance all those with financially competent children or relatives. But the difficulty of ascertaining "financial competence" proved a major loophole for relatives who chose to plead poverty. As with mothers' pensions, fairly onerous restrictions were imposed. Some states required residency of 15 years or more, and elderly of questionable character were excluded. Also, southern states were clearly underrepresented (Social Security Board, 1937, p. 159).

Why did support for these programs emerge in the 1920s, culminating in the federal old age security provisions of the Social Security Act of 1935? If the combination of savings, pensions, and family support was simply inadequate, we might explain the new legislation as a response to "market failure" and "family failure." But if the elderly as a group were actually faring well, we might explain the new legislation as a form of rent-seeking behavior that reflected the growing power of the elderly as an interest group. While these two explanations are not mutually exclusive, a better understanding of their relative importance is crucial to the history of the welfare state.

My second question, concerning the role of changes in the labor force between 1900 and 1940, bears directly on the relative importance of company-provided pensions, as well as other issues. One of the strong points of "Inventing Pensions" is its lucid explanation of the connection between internal labor markets, age discrimination, and pensions. But the discussion focuses primarily on industrial workers and a particularly industrialized sector of transportation, the railroads. Together, these sectors comprised only about 23% of the paid labor force between 1900 and 1940 (U.S. Bureau of the Census, 1975, p. 139). Furthermore, many of these workers were not employed by the large enterprises that established internal labor markets. Were the workers who enjoyed pensions during this period part of an "aristocracy of labor?"

The authors' discussion of pensions and pension recipients gives the impression that financial and labor management innovations contributed to change in the average "life-cycle." But one countervailing trend in the paid labor force as a whole may have been the declining importance of self-employment, a theme emphasized by earlier historical treatments of retirement in the United States (Achenbaum, 1978; Fischer, 1978). The effect of selfemployment on retirement varied by income level. Highly successful farmers or small businessmen were able to accumulate assets and retire at an earlier age (Parsons, 1991, p. 665). On the other hand, the less successful self-employed who could not afford to retire could, unlike most wage earners, adjust their work effort to match their declining physical capacities.

Did the proportion of wage earners in the labor force grow faster than the proportion of wage earners with access to pensions? If so, the net effect of changes in the labor force may have been to increase the level and/or the variance of economic vulnerability in old age. Also relevant is the effect of changes in women's work. Between 1900 and 1940, married women's participation in paid employment increased significantly, from about 6% to over 15% (U.S. Bureau of the Census, 1975, p. 133). Since men often marry younger women, it seems likely that their retirement decisions, and their income in retirement, would be affected by their wives' labor force status. Yet virtually all empirical studies of retirement to date ignore this possibility (Parsons, 1991; Gratton, 1987, 1988).

If married women's entrance into wage employment increased their economic independence and their overall contributions to family welfare, it might have diminished their husbands' demands for both old age pensions and survivor's benefits. But many recent studies suggest that married women may have become more economically dependent after 1900, and especially after 1920, because of the constriction of opportunities for earning income within the home through industrial homework or sale of services to boarders (Folbre, forthcoming; Abel and Folbre, 1990). Also, the costs of children increased along with greater education requirements and restrictions on child labor. A concern for the economic circumstances of widows with children fueled the state Mothers' Pensions programs that developed alongside the state old age pensions. Similar concerns may well have shaped the demand for private pensions.

My final question addresses the relationship between internal labor markets and gender relations. Ransom, Sutch, and Williamson offer a number of reasons why workers accepted seniority-based pay schemes that effectively redistributed income from young to old. One possibility they fail to mention is that internal labor markets stabilized the gender division of labor. In a sense, older men and employers offered young men something in return for lower earnings—protection from the competition of young women. New personnel practices in many firms institutionalized occupational segregation, marriage bars, and lower pay for women (Goldin, 1990).

More attention needs to be devoted to the gender bias implicit in many early pension plans. Women workers were almost certainly less likely than their male counterparts to enjoy coverage, especially since it was often linked to long-term employment. Many women who pursued careers lucrative enough to offer benefits never married, and were disproportionately penalized by plans that offered greater benefits to married than to single workers. Female college professors complained of such inequities in 1918 (Hewes, 1918). The Social Security Act of 1935 provided survivors' benefits for spouses of male, but not female workers. Did private pension plans also discriminate in this way?

Ransom, Sutch, and Williamson have told a compelling story about the invention of company-provided pensions. To fully assess its importance, we need a broader narrative; we can hope to see this emerge from their further research.

## REFERENCES

Abel, M., & Folbre, N. (1990). Women's market participation in the late nineteenth century: A methodology for revising estimates. *Historical Methods, 23*(4), 167–176.

Achenbaum, W. A. (1978). *Old Age in the new land.* Baltimore: Johns Hopkins University Press.

Epstein, A. (1922). *Facing old age: A study of old age dependency in the U.S. and old age pensions.* New York: Alfred A. Knopf.

Fischer, D. H. (1978). *Growing old in America.* New York: Oxford University Press.

Folbre, N. (1992). Informal market work in Massachusetts, 1875–1920. *Social Science History.*

Goldin, C. (1990). *Understanding the gender gap: An economic history of American women.* New York: Oxford University Press.

Gratton, B. (1987). The labor force participation of older men: 1890–1950. *Journal of Social History, 20,* 689–710.

Gratton, B. (1988). Thc new welfare state: Social Security and retirement in 1950. *Social Science History, 12*(2), 171–196.

Haber, C., & Gratton, B. (1993). *Old age and the search for security: An American social history.* Bloomington: Indiana University Press.

Hewes, A. (1918). Dependents of college teachers. *Journal of the American Statistical Association, 16,* 502–511.

Lubove, R. (1968). *The struggle for Social Security, 1900–1935.* Cambridge: Harvard University Press.

Massachusetts Commission on Old Age Pensions. (1910). *Report of the Commission on Old Age Pensions, Annuities, and Insurance.* Boston: Wright and Potter Printing Company, 1910.

Parsons, D. O. (1984). The economics of intergenerational control. *Population and Development Review, 10,* 41–54.

Parsons, D. O. (1991). Male retirement behavior in the United States, 1930–1950. *The Journal of Economic History, 51*(3), 672–674.

Smith, D. S. (1979). Life course, norms and the family system of older Americans in 1900. *Journal of Family History, 4*(3), 285–298.

Social Security Board. (1937). *Social Security in America.* Washington, DC: U.S. Government Printing Office, 1937.

United States Bureau of the Census. (1975). *Historical statistics of the United States, colonial times to 1970.* Washington, DC: Government Printing Office, 1975.

# CHAPTER 2

# The Creation of Retirement

## Families, Individuals, and the Social Security Movement

**Brian Gratton**

The transforming consequences of Social Security in the lives of young and old Americans have inspired a variety of theoretical explanations for the rise of the welfare state. These theories, although approaching a very large number, hinge on a single turning point, the advent of an industrial society destructive to the familial and occupational status of older men and women. Scholars who blame the labor policies of corporate capital or its distorting effect on national welfare policy, begin their account in the late nineteenth century factory system, as do historians who think a virulent antagonism to old people sprang forth in American culture during this period. Others, convinced that the state and its experts governed the evolution of welfare, remark upon the conservative response of Social Security architects to the pauperization of the aged in an urban, wage-earning society (Achenbaum, 1978; Graebner, 1980; Orloff & Skocpol, 1984; Quadagno, 1984, 1987, 1988). These scholarly arguments echo the appeals of the first advocates of public pensions, who claimed that the dependency of the aged had risen to alarming levels in the industrial era. Pension advocate Abraham

Epstein (1922) concluded that the aged in industrial society were likely "to drag out their final days, physically exhausted, friendless and destitute, in the wretched confines of a poorhouse, or to receive some other degrading and humiliating form of pauper relief" (p. 1). Three-quarters of a century later, the impoverishment model still carries analysis before it. Engaging in the new sport of attacking generational inequities, Michael Hurd (1989) has criticized current welfare for excessive generosity to the affluent aged, but affirms that, "[d]uring most of history, to be old was to be poor" (p. 663).

This essay proposes a different model for understanding the origins of Social Security and the strength of the movement for public pensions. It maintains that the aged have always been more affluent than younger people; further, their economic well-being improved between 1890 and 1930, the core of the industrial era. Until the Social Security Act, however, the good fortune of older men and women depended in large part on a familistic, rather than individualistic economic strategy. This strategy led to considerable accumulation of wealth in the industrial period and the dependency of older persons was undoubtedly lower in the 1920s than at any previous time in American history. Although the origins of Social Security cannot reasonably be located in increases in poverty, family-based economic strategies created intergenerational conflicts which prompted all age groups to support public transfers to the elderly. The Depression offered a unique opportunity to achieve this highly popular goal. Social Security benefits met a strong cultural desideratum by allowing the old to retire and the young and old to set up independent, separate households.

## THE WEALTH OF THE AGED

Wealth measurements attest to the superior circumstances of older men throughout American history. Comparative wealth indices, displayed in Figure 2.1, show that the aged possessed considerably greater assets than the young in the colonial, mid-nineteenth, and twentieth centuries. Peaks in mean wealth were reached in late middle age, then declined slightly (Figure 2.1).[1] Using probate records from the 1770s, Alice Hanson Jones (1980) found that the wealth of men rose "up to a peak around age 60, or a plateau from about age 60 to 65 or even older. Thereafter, there is some dropping off in average wealth in later years" (p. 214). Examining eighteenth century evidence, Jeffrey Williamson and Peter Lindert (1980) discovered the same rule of reward to age in different colonies and states. They found a "remarkable consistency over time and across regions" in the relationship between age and wealth, eighteenth century results being "much like mid-nineteenth and twentieth-century patterns" (p. 26). Jackson Turner Main's

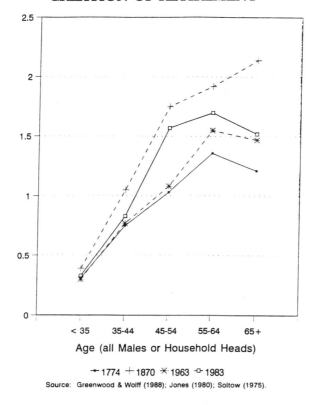

2.5

2

1.5

1

0.5

0

< 35    35-44    45-54    55-64    65+

Age (all Males or Household Heads)

 ⁻ 1774  + 1870  ✳ 1963  ⁻ロ⁻ 1983

Source: Greenwood & Wolff (1988); Jones (1980); Soltow (1975).

**Figure 2.1. Wealth relative to mean.**

(1985) study of seventeenth- and eighteenth-century Connecticut, which has the virtue of measuring consumption needs and standards of living in the period, finds that elderly men fared well in this agricultural economy; only a small proportion fell into poverty in their old age. These advantages extended to an important degree to married women and to widows well provided in estates; the difficulties of other older women, however, prove the importance of gender in determining economic well-being in old age (Haber & Gratton, 1993). Despite the elderly's relative affluence, mean values disguise a highly skewed allocation of slim resources. In Jones's data from decedents in New England in 1774, the mean net worth of men in their 70s was nearly twice that of men of all ages, but ranged from 10 times the average to a negative value. Most older men had relatively little wealth, and even among the more affluent, accumulation was modest by modern standards. Colonial Americans continued to be quite poor in their old age. As Main (1985) notes, "luxury, in Connecticut, rarely existed regardless of age" (p. 142).

Census records from 1850–1870 confirm the persistent, positive relationship between age and wealth, its uneven distribution in the population, and the relative poverty of all Americans prior to the industrial era. Lee Soltow (1975) concludes that the "average individual experienced handsome gains in real wealth as he progressed through life," during the mid-nineteenth century (p. 180). Possession of some real estate or personal assets rose from near 0% among 20-year-old men, to 80% of men in their 50s, then fell slightly after age 60. The value of estates also increased across the lifespan. In 1850, men 70 to 99 held real estate with a mean value of $2439, ten times the value of the estates of men 20 to 29. In 1870, the mean wealth of men 65 and over exceeded that of any other age group. Wealth accumulation in preceding eras also led to generous bequests, hence to greater levels of wealth in the middle and old age of succeeding generations. High mean wealth again obscured general poverty. About 30% of white men 65 and over owned less than $100 in assets, and 70% less than $750. Still greater extremes of poverty characterized certain regions and classes. Per capita wealth in the mid-nineteenth century in the South remained less than half that reported in non-Southern states in 1880, and blacks commanded much less than this share (Atack & Bateman, 1987). Thus, while age led to greater wealth, for the majority the sum total remained insignificant.

As the next section will demonstrate, industrialization did not disturb the accumulation of wealth among the aged, but, instead, raised the real value of their assets and broadened the range of the population likely to possess considerable savings. In very recent decades, the life-cycle pattern mimics pre-industrial examples. Figure 2.1, which compares wealth-holding at specific ages against an overall mean, indicates that wealth in 1963 and 1983 follows eighteenth- and nineteenth-century age patterns, although at considerably greater real value. In 1983, households headed by persons 65 and over held mean assets of $227,464, while those under age 65, had $133,820. Because older households tend to be smaller, elderly individuals possess still greater resources. Even after exclusion of the present value of pensions and certain nonliquid assets, in 1983 "the elderly were more than twice as rich in terms of individual wealth as the average individual" in the United States (Greenwood & Wolff, 1988, p. 137).

Inequality of distribution still holds within the aged population. In 1983, the top 5% of elderly households owned more than half of its cohort's wealth (a level of inequality characteristic of other age groups as well). As in other historical eras, a rather large number of elderly women and aged members of minority groups continue to be impoverished. Nonetheless, median wealth in aged households reached $64,000, versus the median for all households of about $40,000 (Greenwood & Wolff, 1988). These sums do not include the present value of the elderly's Social Security and private pension benefits (i.e., the wealth necessary for annuities equal to such benefits). Given the improvement in pension benefits during the last four decades, the post-World War II aged have undoubtedly enhanced their advantage over the young in possession of assets. The positive relationship between age and wealth stands out, then, as a constant characteristic in American history, despite radical changes in the economy and in governmental policy.

## THE INDUSTRIAL ERA

Wealth is different than income—it's cooled off, less liquid, sometimes frozen. Most assessments of the elderly's economic well-being, especially those which find it inferior, focus on the streams of income available to retired men and women. At present, Social Security and private pension benefits rarely replace earnings fully, and the elderly, however wealthy, receive much lower regular income after they retire. Although little is known about the incomes of older persons in the eighteenth and nineteenth centuries, the conventional impoverishment model assumes that the industrial period led to steep declines in the earnings of aging workers. Was the income of older persons deficient before Social Security?

Data from two cost-of-living surveys in the industrial era suggest the answer is yes. In 1889–1890, the Bureau of Labor surveyed more than 6000 working-class families in nine major industries in the United States. In 1917–1919, the Bureau of Labor Statistics pursued a similar, but more extensive investigation of more than 12,000 households in 92 urban centers. Neither study constituted a random sample of the elderly population; each focused on intact, male-headed families, and the 1917–1919 survey, in particular, underrepresented older populations.[2] But as large detailed samples of industrial populations, they provide an unusual and rich source of evidence on the economic conditions of blue-collar workers of various ages.

Figure 2.2 displays age-earnings profiles for male household heads in each survey, and reveals the inferior income of older workers, a pattern which undoubtedly influenced popular perception of the elderly in industrial society. In both 1889–1890 and 1917–1919, aging household heads saw take-home pay slip below that of very youthful men. Peaks in earnings occurred very early in the life-cycle of these synthetic cohorts, unlike cross-sectional profiles in the present. A synthetic cohort proxies actual career experience by comparing persons of different ages at a single point in time, that is, in cross-sectional data. In contemporary synthetic cohorts, earnings increase

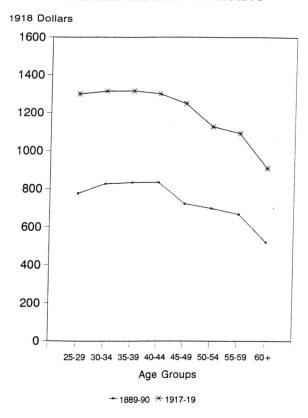

1918 Dollars

Age Groups

← 1889-90  ✳ 1917-19

**Figure 2.2. Median male earnings.**

until men reach their mid-40s and then remain relatively stable until a customary retirement age (Ruggles & Ruggles, 1977). In the industrial era,
however, wage-earners could predict that after age 35 their earnings would
be lower than those of younger men. The expected deficiency influenced
their forecasting about savings, work, and retirement, probably in a conservative way (Owen, 1986). Commentators at the time, as well as more
recent scholars, lament these wage profiles as signs of the parlous circumstances of older workers (Barkin, 1933; Ransom & Sutch, 1986, 1990).

This judgment would be premature on three grounds. First, older blue-
collar workers displayed marked improvement in real income between 1889–
1890 and 1917–1919. In 1917–1919, men 60 and over had 75% greater real
earnings than in the nineteenth-century survey ($910 to $521 in 1918 dol-

lars), compared to an increase of 67% for all men. Second, the synthetic life-cycle presented in cross-sectional data falsely conveys the actual experience of workers across their careers (Owen, 1986). Contemporary longitudinal data on earnings reveal that workers reach peak earnings years later than synthetic cohorts indicate. It cannot readily be determined if or how much the lower wages of older men in the industrial era reflected life-cycle effects, that is, declining productivity or the desire for more leisure in old age (i.e., true declines from a peak), and how much was due to cohort effects, such that older workers' wages had not fallen, but younger men had entered more lucrative occupations. The strong secular growth in the period made cohort effects very powerful; the youngest age group in 1917–1919 earned more than the peak group in 1889–1890. Indeed, it lifted all boats: Men 60 and over earned more in 1917–1919 than their age cohort had in 1889–1890, at 30 to 34 years of age, rising from $828 to $910 per year. The result was that older men knew two truths: They had experienced impressive gains in real income, perhaps across the entire life-cycle, but they still fell behind younger men, who were meeting new standards of living which every family sought to enjoy.

## THE FAMILY ECONOMY

The third error in reading age-earnings profiles too darkly lies in the assumption that men and women made judgments about their condition based on individual earnings. Blue-collar workers in the industrial era relied on a family-based economic strategy; decisions were played out in these settings, rather than in the individualistic terms common to research on work and retirement. Working-class populations often resorted to the collective effort of family members to pursue success, subordinating individual desires to the needs of the family. Family members' wages flowed into the "family fund," and family expenditures out of it (U.S. Bureau of Labor Statistics, 1924, p. 1). The cost-of-living surveys demonstrate the normality of this conception; they were designed to study the family as an economic unit, each describing family income and expenditure in rather numbing detail. The notion that "household members pool and share their economic resources" constitutes an integral part of economic analysis today (Sorensen & McLanahan, 1989, p. 7; Palmer, Smeeding, & Jencks, 1988). A persuasive scholarship attests to the prevalence of family strategies in the industrial era. John Bodnar (1982, 1985) has shown that industrialization did not snuff out the family collective. Bodnar's work describes the familistic *mentalité* in the immigrant working class populations of the early twentieth century. Mark Stern's (1987) study of late nineteenth-century Erie County,

New York, confirms Bodnar's findings, as has Ewa Morawska's (1985) examination of ethnic groups in Pennslyvania at the turn of the century.

The success of a familistic approach depended on tapping children's wages. The maturing and "useful child" (Zelizer, 1985, p. 58) fit the needs of the families of Erie County, for whom "the relative cheapness of raising children and their early entry into productive labor [made] them a natural asset" (Stern, 1987, p. 15). Bodnar's (1982) oral histories recall parents "eager to increase the income of their household" by encouraging children to work, and children proving their "deep obligation" to the family by "turning their wages over to their parents in an almost ritualistic manner" (pp. 167, 176). The narrative history offers abundant testimony about the pressure placed on working-class children to work, even at great personal cost. Stacia Treski recalled that her "'parents wanted fifteen dollars a month from me. . . . They wanted it every month'" (Bodnar, 1982, p. 22). It was expected that "'When you work . . . you used to bring your pay home and give it to your parents. And whatever they feel they want to give you, they decide'" (Bodnar, 1985, p. 73).[3]

The difference between an individualistic and family accounting appears in Figure 2.3. Total income curves differ markedly from those of personal earnings. Household income from all sources rose across the life course and peaked when the head was in his 50s, twenty years after his own acme. Male age-earnings profiles warned working-class families that the household head's earnings would be relatively low in middle-age, a period of high consumption demands in the family. To meet the expected shortfall, households could rely on children's wages, and to a lesser degree, other sources. In households headed by young men, more than 90% of the family's total income came from their earnings. Older men provided a much smaller percentage of the total. In 1889–1890, men 40 to 44 contributed 75%, children 18%, and the remainder came from "other" sources. Men 60 and over earned less than half of family income; children contributed one-third of the total income, and "other" sources provided nearly a fifth.

Children's earnings had become substantially less important in the 1917–1919 survey, one very obvious product of income advances across the industrial era. Rising real income meant that all but the oldest households had approached the ideal state in which the *paterfamilias* earned a "family wage," sufficient to support children in school and wife at home (Rothbart, 1989). In the later survey, men aged 40 to 44 earned 87% of the total, and children contributed only 5%. In the oldest households, however, children still provided nearly 30% of total income. Alternative sources, such as rent, also figured importantly in the oldest households' budgets in this period, making up 10% of the total.

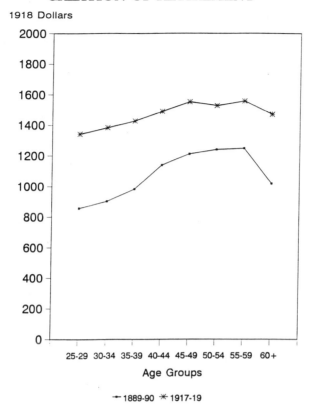

**Figure 2.3. Median household income.**

Children's wages and other sources of income had two important functions in the working-class family economy. First, they met the greater
demands for consumption in maturing families. Household expenditure rose
across the life course of the household head until he was about 50 years of
age. Although his own earnings would never have sufficed, this was also the
moment when total income reached its highest level. The second function
of alternative income was to guarantee surpluses at the end of the year. In
fact, children's wages and other sources increased so much that the amount
of surplus, or savings, generated each year tended to rise during the life
course. Figure 2.4 displays median surpluses for each survey.[4] Surpluses
reached substantial levels in the household head's middle age, and were
maintained into his 60s. Between the nineteenth and twentieth centuries
surpluses also rose in real value. In households headed by men 60 and over,
annual median surpluses had increased from $53 to $89, and mean savings

1918 Dollars

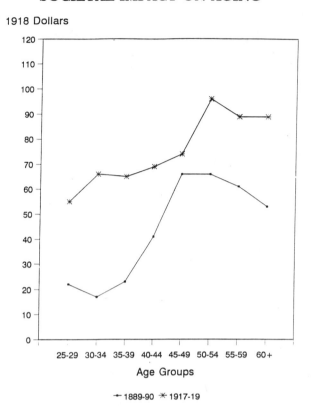

Figure 2.4. Median surplus.

from $134 to $152. In both surveys, the oldest households had lower than average proportions reporting deficits.

Children's wages were instrumental to generating surpluses, but it is debatable whether working sons or daughters were "exploited." Even if we ignore the long stream of consumption costs for children before they reached working age, most older men and women would have profited by having no offspring. If they had only their own expenditure needs to meet, a couple would generally have achieved equal or greater surpluses using the head's wages alone. Nonetheless, if a family included any children, their wages were essential to maintaining both high consumption levels and savings. This meant that families often endured periods of privation when children were young, but looked forward to a dramatic shift. When sons and daughters reached working age, "families changed their economic status radically with the addition of children's earnings" (Ware, 1935, p. 66).

Modest annual surpluses promised considerable accrual of assets in the last stage of the life course. A simple summation of median savings between age 25 and 65 in 1889–1890 yielded assets of $1745, *sans* interest. The same calculation in 1917–1919 produced $3015. Mean surpluses yielded about $5000 in each survey. A man aged 33 in 1889, and 63 in 1919, had accumulated at least $5000 by 1919 if he saved at the mean level and stuffed the surplus under the mattress. These calculations ignore investment returns or interest, as well as the positive impact of inheritance for families fortunate enough to receive bequests. Although older women faced much more hazardous futures, the spread of community property statutes strengthened the rights of widows to these resources built up in the marriage, and women might employ the same familistic strategies with success after a husband's death (DeVault, 1990; Carter, 1988; Grigg, 1989; Shammas, Salmon, & Dahlin, 1987). Thus, by the early twentieth century, working-class couples who relied on family strategies and did not suffer severe misfortune could expect to accrue between $2500 and $5000 in assets by the time the head of household reached his mid-60s.

The wealth reported for older people in industrial states in the mid-1920s corresponds well with the levels inferred from cost-of-living studies. Two studies in that decade offer a convenient test of accrual. Departing from the tradition of surveying the impoverished, the Massachusetts Commission on Pensions (1925, p. 9) conducted "a representative sample of the entire non-dependent population" of the state, excluding those institutionalized (4.4%), those receiving charity (3.2%), and military or civil pensioners (8%). Interviewing 17,000 persons 65 and over, the Commissioners found that 41% possessed assets worth $5000 or more ($4245 in 1918 dollars). Another 20% owned property and other items valued between $1000 and $4999. In 1926–1927, the National Civic Federation (1928) employed the same research director and similar methods to survey 15,000 persons 65 and over in urban areas of the Northeast. Over 40% reported wealth of $5000 or more, and 19% reported $1000 to $4999, almost exactly equal to Massachusetts' results.[5] Since assets tend to be underreported (Palmer, Smeeding, & Jencks, 1988), these represent conservative estimates of the level and range of wealth-holding in the older population, and they confirm the accumulation opportunities visible in the cost-of-living surveys.

They also mark a dramatic improvement in the economic fortunes of the aged during the industrial era. Using constant 1918 dollars, only 10% of males 65 and over in 1870 had wealth equal to $2500, the lower boundary of expected accumulation in 1917–1919 (Soltow, 1975, Chart 4.3). Two-thirds of older men in the mid-nineteenth century had estates valued at less than $1000. In the 1920s surveys, only one-third had less than $1000 in assets (Massachusetts Commission on Pensions, 1925, Table 8; National Civic Federation, 1928, Table 5). The $5000 held by at least 40% of the aged in the 1920s surveys could provide a ten-year annuity of $616, meeting an elderly couple's average annual expenditure in the 1917–1919 survey, a level of consumption 40% higher than that for the elderly in 1889–1890. Not only had a large proportion of the aged established considerable savings, but the real standard of living, which expected assets could provide, had been materially raised from that available in the nineteenth century.[6]

These results imply that impoverishment and dependency had declined. Data in the 1920s surveys—which detailed both wealth and current income—indicate that two-thirds of the aged enjoyed good economic circumstances. Combining earnings and potential income from wealth, half the elderly had income that equaled or exceeded $1300, the average yearly earnings for employees in 1926 (U.S. Bureau of the Census, 1975). Another 15% had a combined income between $600 and $1000, equal to or exceeding the expenditure costs for an elderly couple in the 1917–1919 survey. The remaining third split into two approximately equal parts, one at the verge of dependency, the other already dependent on family or charity. Aging jobseekers, widows, single women, and others not enmeshed in familial systems, suffered in the industrial era (Haber & Gratton, 1993). However, such persons probably faced even worse circumstances in previous eras, and poverty among the elderly had diminished.

Taken together, the cost-of-living data and the 1920s surveys make high estimates of old-age dependency extremely unlikely. The primary effect of economic growth should have been to lower the probability of dependency, rather than raising it, and especially because the family economy provided considerable security for older men and women, even when the earnings of older workers fell behind those of the young. However, for every advantage in the family economy, there existed an equal and opposite disadvantage, and hence the power of the movement for Social Security.

## INTERGENERATIONAL CONFLICT AND THE MOVEMENT FOR SOCIAL SECURITY

Since the movement for public pensions began in the same industrial era in which the economic circumstances of older persons improved, impoverishment cannot explain its history. Indeed, in the midst of the nineteenth century, Civil War pensions demonstrated the consistent popularity of state programs for the elderly. Although poverty declined in the ensuing industrial era, a movement for state-financed pensions for all workers gained considerable strength in the highly conservative 1920s (Lubove, 1968). The political strength of this movement lay originally in the working class (Anglim & Gratton, 1987). Strongly supported by ethnic politicians and by the Catholic hierarchy (shepherds of the same working-class constituencies), trade union associations lobbied for noncontributory pensions to be given as a matter of right to "veterans of labor." Their legislation was designed, not for paupers, but for aging workers who could then leave the labor force. Recipients were to be allowed to retain their homes and other personal property, and authorities could not compel children to support aging parents. During the 1920s, politicians such as Governor Franklin Delano Roosevelt discovered that such proposals appealed to a wide spectrum of voters (Haber & Gratton, 1993, Chap. 5). By 1930, 12 states—including New York, Massachusetts, and California—had enacted old age pension legislation. Opposed by business interests and severely restricted in scope, the state old age pension laws of the pre-Depression era nonetheless prefigured Social Security, and demonstrated the growing enthusiasm for public sector transfers to the aged, even in prosperous times.

The Depression strongly encouraged the pension movement and ushered in the Social Security Act, but cannot explain the subsequent history of expansion and liberalization of benefits. More and more generous public transfers to the aged continued after the passage of the initial legislation, well into the era of prosperity after the Second World War. In this process the actual level of need among the elderly was rarely, if ever, measured accurately, because need never constituted the primary motivation behind legislation—political ends were always paramount.[7] The politics of old age did not depend on the small percentage of Americans 65 and over. It sprang from the desires of a broader constituency, that is, Americans of every age, to escape the demands imposed by family economic strategies. Although family strategies ensured both high consumption and the accumulation of savings for old age, it had two negative features. First, it retarded full retirement for older men; second, it provoked considerable intergenerational friction.

Although the labor force activity of older men fell between the agricultural era and the industrial period, recent research has found relatively constant work activity among older men between 1900 and 1930 (Gratton, 1986; Ransom & Sutch, 1986).[8] These flat participation rates—at about 55 to 60% of men aged 65 and over—are curious because of evidence of increasing wealth, somewhat greater private pension coverage, and the traditional argument that older workers competed poorly in the industrial era. But, without a guaranteed retirement income, higher levels of wealth allowed only the most affluent men to leave work permanently, that is, to retire. Even those with considerable savings faced serious uncertainties about the long-term value of assets, expenses in retirement, and longevity. As a result, relatively few severed themselves entirely from the working life. Many men worked at their regular occupations until death, or gradually reduced work effort. Others, facing labor markets hostile to older workers, found only temporary work. Intermittent labor force activity followed the logic of the family economy, in which workers with sufficient wealth and dutiful children could reduce the amount of work they did, or leave the labor force for a time, especially if sick or less physically able. Movement in and out of the labor force characterized older male workers as late as the 1940s (Tuma & Sandefur, 1988). On the whole, it appears that only the wealthiest, the sickest, or the few guaranteed regular income could assume that they had left work forever. At the turn of the century, even men who had not worked in a year did not declare themselves to be retired (Rotondo, 1991).

Older men and women also continued to press their children to contribute to the family fund, repaying in part the years of investment which parents could rightly claim they had made, and preserving or raising the level of savings the family had accumulated, the hedge against older males's low wages, unemployment, or illness. This pressure for a collective effort also sheds light on the surprising increase in the proportion of complex households in the late nineteenth and early twentieth centuries, a phenomenon well described by Steven Ruggles (1987). ("Complex" denotes households extended to three generations, those which include siblings, cousins, or fictive kin of the head, and especially those in which adult children still reside.) Two factors promoted more complex household arrangements. First, declines in child mortality, female mortality, and age at marriage led to richer demographic possibilities. It became more likely that adult children and aged parents would live long enough to form complex households. In the pre-industrial era, these possibilities had been extremely limited. Second, as the cost-of-living studies suggest, complex family arrangements came to serve critical functions for the expanding working class. In late nineteenth-century Massachusetts, urban and industrial growth strengthened, rather than weakened, ties among generations (Chudacoff & Hareven, 1977). In Salem, Lawrence, and Lynn, Massachusetts in 1880, a greater percentage of the elderly headed households inhabited by adult children than had their counterparts in 1860. Moreover, a higher proportion of urban elders lived with their children than did their rural peers: 64% of men and 61% of women aged 55 and over lived with children; in non-urban areas of Essex County the corresponding rates were 47% and 35%. In early twentieth-century New York state, the urban elderly were more likely than the rural aged to reside with an adult child (Weiler, 1988). In the 1920s, 40% of the state's rural elderly lived with children in their homes; in the cities, 60% resided with offspring.

In addition to its economic role, complex households met an important cultural norm in American society: the duty to sacrifice oneself for one's family. In the mid-nineteenth century, middle-class sentiment proclaimed the family as the foundation of all social order, responsible for the development of an individual's personality, values, and character. The care of the dependent relative, and especially the widowed mother, was a moral obligation that went beyond economic considerations, and the middle class often had the economic wherewithal to meet this obligation (Deglar, 1980; Ryan, 1981). In the 1900 Census, the middle classes appeared to have been more likely than poorer families to provide housing to aid relatives. While 68% of all urban middle-class individuals age 55 and older resided with at least one offspring, among the urban working class, the proportion was 61% (Smith, 1979, 1982, 1986).

By the second decade of the twentieth century this sentiment's force weakened. Fewer middle-class families accommodated complex households. In 1880, 41% of all families with servants in Erie County, New York, lived with extended kin; in 1915, the proportion was only 20% (Ruggles, 1987). The increasing prevalence of nuclear families reflected Americans' attention to a competing familistic ideal, as well as the means to sustain it; still greater wealth now allowed middle-class families to realize a cultural norm favoring separate dwellings for different generations. Prosperous elderly individuals could afford to live independently, without depending on their children's wages or assistance. Their children could also afford to obtain housing and reside by themselves.

Although sanctioned in some respects in middle-class culture in the nineteenth century, the ideal of separation received more and more prominence in popular media and advice literature as the middle class grew prosperous enough to honor it (Haber & Gratton, 1993, Chaps. 1 & 6). In the twentieth century, this preference began to find expression as a "modern" cultural prescription. The small private household was favored by social critics and advocates of proper family behavior. They argued that children who stayed in aging parents' households interrupted their education and missed their own opportunities in life. Middle-aged adults were forced to make irreconcilable economic judgments over the allocation of valued resources. In supporting an aged mother, they robbed the young; in providing for their children, they were dismissing the long-standing obligations they owed to their elders.

According to critics, members of complex families seemed to be faced with an insurmountable predicament: either they nurtured children's growth and education or they saved older members from dependency. "Because of the necessity of supporting the aged," wrote the editors of *The Worker in Industrial Society* in 1923, "the children are frequently doomed to under-nourishment; and to a life in the midst of crowded and unsanitary quarters; to leave school early in life and in their turn to join the ranks of the unskilled" (Douglas, Hitchcock, & Atkins, 1923, p. 465). Politicians picked up the appeal of this argument. According to David I. Walsh (1927), Senator from Massachusetts, the family economy created a vicious cycle of impoverishment: "Many married sons and daughters, in order to spare their aged parents the disgrace and bitterness of pauperism, assume burdens which cannot be borne except at the cost of depriving their own children of the rights of childhood and the opportunities of success, and of dooming themselves in turn to an old age of helpless dependence" (p. 224). Given such fears, family experts and welfare advocates came to view the family economy and its non-nuclear households with increasing hostility. Only the poor and the immigrant, they argued, would choose to live in such households; better families would follow the model of independent residences.

Even as the middle class rejected complex households, increasing proportions of the working class had turned to them. As we have seen, working-class parents relied upon the wages of the young, and still believed that "a child ought to sacrifice his own interest or ambition to promote the welfare of the family" (Ware, n.d., n.p.). As the average income levels of the working class rose to the standards that the middle class had achieved in the nineteenth century, more workers secured wealth sufficient to provide housing and support for relatives, in exchange for assistance. The "luxury" of kinship co-residence, once only available to the middle class and skilled workers, now became a pattern among laborers. Moreover, these practices raised the financial well-being of the group. In 1880, in Erie County, New York, for instance, the inclusion of extended family among the unskilled generally corresponded with lower family wealth (Ruggles, 1987). By 1915, this loss of average income was no longer the case. The extended family, in fact, was linked to an improvement in economic status.

For working-class families, complex households continued to have a clear economic purpose, one hard to abandon. Nonetheless, it appears that most blue-collar families would have preferred to ease intrafamilial pressure. Between 1889–1890 and 1917–1919, the average number of children working in households headed by men 40 and over fell from 1.2 to .7. Only in the oldest households in the twentieth-century survey did reliance on children's wages come close to the nineteenth-century levels. Insofar as the household head's earnings would allow, families resisted forcing children to interrupt schooling for work. During the prosperous 1920s it seems likely that reliance on children would have continued to fall, as rising wages made it possible to reduce the conflicts inherent to intrafamilial exchange.

Co-residency and sharing of wages provided a route to life-cycle security, but at great cost. Within complex households the lines of authority often led to conflict and dissension. Although sanctioned by a strong normative principle of familial duty, the pressure on other family members to contribute their wages to the family fund engendered considerable friction. These conflicts manifested themselves in working-class narratives. Bodnar's (1982) summary of oral histories notes the presence of "intergenerational friction" and "tension and discord" (pp. 175–76). Young women "eagerly sought a marriage partner [*sic*] in order to escape their families of origin and the employment burdens they had endured as young people" (p. 176). Loss of educational opportunities for the young and pooling of funds caused discord within the family unit, especially because surpluses tended to become part of the assets of the aging couple (Gabaccia, 1988; Hall et al., 1988; Hareven, 1982).

Isolated middle-class households also faced problems, these presented by declines in fertility. School laws, occupational requirements and restrictions, and a new view of children as precious, rather than as potential assets, made them more expensive to raise, encouraging couples to limit offspring. Fewer siblings increased the probability that a child would bear prime responsibility for caring for, or housing, an aging parent. The aged could not select the most congenial environment, nor could the children decide which of many siblings would remain in the household or provide primary care for the old. Many more adult daughters, the most likely descendants to care for old parents, faced difficult and demanding decisions (Gratton, 1986; Kobrin, 1976; Rubinow, 1930; Treas, 1977). The antagonisms created by sharing households found expression in the magazine articles of the early twentieth century, and in the recollections of children who lived in these intergenerational homes. Conflict replaced "harmony," and the "intrusion" of old parents threatened to lead to "divorce, and certainly [to] marital unhappiness and problems in children" (Anon., 1931, pp. 712–18; Gratton, 1986; Heaton & Hoppe, 1987).

The Depression of the 1930s dramatically exposed the utility and disutility of the family economy. The dramatic rise in unemployment and the long duration of the depression magnified the internal pressures for American families of every class. Older men and women faced the failure of their businesses, or of the firms they worked for, or of the insurance companies and pension funds upon which they depended. The best-conceived arrangements for security in old age came apart in the stock market crash and subsequent depression. The loss of nine million families' life savings in bank failures was a severe blow for the middle-class elderly in particular. Among working-class Americans and farmers, on the other hand, real estate had often served as the only important asset. These assets became decidedly illiquid in the fall of values accompanying the depression. Others lost even this defense against impoverishment. Urban dwellers, unable to pay their debts, had to forfeit their homes. By 1934, more than half of all homeowners in Indianapolis, Indiana and Birmingham, Alabama, had defaulted on their loans (Mintz & Kellogg, 1988). In rural areas, thousands of farmers who could not pay mortgages, or even taxes, experienced the repossession and auction of family farms.

Families responded in the traditional fashion to this economic disaster: Children quit school to find work; the elderly who had been independent found themselves again relying on their children and other relatives to underwrite family income. These difficult choices reveal themselves dramatically in data for family economies. Between 1889 and 1917 the percentage of total family income accounted for by older male heads' wages had risen; that drawn from children's wages had diminished, indicating more opportunity for schooling or other choices. But, in the 1930s this trend was reversed; families found themselves falling back toward nineteenth-century standards. As an example, in households headed by men 60 to 64, the proportion of family earnings contributed by the head rose from 63% to 67% between 1889 and 1917, then fell back to 64% in 1939 (Gratton & Ito, 1991).

Children stayed home rather than setting up their own households. In Massachusetts in 1940, over half of all males and females aged 20 to 29 resided as "children" in the homes of their parents, a figure substantially higher than nineteenth-century rates or those obtained ten years later, in 1950 (Gratton, 1986). In many cities families "doubled up" to cut the cost of expenses, relinquishing again the ideal of separate households they had so recently achieved (Cohen, 1990). Ruby and Elton Cude of San Antonio, Texas illustrated well the plight of the suddenly impoverished middle class (Blackwelder, 1984). From 1932 to 1936 the Cudes and their two young children struggled to live independently in their own home. By 1936, however, the financial burdens had became too great, and they were forced to return to her parents' residence. The house sheltered not only Ruby's parents but her two younger sisters, an unemployed uncle from Mississippi, another uncle with his wife and two children, and a boarder. Having experienced a gradual easing of pressures on the family, Americans resented the reimposition of burdens. As the Republican party was to learn, albeit slowly, the middle class had joined the working class in "the overwhelming judgment of the American people" that all families deserved protection from the insecurities of the marketplace (Holtzman, 1963; Republican Program Committee, 1939).

## SOCIAL SECURITY: MASS RETIREMENT, ISOLATED HOUSEHOLDS

Social Security directly addressed the broad desire for residential autonomy, and led to mass retirement. More efficient risk sharing in national social insurance had advantages over family security systems, and its neutral, extra-familial process reduced tension between kin over fairness. Guaranteed monthly checks, even at levels which appear low, eased the calculation of how much savings were necessary to support old age. Almost immediately the labor force participation of aged men began to drop, due principally to benefits from Old Age Assistance (OAA), Title I in the Social Security Act. In 1935 the Roosevelt administration's Social Security program rode to victory on this title. Martha Derthick (1979) argues that "in 1935 congressmen would probably have chosen OAA grants and OAA grants only. . . . But for being linked to this highly acceptable program, old age insurance would surely have been unacceptable to the legislature" (p. 220).

A noncontributory relief program, OAA followed the model proposed by working-class groups in the 1920s and Townsendites in the 1930s, although at first much less generously than they had hoped. Even before the Social Security Act, the popularity of what were called "flat" pensions (i.e., not based on contributions) was manifest. Fifteen states passed statutes between 1929 and 1933, and in a more generous fashion than in earlier laws. The number of older persons receiving benefits expanded rapidly before national programs were in place. After the passage of Social Security legislation, the Federal government gave matching grants for "needy" persons 65 and over who withdrew from work, but left it to the states to define need. Many states found it expedient to give OAA to very large proportions of the elderly and to provide large benefits. Social Security analysts noticed that in certain states "the influence of strong pension movements has been important in developing old-age assistance programs with assistance and eligibility standards broader and more liberal" than elsewhere (Gratton, 1988; *Social Security Bulletin*, December 1949, March 1951, p. 15).

To view OAA as need-based poor relief would do violence to the truth. In states with a "pension philosophy," the popularity of flat grants—and their consequent appeal to politicians—led to very liberal eligibility criteria, including exclusion of certain assets and repudiation of relatives' responsibility for aged family members (Gagliardo, 1949, p. 67). Many states financed high grants, and, in some, pensions were issued to two-thirds of persons 65 and over, ridiculing the idea that need was the criterion for OAA. As the aging pension advocate Abraham Epstein (1939) remarked to William Haber, OAA was "definitely political in texture . . . and the number of aged recipients in those states does not at all represent the actual extent of need" (n.p.). From 1936 to 1950, OAA provided benefits to more persons than OAI and its average grant was substantially higher than that available in the insurance program. At the end of the decade, combined Federal and state expenditure for OAA was $1.6 billion, versus about .7 billion in transfer payments for Old Age Insurance (OAI). OAA accounted for 62% of Federal, state, and local expenditure on public assistance (Derthick, 1979; Gratton, 1988). Despite a decade of prosperity and the presence of OAI, OAA rolls began to increase in the late 1940s. Social Security administrators and other government officials grew alarmed over the increasing liberality of state eligibility regulations, including relaxation of lien laws and relatives' responsibilities (Social Security Bulletin, December 1949, July 1950, November 1951; Burns, nd).

By 1950, OAA supported nearly 25% of the older population (twice the percentage on OAI). The average replacement rate across all the states was about 20% of an industrial worker's income. But spouses could also receive grants, and states differed sharply in generosity; in some states nearly half of median family income could be replaced. The political appeal of OAA led to Federal legislation which raised benefits more rapidly than the cost of living, and made it attractive to states to provide grants. Between 1940 and 1950 the average OAA benefit increased in real value, while the real value of OAI declined (Gratton, 1988; Social Security Bulletin, October 1948, March 1951, November 1951, January 1952, September 1952.)

Given liberal rules on property and assets, OAA offered an alternative to work for many older people; the consequences can be readily observed in the labor market decisions of older men. The labor force participation rate (LFPR) of men 65 and over fell much more rapidly after 1930 than before, declining 20% in two decades. While most economists argue that Social Security benefits were not large enough before the 1950s to induce retirement, their analyses ignore the OAA program (Clark, Kreps, & Spengler, 1978; Danziger, Haveman, & Plotnick, 1981; Tuma & Sandefur, 1988).

In fact, OAA rewrote the rules for labor force decision-making in old age. The labor force activity of men 65 and over at the state level displays a striking change after 1930, a shift directly connected to Social Security, and to OAA in particular. In 1890 and 1930 a variety of ethnic, racial, and economic specifications explain differences among states in the aggregate labor force participation rates of men 65 and over, as well as differences in the propensity of individual older men to remain in the labor force (Gratton, 1987; Whaples, 1989). By 1950 a new determinant dominated labor force decisions. In states where Social Security benefits were high, fewer older men worked. The strongest variable in explaining decline in the elderly's labor force activity between 1930 and 1950 was the ratio of OAA payments to median income. Where assistance payments came closest to replacing income, the labor force activity of older men fell rapidly (Gratton, 1987). These results, based on aggregate data, are confirmed when evidence for individuals is examined. In a sample of older men from the 1950 United States Census, those who lived in states in which OAA benefits compared favorably to income had a much lower probability of being in the labor force (Gratton, 1988).[9]

The replacement ratio of OAA to income emerged as the dominant new element in labor force decision-making. Men were less likely to be in the labor force if they lived in states where OAA benefits compared favorably to income. Workers previously hesitant to retire and to depend on savings could choose to leave the labor force, confident of a regular income. In 1930, 54% of men 65 and over were in the labor force; by 1950, about 42%. During its initial years, Social Security undoubtedly had its greatest impact on the aged in marginal jobs or looking for work. Expansion and liberalization of the OAI program after 1950, however, led to broader inducements to retire, even among healthy workers. Since private pensions became more common during the same period (covering more than half of all workers), retirement appeared as an attractive option, even among more secure and advantaged older employees (Bowen & Finnegan, 1969; Quadagno, 1988; Barfield & Morgan, 1969; U.S. Bureau of the Census, 1988).

In their increasingly generous provision, Social Security benefits had another striking consequence, permitting most Americans to achieve what social gerontologists call "intimacy at a distance" (Rosenmayr & Kockeis, 1963). Favored by the middle class in the twentieth century, the independent isolated household now came within the grasp of all but the poorest Americans. After the Second World War, rising real incomes and higher Social Security benefits released many from the prerequisites of the family economy, which had demanded continued coresidence with children. In the 1950s Social Security recipients began to establish a pattern of separate residences (Schorr, 1958). Even the working class could retire and live alone or with only a spouse, secure that a regular income would be received.

The consequent change in typical household structure was profound. Since the 1940s, the trend toward greater complexity has been reversed and replaced by the rise of the independent autonomous household. In Massachusetts, the percentage of persons 20 to 29 who lived as "children," fell from 52% to 38% between 1940 and 1950, and for the nation, the rate fell 10% from 1940 levels. During this first decade of full Social Security benefits, a movement to small independent units characterized all Americans. Decline in the mean size of households and families exceeded 10% for all age and gender groups. Changes for older women can be attributed largely to important shifts in the living arrangements of widows, and especially in the increase in the proportion who live alone in their own residences, or in small boarding and lodging houses. The percentage of these "primary individuals" among non-widowed older women actually declined between 1940 and 1950, while it increased by 18% for widows (Gratton, 1986; U.S. Bureau of the Census, 1983, 1984).

Still more dramatic change since 1950 means that, among women, the solitary household has replaced dependent status in the homes of children. The proportion of women who lived as mother to the household head fell from 22% in the late nineteenth century, to 14% in 1950, and to 4% in 1980 (Kobrin, 1976; Mindel, 1979; Smith, 1982). In 1900, more than 60% of all persons aged 65 and older resided with their children, as household heads or as dependents. By 1962, the proportion of the old that lived with their children had dropped to 25% and by 1975 to only 14% (Haber & Gratton, in press, Chap. 2; Smith, 1982). Whereas less than 10% of the elderly lived alone in 1900, more than 40% of women and 15% of men now do so. The trend to independent households has affected men, but the most significant transformation has obviously occurred in the residence pattern of widowed and single women. In 1940, 58% of elderly women who were not living with husbands resided with kin; by 1970, only 29% of these individuals shared homes with other family members (Heaton & Hoppe, 1987; Kobrin, 1976). The preference for separate households fostered the demand for Social Security, and Social Security allowed the preference to be fully expressed.

## CONCLUSION

In 1938 the National Association of Manufacturers journal, *Social Security*, cautioned that OAA was not being distributed to the truly needy, but to those who had never received public funds. There had "'developed a new psychology and pensions are being received with the attitude that it [*sic*] is something due. Thousands accept pensions now who formerly were unwilling to accept direct relief'" (Wood, 1938). Millions believed that pensions were a very good idea, and Americans of all ages regularly endorsed Social

Security by large majorities (Schiltz, 1970). Recent scholarly debate over the origins of the American welfare state has the great merit of bringing the Social Security Act to its proper place as a turning point in the history of the twentieth century. These accounts contain more than a measure of truth. Nonetheless, each, in a different manner, diminishes the content of the legislation by focusing on the destructive impact of industrialization upon the aged. Social Security then becomes a reform crafted by one elite or another to rescue the impoverished and dependent elderly.

Such interpretations underestimate the force of popular will expressed in the evolution of policy, as well as its transforming impact on work and family, in part because of a failure to consider the possibility that public welfare was devised for a relatively prosperous group. The advantageous economic circumstances of the American elderly seem incongruous in the periodization of Social Security. There is good reason to believe that the aged were relatively privileged on the whole, and that their conditions improved between the mid-nineteenth and early twentieth centuries. They participated in the substantial economic gains which occurred under the yoke of the machine, enjoying in the 1920s a standard of living unimaginable in the nineteenth century.

Although it generated the levels of wealth necessary for affluent old age, industrialization relied on wage employment, which sharply elevated the difficulty of calculating economic needs in old age, and led to reliance on a familistic strategy. By capturing some of the earnings of other family members, aging couples were able to maintain surpluses in the face of faltering personal income. Extensive evidence exists that this was the conscious strategy of working-class families. Wealth tended to accrue to the aged, but only through the use of the income of family workers.

Such use of family members' earnings surely represents a retirement tax. The same penalty, in another form, occurred when adults took aging mothers, fathers, aunts, or friends into their homes. In concert with findings in contemporary social gerontology, historical evidence shows that both impositions engendered controversy and strife within families, especially when they abruptly ended education for children, compelled coresidence of generations, and restrained the life choices of younger persons. As the birthrate declined, the risk of familial taxation and conflict increased for all adults. In the Depression, the insecurity of private defenses against these threats became abundantly clear to both the working class and the middle class.

From this perspective, Social Security not only offered an attractive alternative, but one whose appeal was centered in the politically appropriate group—the mass of the working and voting population. The aged themselves never represented a large enough voting bloc to have forced taxation on the young. Instead, different generations shared a desire to escape the internal pressures of family strategies, and to substitute for them an intergenerational exchange which reduced insecurity about regular income in old age. The reasons can be read in the consequences: mass retirement, separate households, and the abandonment of the family economy. By giving older people something the private market would not provide—a guaranteed income in old age—Social Security released older men from work and all Americans from intrafamilial tensions. These desires existed well before the Social Security Act, and, after its enactment, were the spirit behind expansion of benefits. Intimate conflicts were replaced with intergenerational burdens, whose full weight was not immediately apparent.

## NOTES

[1]Deficiencies in historical evidence compound the known difficulties in assessing the well-being of elderly persons (Espenshade & Braun, 1983). In particular, cross-sectional data, used to infer life-course characteristics, actually reflect differences among individuals of different ages at a single moment of time.

[2]The data for *Cost of Living of Industrial Workers in the United States and Europe, 1888–1890* and *Cost of Living in the United States, 1917–1919* can be accessed in machine-readable format from the Inter-University Consortium for Political and Social Research in Ann Arbor, Michigan. Men 45 and over made up 32% of all males 25 and over in the 1889–1890 study; such men constituted 38% of the male population aged 25 and over in the United States. In the second study, older men were only 20% of adult males, versus 38% in the population as a whole. The criteria for each study tended to exclude both the affluent and the impoverished aged. For a more complete discussion and analysis of the data, see Gratton and Rotondo (1991).

[3]Conflict was endemic to such exchanges and scholars have recently turned their attention to the dynamics of dominance and distribution within family units ("Family Strategy," 1987).

[4]For the calculation of surplus in each survey, see Gratton and Rotondo (1991). Savings are overestimated in 1889–1890, and residual estimates of surplus (i.e., income minus expenditure) may exaggerate actual savings. Additional data, described below, confirm the plausibility of these estimates.

[5]The surveys used a mix of random and convenience sampling methods; certain polling districts in each were chosen as typical or representative, rather than by lot. In survey reports, married couples shared assets and husband and wife would be reported at the same level of wealth. This procedure inflated individual averages, but is equivalent to the household measurement presented in the cost-of-living data. Roundly criticized by pension advocates, the surveys are demonstrably superior to others in the period. Using National Civic Federation and other data for New York State, N. Sue Weiler (1988) concludes that the elderly enjoyed relatively good economic conditions in the 1920s.

[6]For annuity calculations (at 4% interest) and per capita expenditure, see Gratton and Rotondo (1991). These are hypothetical calculations, since assets have varying degrees of liquidity (a point often made about the wealth of the contemporary aged). But investments common to the working class, such as real estate, suggest a similar annuitization of assets.

[7]The lack of accurate estimates of dependency extended to the justification of the Social Security Act in the Supreme Court. In the opinion upholding the constitutionality of the Act, Justice Benjamin Cardozo (*Helvering v. Davis*, 1937) cited data in the government brief as proof of the dependency of the elderly in modern industrial society. The Justice relied on the report *Economic Insecurity in Old Age* (U.S. Social Security Board, 1937), by Marjorie Shearon, a staff member on the Social Security Board. Shearon estimated that 65% of those 65 and over were completely dependent. Her figure rested on several questionable calculations, the most important being the decision to make all spouses of self-supporting men and women "dependent."

[8]Ransom and Sutch (1986) argue that "retirement" was very common in the nineteenth century and no decline occurred between 1870 and 1930. Confusing retirement with labor force and unemployment measures does not aid their case, nor does an arbitrary treatment of data and evidence. Jon Moen's more plausible series shows rather steep declines in gainful employment until 1910, then stability (1988, 1991).

[9]The reader should note that the 1950 data set did not provide information on OAA benefits for individuals; instead, the mean benefit in a state was assigned as a characteristic of men from that state.

## REFERENCES

Achenbaum, W. A. (1978). *Old age in the new land: The American experience since 1790.* Baltimore: Johns Hopkins University Press.

Anglim, C., & Gratton, B. (1987). Organized labor and old age pensions. *International Journal of Aging and Human Development, 25*, 91–107.

Anonymous. (1931). Old age intestate. *Harper's Magazine, 162*, 712–18.

Atack, J., & Bateman, F. (1987). *To their own soil: Agriculture in the antebellum north.* Ames, IA: Iowa State University Press.

Barfield, R. E., & Morgan, J. N. (1969). *Early retirement: The decision and the experience.* Ann Arbor, MI: University of Michigan Press.

Barkin, S. (1933). *The older worker in industry: A study of New York state manufacturing industries.* Albany: State of New York.

Blackwelder, J. K. (1984). *Women of the depression: Caste and culture in San Antonio, 1929–39.* College Station, TX: Texas A&M University Press.

Bodnar, J. (1982). *Workers' world: Kinship, community, and protest in an industrial society, 1900–1940.* Baltimore: Johns Hopkins University Press.

Bodnar, J. (1985). *The transplanted: A history of immigrants in urban America.* Bloomington: Indiana University Press.

Bowen, W., & Finnegan, T. A. (1969). *The economics of labor force participation.* Princeton, NJ: Princeton University Press.

Burns, E. (n.d.). The Papers of Eveline Burns, Social Welfare History Archives, University of Minnesota, Box 8, Folder Government Committee and Aging Work 1936–1943. Minneapolis.

Carter, H. S. (1988). Legal aspects of widowhood and aging. In A. Scadron (Ed.), *Widows and widowhood in the American southwest: 1848–1939.* Urbana: University of Illinois Press.

Chudacoff, C., & Hareven, T. (1977). From the nest egg to family dissolution. *Journal of Family History, 4,* 69–83.

Clark, R., Kreps, J., & Spengler, J. (1978). Economics of aging: A survey. *Journal of Economic Literature, 16,* 919–962.

Cohen, L. (1990). *Making a new deal: Industrial workers in Chicago, 1919–1939.* Cambridge: Cambridge University Press.

Danziger, S., Haveman, R., & Plotnick, R. (1981). How income transfer programs affect work, savings, and the income distribution: A critical review. *Journal of Economic Literature, 19,* 975–1028.

Deglar, C. (1980). *At odds: Women and the family in America from the revolution to the present.* New York: Oxford University Press.

Derthick, M. (1979). *Policymaking for social security.* Washington: Brookings Institution.

DeVault, I. A. (1990). *Sons and daughters of labor: Class and clerical work in turn-of-the-century Pittsburgh.* Ithaca: Cornell University Press.

Douglas, Paul H., Hitchcock, C. N., & Atkins, W. E. (Eds.), (1923). *The worker in industrial society.* Chicago: University of Chicago Press.

Epstein, A. (1922). *Facing old age: A study of old age dependency in the United States and old age pensions.* New York: Knopf.

Epstein, A. (1939). Letter to William Haber, 9 January 1939. Papers of William Haber, Michigan Historical Collections, Bentley Historical Library, University of Michigan; Box 1, Folder Correspondence, Epstein, Abraham. Ann Arbor.

Espenshade, T. J., & Braun, R. E. (1983). Economic aspects of an aging population and the material well-being of older persons. In *Aging in society: Selected reviews of recent research.* Hillsdale, NJ: Lawrence Erlbaum Associates.

Family strategy: A dialogue. (1987). *Historical Methods, 20,* 113–25.

Gabaccia, D. (1988). The transplanted: Women and family in immigrant America. *Social Science History, 12,* 247–249.

Gagliardo, D. (1949). *American social insurance.* New York: Harper and Brothers.

Graebner, W. (1980). *A history of retirement: The meaning and function of an American institution.* New Haven, CT: Yale University Press.

Gratton, B. (1986). *Urban elders: Family, work, and welfare in Boston 1890–1950.* Philadelphia: Temple University Press.

Gratton, B. (1987). The labor force participation of older men, 1890–1950. *Journal of Social History, 20,* 689–710.

Gratton, B. (1988). The new welfare state: Social security and retirement. *Social Science History, 12,* 171–96.

Gratton, B., & Ito, R. M., II. (1991). The family economy in the American working class: 1889–90, 1917–19, 1939. Paper delivered at the Meeting of the Gerontological Society of America, San Francisco.

Gratton, B., & Rotondo, F. M. (1991). Industrialization, the family economy, and the economic status of the American elderly. *Social Science History, 15,* 337–62.

Greenwood, D. T., & Wolff, E. N. (1988). Relative wealth holdings of children and the elderly in the United States, 1962–83. In J. L. Palmer, T. Smeeding, & B. B. Torrey, (Eds.), *The vulnerable*. Washington: Urban Institute.

Grigg, S. (1989). Women and family property: A review of U.S. Inheritance studies. *Historical Methods, 22,* 116–22.

Haber, C., & Gratton, B. (1993). *Old age and the search for security: An American social history*. Bloomington: Indiana University Press.

Hall, J. D., Leloudis, J. Korstad, R., Murphy, M., Jones, L. A., & Daly, C. B. (1988). *Like a Family*. Chapel Hill: The University of North Carolina Press.

Hareven, T. K. (1982). *Family time and industrial time*. Cambridge: Cambridge University Press.

Hareven, T., & Chudacoff, C. (1978). Family transitions in old age. In T. Hareven, (Ed.), *Transitions*. New York: Academic Press.

Heaton, T. B., & Hoppe, C. (1987). Widowed and married: Comparative change in living arrangements, 1900-1980. *Social Science History, 11,* 261–280.

*Helvering v. Davis*. 1937. No. 0–301, U.S. 619, Fall Term, U.S. Supreme Court. Washington.

Holtzman, A. (1963). *The Townsend movement: A political study*. New York: Bookman Associates.

Hurd, M. (1989). The economic status of the elderly. *Science, 244,* 659–664.

Jones, A. H. (1980). *Wealth of a nation to be: The American colonies on the eve of the revolution*. New York: Columbia University

Kobrin, F. E. (1976). The fall in household size and the rise of the primary individual in the United States. *Demography, 13,* 127–138.

Lubove, R. (1968). *The struggle for social security: 1900-1935*. Cambridge, MA: Harvard University Press.

Main, J. T. (1985). *Society and economy in colonial Connecticut*. Princeton: Princeton University Press.

Massachusetts Commission on Pensions. (1925). *Report on old-age pensions*. Boston: Commonwealth of Massachusetts.

Mindel, C. H. (1979). Multigenerational family households: Recent trends and implications for the future. *Gerontologist, 19,* 456–463.

Mintz, S., & Kellogg, S. (1988). *Domestic revolutions: A social history of American family life*. New York: The Free Press.

Moen, J. (1988). From gainful employment to labor force. *Historical Methods, 21,* 149–59.

Moen, J. (1991). Rural, nonfarm households: A new view of the labor force participation rate of men 65 and older, 1860-1980. (Unpublished paper). Oxford, MS: University of Mississippi.

Morawska, E. (1985). *For bread with butter: The life-worlds of east central Europeans in Johnston Pennsylvania 1900-1940*. Cambridge: Cambridge University Press.

National Civic Federation. (1928). *Extent of old age dependency*. New York: National Civic Federation.

Orloff, A. S., & Skocpol, T. (1984). Why not equal protection? Explaining the politics of public social spending in Britain, 1900-1911, and the United States, 1890s-1920. *American Sociological Review, 49,* 726–50.

Owen, J. (1986). *Working lives: The American work force since 1920*. Lexington, MA: Lexington Books.

Palmer, J. L., Smeeding, T., & Jencks, C. (1988). The uses and limits of income comparison. In Palmer, J., Smeeding, T., & Torrey, B. B. (Eds.), *The vulnerable*. Washington: Urban Institute Press.

Quadagno, J. S. (1984). Welfare capitalism and the Social Security Act of 1935. *American Sociological Review, 49*, 632–47.

Quadagno, J. S. (1987). Theories of the welfare state. In W. R. Scott, & J. F. Short, Jr. (Eds.), *Annual Review of Sociology, 13*. Palo Alto, CA: Annual Reviews.

Quadagno, J. S. (1988). *The transformation of old age security: Class and politics in the American welfare state*. Chicago: University of Chicago Press.

Ransom, R. L., & Sutch, R. (1986). The labor of older Americans: Retirement of men on and off the job, 1870–1937. *Journal of Economic History XLVI*(1), 1–30.

Ransom, R. L., & Sutch, R. (1990). Retirement: Past and present. Paper delivered at Conference on Retirement, Social Security and the Future, Washington, DC.

Republican Program Committee. (1939). Documents 41 & 42, Box 96, Post-Presidential Subject Files, Hoover Presidential Library.

Rosenmayr, L., & E. Kockeis. (1963). Propositions for a sociological theory of aging and the family. *International Social Science Journal, 15*, 410–26.

Rothbart, R. (1989). 'Homes are what any strike is about:' Immigrant labor and the family wage. *Journal of Social History, 23*, 267–284.

Rotondo, F. M. (1991). Work and well-being: The American elderly in the industrial era. (Master's Thesis). Tempe, AZ: Arizona State University.

Rubinow, I. M. (1972). The care of the aged. In D. J. Rothman, (Ed.), *The aged and the depression*. New York: Arno.

Ruggles, S. (1987). *Prolonged connections: The rise of the extended family in nineteenth-century England and America*. Madison: University of Wisconsin Press.

Ruggles, N. D., & Ruggles, R. (1977). The anatomy of earnings behavior. In F. T. Juster (Ed.), *The distribution of economic well-being*. Cambridge: NBER.

Ryan, M. (1981). *Cradle of the middle class*. Cambridge: Cambridge University Press.

Schiltz, M. E. (1970). *Public attitudes toward social security: 1935–1965*. Washington: U.S. Department of Health, Education, and Welfare.

Schorr, A. L. (1958). *Filial responsibility in the modern American family*. Washington: GPO.

Shammas, C., Salmon, M., & Dahlin, M. (1987). *Inheritance in America: From colonial times to the present*. New Brunswick, NJ: Rutgers University Press.

Smith, D. S. (1979). Life course, norms, and the family system of older Americans in 1900. *Journal of Family History, 4*, 285–298.

Smith, D. S. (1982). Historical change in the household structure of the elderly in economically developed societies. In P. N. Stearns (Ed.), *Old age in preindustrial society*. New York: Holmes & Meier.

Smith, D. S. (1986). Accounting for change in the families of the elderly in the United States, 1900–present. In D. Van Tassel, & P. N. Stearns (Eds.), *Old age in a bureaucratic society*. New York: Greenwood Press.

*Social Security Bulletin*. October 1948; December 1949; July 1950: March 1951; November 1951; January 1952; September 1952.

Soltow, L. (1975). *Men and wealth in the United States 1850–1870*. New Haven, CT: Yale University Press.

Sorensen, A., & McLanahan, S. (1989). Women's economic dependency and men's support obligations: Economic relations within households. [Working Paper #89-26]. Madison: Center for Demography and Ecology.

Stern, M. (1987). *Society and family strategy: Erie County. New York, 1850–1920.* Albany: State University of New York Press.

Treas, J. (1977). Family support systems for the aged. *Gerontologist, 17,* 486–491.

Tuma, N. B., & Sandefur, G. D. (1988). Trends in the labor force activity of the elderly in the United States, 1940–1980. In R. Ricardo-Campbell, & E. P. Lazear, (Eds.), *Issues in contemporary retirement.* Stanford: Hoover Institution.

U.S. Bureau of the Census. (1975). *Historical Statistics of the United States,* pt. 1. Washington, DC: U.S. Government Printing Office.

U.S. Bureau of the Census. (1983). *Census of population: 1940. Public use microdata sample* [machine-readable data file]. Washington: Bureau of the Census [producer and distributor].

U.S. Bureau of the Census. (1984). *Census of population: 1950. Public use microdata sample* [machine-readable data file]. Washington: Bureau of the Census [producer and distributor].

U.S. Bureau of the Census. (1988). Statistical Brief, SB-1-88, Washington, DC: U.S. Government Printing Office.

U.S. Bureau of Labor Statistics. (1924). *Cost of living in the United States.* Bulletin No. 357. Washington, DC: U.S. Government Printing Office.

U.S. Social Security Board. (1937). *Economic insecurity in old age.* Washington, DC: U.S. Government Printing Office.

Walsh, D. I. (1927). *American Labor Legislation Review,* September.

Ware, C. F. (1935). *Greenwich village, 1920–1930.* Boston: Houghton Mifflin.

Ware, C. F. (n.d.). Questionnaires in Carolyn F. Ware Collection, Boxes 51–55. Franklin Delano Roosevelt Library, Hyde Park, NY.

Weiler, N. S. (1988). Industrial scrap heap: Employment patterns and change for the aged in the 1920s. *Social Science History, 1,* 65–88.

Whaples, R. (1989). The 'problem of old age' in America: Older men, retirement, and the industrial scrap heap. Paper delivered at the Annual Meeting of the Social Science History Association, Washington, DC.

Williamson, J. G., & Lindert, P. H. (1980). *American inequality: A macroeconomic inquiry.* New York: Academic Press.

Wood, B. G. (1938). In National Association of Manufacturers Collection, Box 209, Folder US Government Legislation, Social Security Act, General 1938–54, Hagley Archives. Wilmington.

Zelizer, V. (1985). *Pricing the priceless child: The changing social value of children.* New York: Basic Books.

# The Supply and Demand for Retirement: Sorting out the Arguments

## Jon R. Moen

The increase in retirement of older men since the 1930s has fascinated social scientists and historians for several decades. What caused the increase? Why was it so great? Many explanations have been offered, but few have been satisfying, at least from an economist's point of view. Economists like to explain things in terms of supply and demand. Such an approach is useful in sorting out many of the arguments that have been presented to explain the increase in the "quantity" of retirement by older men in the twentieth century. In particular, I shall try to fit (perhaps force is more accurate) Brian Gratton's paper into a simple supply and demand model of retirement, showing what he does and does not try to explain about the increase in retirement.

Gratton begins by challenging several traditional beliefs about older workers and the elderly. The most important is that as a class they were poor, a belief that is still widespread today (e.g., see Hurd 1989). Throughout the eighteenth and nineteenth centuries evidence in the form of probate inventories or census records demonstrate increasing wealth with age. Although wealth was distributed unevenly, it still was the case that only a few people could accumulate enough wealth to retire. Nevertheless, retirement resulting from wealth accumulation was not common even in the midnineteenth century; other factors like urban versus rural residence or health were more important in influencing the decision to retire (Moen, 1987). The elderly may have been wealthier than younger groups, but they were not yet wealthy enough for many to consider retirement.

Moving on to the turn of the century, Gratton looks at two cost-of-living surveys for 1889–1890 and 1917–1919. Although both surveys show declining earnings for men after age 30, drawing conclusions about the course of earnings of older workers from cross-sectional information is misleading. Men 60 and older had higher real earnings in 1917–1919 than did the same age group in 1889–1890. Furthermore, men 60 and older in 1917–1919 also had higher earnings than did men 30 to 39 in 1889–1890. In other words, looking at cohorts rather than cross sections of earnings reveals increasing earnings across time, even though the relative standing of older workers may not have changed much. Claudia Goldin has demonstrated the value of cohort specific data in her studies of female labor force participation, showing little interruption of participation within marriage and generally rising participation rates across cohorts (1983, 1990). In the early twentieth century, it thus appears that the earnings of older workers were increasing rather than deteriorating.

Having established that older workers were not losing ground, Gratton expands his discussion of increasing earnings to include income earned by all family members as the relevant measure of economic welfare. Here is where the "demand" side of the story really begins. He argues that a family-based strategy of wealth accumulation, or savings, in which the earnings of children were a key component, resulted in surpluses above the family's consumption needs, surpluses that increased over time. As family real income rose, the earnings of children tended to go more and more to providing savings for the parents in old age. This conclusion was based on evidence from several surveys done by the Massachusetts Bureau of Pensions in the 1920s. Thus, the cost of living surveys and the Massachusetts surveys cast some doubt on the notion that older workers were becoming increasingly impoverished during industrialization, although they also may have become more financially dependent on other family members (see Gratton and Rotondo, 1991, for more discussion of the family-based strategy).

Closely associated with the family-based strategy of wealth accumulation is the increasing number of "complex" households in the late nineteenth and early twentieth centuries. Steven Ruggles (1987, p. 140) defines an extended *family* as a family with three or more generations of relatives living together (e.g., child, parents, grandparents). Gratton defines "complex" households to include extended families along with other household arrangements that go beyond the simple, nuclear family to include other relatives, adult children, boarders, etc. More precise definitions are not necessary for the overall argument presented here.

Extended families and complex households arose for several reasons. Demographic factors seem to be important, although how they worked together is not certain. First, there was a significant increase in life expectation at birth or at age 10 starting around 1850 (Preston and Haines, 1991, pp. 53–4; Fogel, 1986, p. 465). Life expectation at age 40 or 60 was also increasing around the turn of the century, although the increase was modest (U.S. Bureau of the Census, 1961). Thus, one could expect to see more, if not older, old people. Parents were living long enough to expect to see their children grow up and have children of their own, and perhaps come and live with them. Declining age at marriage also increased the potential for three generations to be present in the same family.

Complex households in the mid-nineteenth century appear to have been more of a luxury rather than a necessity, with the wealthy being more likely to live in complex households than the middle or working classes. Over the next several decades, the improving financial state of the middle class and skilled craftsmen let them adopt complex households as a means to support older family members. In some instances more affluent middle-class households were able to abandon complex households and support older members in their own homes. By the 1920s the working class was generally able to afford complex households.

Although complex households were an important way for families to accumulate assets and provide economic security over the life-cycle, they also were the source of increasing intergenerational conflict. Older children wanted to begin lives and homes of their own. Often the responsibility of taking care of an older parent fell on the oldest daughter, who was eager to marry and start a home of her own. Even though households were accumulating assets, economic uncertainty in the early twentieth century had prevented all but the most affluent from retiring completely. This can be seen in the relatively constant labor force participation rate of men 65 and older between 1900 and 1930 (Moen, 1988, 1991). Older workers did not divorce themselves from the work force completely. Rather, they may have taken less demanding jobs, or they moved in and out of the work force as their financial situation weakened or strengthened. Children still had some role in supporting their parents in old age, and as Gratton indicates, the combination of increasing household income and continued obligations to support older family members in complex households resulted in rising intergenerational tensions. By the 1920s the evidence of tension is especially clear in working-class families, the last group to adopt complex households. The perception often was that the welfare of children was being sacrificed for the benefit of grandparents or other older family members.

The ability of older workers to move in and out of the work force may not have been as frictionless as Gratton makes it seem. Robert Margo (1991) has shown, using the 1900 Public Use Sample, that the difficulty of reentering the labor force after a spell of unemployment increased with age. Therefore, older workers faced increasing uncertainty about their ability to supplement household income during times of increased financial need. They could just as well become a financial dependent as they could a financial contributor, resulting in continued dependence on complex households and more intergenerational tension.

The Great Depression upset the progress older workers had been achieving early in the twentieth century and encouraged the pension movement to push for federally funded pensions. The middle class had been increasingly able to escape the confines of the complex household. Yet with their savings wiped out, private pension plans and life insurance policies bankrupt, increasing numbers of middle-class families were thrown back into complex living arrangements. Gratton notes that popular support for federally funded pensions could be found at different points in time; witness the widespread support for the Civil War pension. The 1930s was certainly a period when support for a federally funded pension scheme was easily found; many families had gotten used to not having to support older members in the household. If they couldn't finance residential autonomy on their own, they would be glad to let the government try to do so.

The rising number of complex households during the Depression and increased intergenerational tensions explain the increase in demand for federally funded pensions. Borrowing some material from another paper by Gratton (and Carole Haber) helps fill out the supply side of the story of the increase in retirement by older men. Haber and Gratton (1992) argue against the view that older workers were unambiguously and completely degraded and made obsolete by industrialization, being forced into involuntary retirement and relegated to the industrial scrap heap. Substantial changes in the structure of manufacturing and the organization of labor actually prompted employers to offer pension schemes to their workers.

In many industries in the nineteenth and early twentieth centuries the relationship between employer and employee sometimes took on the appearance of something like a general contractor farming work out to several subcontractors. The iron and steel industry is a well-documented example (Montgomery, 1987, Chap. 1). The employer would often contract with a skilled craftsman to operate a blast furnace, who in turn would be responsible for hiring his own crew and paying them out of what the company paid him for his final product. The size and distribution of payments was often guided by union rules.

Under this system of subcontracting, much of production was under the control of the skilled craftsman, a worker who had accumulated detailed knowledge of all aspects of production. He was responsible for training younger workers and passing on his accumulation of knowledge, and he could also hire younger workers to relieve him of the more physically demanding tasks. Under such a system it is not surprising to find rewards for seniority and experience and some degree of respect for senior workers.

As manufacturing developed, assembly lines became more common and jobs became more specialized. Owners were continually trying to reduce the craftsman's control over production. Knowledge of production passed to foremen and scientific managers, reducing the value of experienced older workers. They were being replaced by machines and low-skilled workers knowing only a specialized task.

To many reformers this was clear evidence that older workers were being abandoned, unable to keep up with fast-paced, scientifically managed industry. But to many capitalists new problems began to appear. Hiring of workers had passed from the craftsman to the company foremen, and labor markets had become spot markets in which workers were hired by the week or perhaps even the day. With diminished reward for experience and little reason to expect long-term attachment to any one company, workers were unlikely to develop much loyalty to a firm and instead would shop around for the best wage. High rates of labor turnover had become a costly side-effect of scientific management.

To reduce turnover and the costly retraining expenses it incurred, many industries attempted to install "seniority-based" systems of promotion. These systems attempted to recreate the positions of skill and authority that older workers achieved over time, when production was "craft" oriented and premiums were paid for the skills older workers had accumulated. The older craft system of production had imposed some order and discipline in the factory. With assembly line production and specialization of tasks, older workers tended to accumulate fewer skills and had become just another hired laborer who could be easily replaced. The order of the old craft system broke down with the rise of specialized tasks.

Seniority-based systems of promotion "promised" increasing wages over time if the worker remained loyal to the firm. Firms realized after a time that they were paying older workers more than their marginal product. To a profit-maximizing firm such a situation could not go on for long. But the firm could not simply fire the older worker, for that would upset the workings of the seniority-system: younger workers would see that at the end of their careers there was no ultimate reward for loyalty, so why be loyal in the first place? Therefore, firms would install mandatory ages of retirement, but they would also provide the retiree with a modest pension as a reward for years of service. Ransom, Sutch, and Williamson (1991) argue that the increased productivity caused by the reduced turnover was more than enough to pay for these pensions.

Unions as well as employers had some incentive to install "seniority-based" systems of promotion and hiring. Unions wanted to increase job security and therefore the security of the union itself, while employers were eager to reduce high levels of worker turnover that reduced efficiency. Firms recognized that even though wages may have increased with age, productivity necessarily did not. Seniority rules eventually resulted in age limits in making new hires and mandatory retirement around age 65.

Early private pensions were generally funded by the company rather than by employee contributions and were considered a cost of doing business. Greenough and King (1976) and Haber (1983) argue that the pensions were primarily a device to control and manipulate the labor force, not a guaranteed benefit for years of loyal service. They were provided at the discretion of the company; any behavior that was inappropriate on the part of the employee would result in forfeiture of any benefits. For example, striking, extended unemployment, and criminal behavior were a few of the reasons a company could deny pension benefits. In general workers had no legal rights to the early, company-sponsored pensions, most of which were non-contributory plans.

Union-sponsored plans were no more reliable than company plans. They were funded out of general assessments on union members, which increased as the number of older members grew and competition for alternative uses of union funds stiffened (Greenough and King, 1976, pp. 41–2). The Great Depression bankrupted most union plans.

Seniority-based systems of promotion and retirement eventually produced internal labor markets that helped workers *within* the firm but did little to help those who fell out of the system. Margo's results showing increasing difficulty of reentering the labor force at older ages may partly reflect the effects of hiring age limits. At any rate, Gratton and Haber make the case that industrialization was not harmful to all older workers in general, just those who slipped through the cracks (which at times could be very wide). Thus it seems that structural changes in labor markets involving transitions from craft to spot to internal labor markets were responsible for the increase in supply of pensions and, hence, retirement.

Before the Great Depression, both the supply and demand for pensions were increasing. But why was the increase in the number of privately sponsored pensions so small? According to Murray Webb Latimer (1932, p. 47), 397 plans were in operation in 1929, covering less than 10% of the work force. One reason might be that the period during which private pensions were being established was actually quite short. Richard Edwards (1975) argues that before 1919 the probability of a corporation failing was much higher than after 1919, a time of consolidation and business mergers. Higher turnover among businesses would reduce the probability that a pension plan would be established, or at least be around long enough to support many retired workers, as it is by nature a long-term obligation on the part of a company. Even though pensions may have been gaining ground in the 1920s, the Great Depression stopped further progress.

Company-sponsored pension plans may have helped some older workers during normal economic times, but there was no guarantee that they would be there during economic downturns. Seniority and pensions were of little value if the firm went broke, as more than a few did during the Great Depression. If the demand for pensions had been increasing slowly before the Depression, it grew rapidly during that time. The supply from private sources, however, did not. Eventually the Social Security Act was passed to aid the increasing number of older workers—and their dependents—who had been thrown out of work.

Gratton (1988; Gratton & Rotundo, 1991) and Moen (1987) argue, however, that it was not the Old Age Insurance (OAI) program (Title II) payments that could have immediately helped older workers. Not all workers were covered, the value of benefits was initially not great, and the first payments were not made until 1940. Gratton argues that it was the Old Age Assistance (OAA) program (Title I) that benefited the destitute elderly. The benefits were reasonable, although they varied across states, and they started immediately. Initially the OAA program was larger than the now more familiar OAI program, and Gratton demonstrates that it caused an increase in retirement of older workers between the mid 1930s and 1950. After 1950 OAI expanded in coverage and eclipsed OAA as the main program under Social Security. Until very recently, few if any economists seem to have recognized this (Parsons, 1991).

I believe there is an analogy to be drawn. Social Security was referred to as an *insurance* program. At roughly the same time the Social Security program was being developed, bank deposit insurance through the FDIC was created to protect depositors from the large number of bank failures of the early 1930s. The Federal Reserve did not know what to do to help failing banks, or at least did nothing to aid them up through 1933. In general, American banking history has shown that private or state sponsored deposit insurance schemes have always failed; they had no power to create money. The FDIC provided an authority outside of the system to protect workers' bank deposits.

Like private deposit insurance, privately funded pension plans also failed. Through Social Security the federal government provided an authority outside of the system to protect workers' retirement; the government had the power to tax to back up their guarantee.

Until recently the FDIC seemed to work; until recently Social Security seemed to work, although there are more and more signs of problems down the road as the work force continues to age. As Gratton (1988) has demonstrated, the federal government was responsible for much of the increase in retirement after 1950. Whether or not it has the ability (or will) to let it continue remains to be seen.

Gratton's paper thus shows that the increasing demand for pensions, fueled by rising earnings of workers, made itself apparent through an increase in the demand for separate households for older workers. A family-based strategy of supporting older workers, while successful in many instances, produced intergenerational conflict that hastened the search for ways to support older family members that were physically as well as financially separate from their children. Other work by Gratton and Haber and by Ransom, Sutch, and Williamson and others shows how firms slowly increased the supply of pensions and retirement to further their own interests in response to changing compensation schemes and the rise of internal labor markets. Both the supply and demand for pensions slowly increased in response to independent forces in the early twentieth century. After the Great Depression they increased because of Social Security.

## REFERENCES

Edwards, R. (1975). Stages in corporate stability and the risks of corporate failure. *Journal of Economic History*, 428–57.

Fogel, R. (1986). Nutrition and the decline in mortality since 1700: Some preliminary findings. In S. Engerman & R. Gallman (Eds.) *Long-Term Factors in American Economic Growth*, vol. 51 of Studies in Income and Wealth (NBER).

Goldin, C. (1983). The changing economic role of women: A quantitative approach. *Journal of Interdisciplinary History*, Spring, 707–33.

Goldin, C, (1990). *Understanding the gender gap: An economic history of American women*. New York: Oxford University Press.

Gratton, B. (1988). The new welfare state: Social Security and retirement in 1950. *Social Science History*, Summer, 171–96.

Gratton, B., & Rotondo, F. (1991). Industrialization, the family economy, and the economic status of the American elderly. *Social Science History*, Fall, 337–362.

Greenough, W., & King, F. (1976). *Pension plans and public policy*. New York: Columbia University Press.

Haber, C. (1983). *Beyond sixty-five: The dilemma of old age in America's past*. New York: Cambridge University Press.

Haber, C., & Gratton, B. (1993). *Old age and the search for security: An American social history.* Bloomington, IN: Indiana University Press.

Hurd, M. (1989). The economic status of the elderly. *Science, 244,* 659–64.

Latimer, M. W. (1932). *Industrial pension systems.* New York: Industrial Relations Counselors.

Margo, R. (1991). The labor force participation of older Americans in 1900: Further results. Working paper no. 27 in NBER Series on Historical Factors in Long Run Growth.

Moen, J. (1987). *Essays on the labor force and labor force participation rates: The United States from 1860 to 1950.* Unpublished Ph.D. dissertation, University of Chicago.

Moen, J. (1988). From gainful employment to labor force: Definitions and a new estimate of work rates of American males, 1860 to 1980. *Historical Methods,* Fall, 149–59.

Moen, J. (1991). Rural, nonfarm households: A new view of the labor force participation of men 65 and older, 1860–1980. Unpublished manuscript, University of Mississippi.

Montgomery, D. (1987). *The fall of the house of labor.* New York: Cambridge University Press.

Parsons, D. (1991). Male retirement behavior in the United States, 1930–50. *Journal of Economic History,* September, 657–74.

Preston, S., & Haines, M. (1991). *Fatal years: Child mortality in late nineteenth-century America.* Princeton, NJ: Princeton University Press.

Ransom, R., Sutch, R., & Williamson, S. (1991). Inventing pensions: The crisis of 1906, age discrimination, and the search for old-age security in industrial America, 1900–1940. University of California History of Retirement Project working paper.

Ruggles, S. (1987). *Prolonged connections: The rise of the extended family in nineteenth-century England and America.* Madison, WI: University of Wisconsin Press.

U.S. Bureau of the Census. (1975). *Historical statistics, series B116–125.* Washington DC: Government Printing Office.

# Family Structure,
# Family Income,
# and Incentives to Retire

## Emily S. Andrews

Labor–leisure trade-offs are determined by individual preferences given a wage rate and other financial resources. The impact of spousal income and work patterns over time have also been incorporated to extend this analysis. Most economic studies of the retirement decision fall within this framework.[1]

Brian Gratton's chapter investigates issues of considerable interest to economists but deviates from the pattern just described in several ways. In so doing, he expands and augments the sometimes narrow horizons of the economics profession. Gratton bolsters his arguments by combining narrative history and survey statistics. Economists typically lose sight of the importance of nonquantitative material in signaling economic trends.

Gratton's study spans a wider horizon than the work of most economists. He discusses trends in real income and changes in family structure that emerge in the late nineteenth century and continue into the twentieth. This broad perspective should be considered by researchers and policy makers today, particularly since actuarial and economic forecasts of the Social Security system project benefit payments well into the 21st century. A backward look can serve as a cautionary reminder about the possibility of unanticipated outcomes. The Great Depression of the 1930s and World War II would fit into this category.

Gratton argues, in part, that changes in family structure led to the development of the Social Security system. He then suggests that the key to increased retirement among older workers during the 1930s was old age assistance (OAA), provided under the Social Security Act, rather than old age and survivors insurance (OASI). His arguments are founded on a wealth of survey data from numerous sources.

Gratton develops a picture of earnings, income, and assets within a life-cycle context. His evidence on earnings profiles is intriguing because it suggests that earnings used to peak at a rather young age at the turn of the century. Gratton also provides evidence that the family income enjoyed by households peaked somewhat later. The continued increase in family income, despite the aging of the household head, was the result of supplementary income from other family members—in particular, from children in the household.

Gratton indicates that this pattern was changing by the 1920s as a result of two trends. First, the earnings of household heads started to peak later in life. Second, the modern nuclear family was emerging, with younger children less likely to augment family earnings and older children more likely to live in separate households. These changes took place during several decades of economic growth and changing technology.

Gratton hypothesizes that the popularity of Social Security was an outgrowth of changes in family structure and family income. In particular, he suggests that the disintegration of the extended family created a societal demand for retirement income provision that would shift the burden of supporting the elderly from individual families to all workers.

In addition to data on earnings, Gratton provides a series of snapshots of savings and wealth. His data indicate that the distribution of wealth among the aged has been, and continues to be, highly skewed. I regard his findings on savings with some suspicion, however. Calculations of savings that are derived from the difference between income and consumption may be highly unreliable if consumption expenditures are underestimated. Even today, the calculation of savings as a residual is likely to be subject to significant error.

Furthermore, the generally optimistic tone of Gratton's evaluation of the income of the elderly prior to Social Security seems somewhat discordant in view of the empirical evidence presented. In particular, while Gratton indicates a dramatic improvement in the economic fortunes of the aged by the 1920s, he also reports that, based on a survey conducted in 1917–1919, one-third of elderly couples were at the verge of dependency or dependent on family or charity.

His qualitative appraisal awaits the development of a poverty rate similar to that currently employed by the Census Bureau. Based on poverty levels calculated for 1959, over one-third of all elderly persons were in poverty. An area for future research would be to develop a poverty measure applicable to a longer time span to determine whether poverty among the aged could have actually risen between 1920 and 1960, as the data presented by Gratton suggest.

The remainder of Gratton's paper focuses on the role of OAA in retirement, following the enactment of Social Security legislation but prior to universal OASI benefit recipiency. Since the preponderance of economic studies have sought to measure the impact of OASI benefits on retirement during the 1970s, Gratton's findings add a new perspective to current debates on the determinants of retirement age.

## THE FAMILY ECONOMY

Gratton develops the hypothesis that during the twentieth century, the relevant household economic unit shifted from the extended family to the nuclear family. The effect of this change was twofold. First, unmarried children no longer made significant economic contributions to their parents and, second, persons of working age became less willing to provide income for their elders.

Demographic factors may have, in part, supported this outcome. Family support of the elderly is less of a financial burden for families in which many siblings are present. Either siblings can share in the support of their elderly parents as needed, or one sibling may be selected for that task. In any event, *ceteris paribus*, the likelihood of financial burden is higher in a society averaging two children per couple than in a society averaging seven.

The data suggest that over the period 1900 to 1950, the number of working-age children per elderly person declined. As a rough approximation, a reverse dependency ratio shows the number of persons age 35 to 65 per persons age 65 and over (Table 2.1). Individuals age 35 to 65 would be most likely to have elderly parents that they could be called upon to support.

### Table 2.1 Reverse Dependency Ratios

| Year | Ratio of age 35–65 to age 65 plus | Ratio of age 14–65 to age 65 plus |
|------|-----------------------------------|-----------------------------------|
| 1900 | 7.37 | 16.6 |
| 1910 | 7.35 | 16.2 |
| 1920 | 7.39 | 15.2 |
| 1930 | 6.79 | 13.3 |
| 1940 | 5.95 | 11.3 |
| 1950 | 5.27 | 9.2 |

Source: Compiled from U.S. Bureau of the Census. *Historical Statistics of the United States: Colonial Times to 1957.* (1961), Series A, 22–33, page 8.

That ratio fell from 7.37 to 5.27 between 1900 and 1950. The decline in the ratio was well underway prior to the enactment of Social Security.

The ratio of persons age 14 to 65 per persons age 65 and older was more favorable, although it decreased from 16.6 in 1900 to 9.2 in 1950.[2] Nonetheless, in 1930, the ratio of the full working-age population (age 14 to 65) to the elderly was more than 13 to one, while fewer than 7 adults age 35 and older were available to support those age 65 and over. In other words, although the burden of retirement support was growing greater for older working-age children, by starting a Social Security program, younger people could be brought into the support network. Thus, the income of younger workers would, once again, provide family support within the new context of social insurance.

## SOCIAL INSURANCE AND ECONOMIC GROWTH

Perhaps the reason that social insurance became popular in the 1930s was due to the conjunction of the demographic trends outlined above and poor cyclical economic performance. Per-capita Gross National Product (GNP) had grown consistently from the turn of the century through the 1920s (Table 2.2). However, in real terms, GNP per capita fell from $781 per person in 1925 to $590 per person in 1933. These data reflect the severe decline in output during the Great Depression.

**Table 2.2 Real Per-capita GNP and Labor Force Participation Rates**

| Year | Per capita GNP 1929 Dollars | Labor force participation men age 65 and older |
|------|------|------|
| 1897–1901 | $496 | 63.1% |
| 1902–1906 | $569 | |
| 1907–1911 | $608 | |
| 1912–1916 | $632 | |
| 1920 | $688 | 55.6% |
| 1925 | $781 | |
| 1930 | $772 | 54.0% |
| 1931 | $721 | |
| 1932 | $611 | |
| 1933 | $590 | |
| 1934 | $639 | |
| 1935 | $718 | |
| 1940 | $916 | 44.2% |

Source: Compiled from U.S. Bureau of the Census. *Historical Statistics of the United States: Colonial Times to 1957.* (1961), Series D, 13–25 and F, 44–48, p. 71 and p. 140.

Perhaps the combination of declining resources, coupled with an increasing burden upon the older working-age population to take care of their elderly parents, strengthened the call for a social insurance retirement program.

At first blush this solution would not appear to be favorable to younger persons, however, who would not be facing immediate obligations to provide parental support. Nevertheless, during the Great Depression, younger workers would also have an economic incentive to support social insurance. During the 1930s the unemployment rate on average exceeded 20%, compared to rates of around 5% during the 1920s. Nonetheless, labor force participation rates maintained levels of 55 to 56% during both decades. If unemployment tended to be higher for younger workers (as it has been in recent years), then younger workers would have an incentive to encourage older workers to leave the labor force and "surrender" their jobs.

## OLD AGE ASSISTANCE: CAUSE OR EFFECT?

Gratton's research indicates that OAA had a significant impact on the labor force participation of older men (Gratton, 1987, 1988). In fact, OAA recipiency rose from 8.1% of those age 65 and over to 21.7% of the population, the year that OASI benefits first became available (Table 2.3). In 1940 average OAA benefits and OASI benefits were virtually identical.[3] Economic theory indicates that the increased availability of pension income should lead to lower labor force participation rates.

Nonetheless, the determinants of retirement remain illusive. In particular, the interaction of other economic factors, including real wages rates and unemployment, in conjunction with the availability of retirement income demands further research.

The labor force participation rate of older men declined from 63.1% over 1897–1901 to 55.6% in 1920 (Table 2.2). This 7.5 percentage point drop took place prior to the enactment of Social Security. By contrast the labor force participation rate of older men remained virtually unchanged between 1920 and 1930. Presumably these trends were affected by changes in real wages, changes in the structure of industry and, possibly, the availability of pensions. More empirical research is needed on these issues, however, before any conclusions can be drawn.

The fact that the labor force participation rate for men age 65 and older did not decline significantly between 1940 and 1950 is somewhat surprising (Table 2.3). In fact, their labor force participation actually rose to over 50% in both 1944 and 1945 during the height of World War II. Nonetheless, OASI benefits, which were first paid in 1940, covered over 14.9% of those age 65 and older. Thus, by 1950, 37.5% of the elderly received either

Table 2.3 Social Security Recipiency and Labor Force
Participation Rates (percentages)

| Year | Recipiency rates | | | Labor force participation, men age 65 and older |
|------|------|------|------------|---------------------------------|
|      | OAA  | OASI | OAA or OASI |                                 |
| 1936 | 8.1  | –    | –    |      |
| 1937 | 15.6 | –    | –    |      |
| 1938 | 19.4 | –    | –    |      |
| 1939 | 21.0 | –    | –    |      |
| 1940 | 21.7 | 0.7  | 22.4 | 44.2 |
| 1941 | 23.3 | 2.1  | 25.4 | –    |
| 1942 | 23.4 | 3.2  | 26.6 | –    |
| 1943 | 21.9 | 3.8  | 25.7 | 49.5 |
| 1944 | 20.5 | 4.6  | 25.1 | 50.9 |
| 1945 | 19.4 | 5.7  | 25.1 | 50.8 |
| 1946 | 19.4 | 8.0  | 27.4 | 47.4 |
| 1947 | 20.2 | 9.7  | 29.9 | 46.8 |
| 1948 | 20.5 | 11.3 | 31.8 | 45.7 |
| 1949 | 21.8 | 13.3 | 35.1 | 45.9 |
| 1950 | 22.6 | 14.9 | 37.5 | 44.7 |

Source: Compiled from U.S. Bureau of the Census. *Historical Statistics of the United States: Colonial Times to 1957.* (1961), Series D, 13–25 and H, 207–221, pages 71 and 201.

OAA or OASI. Since these benefits were predicated on a work test, recipients could not report significant labor force activity.

These facts raise an interesting issue. If recipiency rates increased without a diminution of work effort among the population age 65 and over, logic suggests that Social Security benefits were received by individuals who would have retired anyway. What their sources of retirement income would have been in the absence of these benefits remains a mystery.

Furthermore, if the increased prevalence of benefit recipiency did not lower labor force participation rates during the 1940s, how can we be sure that OAA led to increased retirement during the 1930s?[4] Since correlation is not causality, other hypotheses should be investigated. Published historical sources unfortunately do not provide information on the labor force participation rates of older men on a year-to-year basis throughout the 1930s.[5] Thus, the labor force participation rate of older men may have declined prior to 1936, the first year in which OAA benefits were paid. In that case, the apparent increase in the prevalence of retirement may actually represent disguised unemployment.

Without time series data on both unemployment rates and labor force participation rates, the respective effects of OAA benefits and poor economic conditions on retirement will be difficult to unravel. In the absence of such information, one reasonable hypothesis may be that OAA primarily served to transfer income to unemployed older workers who otherwise would have had to fall back on their families or charity.

## CONCLUSIONS

Gratton's paper provides insight into a number of issues and raises questions about them as well. In particular, further research on three topics would be of considerable interest. First, to what extent did the disintegration of the family economy create a demand for Social Security? Second, in what ways did the Great Depression interact with changes in family life? And, third, how can we explain declines in labor force participation among the elderly within a wider context? Further research on the past cannot but help us understand our uncertain future.

### NOTES

[1]See Quinn, Burkhauser, and Myers (1990) for a review of much of this literature.

[2]This second dependency ratio, which includes younger persons, would be affected by immigration between 1900 and 1920. Since immigrants tend to be younger, the first dependency ratio would not be affected as much.

[3]In that year, both benefits averaged $43. Subsequently, OASI benefits rose substantially in real terms while OAA benefits (and subsequent benefits from the Supplemental Security Insurance (SSI) program remained relatively constant.

[4]Studies of the impact of Social Security on retirement during the 1970s are not likely to be affected by the problems indicated above. By the 1970s eligibility for benefits was widespread. Hence, the amount of benefits received, rather than eligibility, would affect the retirement decision. Furthermore, by the 1970s virtually all retirees received Social Security benefits (except for federal and some state and local retirees). Hence, Social Security payments could no longer substitute or be additions to other sources of income for already retired (or retiring) workers.

[5]That is narrowly defined as material published in the U.S. Bureau of the Census, *Historical Statistics of the United States* (1961) or cited by Gratton.

### REFERENCES

Gratton, B. (1987). The labor force participation of older men: 1890–1950. *Journal of Social History, 20,* 689–710.

Gratton, B. (1988). The new welfare state: Social security and retirement in 1950. *Social Science History,* 171–196.

Quinn, J. F., Burkhauser, R. V., & Myers, D. A. (1990). *Passing the torch: The influence of economic incentives on work and retirement.* Kalamazoo, MI: W. E. Upjohn Institute.

U.S. Bureau of the Census. (1961). *Historical statistics of the United States: Colonial times to 1957.* Washington, DC: U.S. Government Printing Office.

# CHAPTER 3

# Over the Hill to the Poorhouse

## Rhetoric and Reality in the Institutional History of the Aged

Carole Haber

In June 17, 1871, Will M. Carleton's "Over the Hill to the Poorhouse," was published on the cover of *Harper's Weekly*. The poem told the story of an honorable widow of seventy who was passed from child to child until she was relegated to the poorhouse. In the final verse she bemoaned her plight:

> *Over the hill to the poor-house–my childr'n dear, goodbye!*
> *Many a night I've watched you when only God was nigh:*
> *And God'll judge between us; but I will al'ays pray*
> *That you shall never suffer the half I do to-day (Carleton, 1871).*

Three years later David Braham and George L. Catlin wrote a companion piece as a popular song. In their version of "Over the Hill to the Poor House," it was an elderly man, rather than a woman, who suddenly found himself forsaken by his children. Completely deprived of their support, his destiny seemed clear: he had few alternatives but to enter a poorhouse. In the refrain of the song, the old man lamented:

*For I'm old and I'm helpless and feeble,*
*The days of my youth have gone by,*
*Then over the hill to the poor house,*
*I wander alone there to die (Braham & Catlin, 1874).*

The authors of both versions of "Over the Hill to the Poorhouse" were not alone in portraying the almshouse as the inevitable fate of large numbers of upstanding and industrious Americans. In his 1911 film *What Should We Do With Our Old?* D. W. Griffith depicted a hardworking elderly man who was displaced at the line by a younger worker and immediately became impoverished at home. As his poverty-stricken condition led to the death of his wife, he faced the certainty of institutionalization.

A discussion of the seemingly inevitability of almshouse residency for the old was not limited to poem, song, or film. By the early twentieth century, welfare reformers constantly evoked the symbol of the ominous and inevitable almshouse. Its existence, pension advocates claimed, proved the powerlessness of old age in the industrial era. According to their studies, the number of elderly people in institutions was on the rapid increase. The far reach of the asylum, such aging "experts" claimed, proved that even the once middle-class old faced the terror of institutionalization. Without direct intervention, most old people would end their lives confined to the poorhouse.

The precise figures produced by aging advocates, however, depicted a far different reality. While the proportion of elderly individuals *within* the asylum was on the rise, the percentage of society's institutionalized elderly remained remarkably stable. Throughout the late nineteenth and early twentieth centuries, only 2% of the old actually found themselves confined to an asylum (Achenbaum, 1978; Gratton, 1986; Manard, Kent, & Van Gils, 1975). Yet the threat of the almshouse clearly reached beyond this limited number. The continual and widespread fear of asylum residency had a dramatic impact upon both public perceptions of the old and on demands that the state provide broadly based assistance.

This chapter will examine how the almshouse came to play such a central role in the history of old age and how it was employed as a powerful symbol in the debate over the nation's elderly. As we shall see, great distance separated the rhetoric of almshouse residency from the reality of its existence. Both in terms of the proportion of elderly people who were incarcerated, and the factors that led to their institutionalization, popular writers and welfare advocates alike greatly exaggerated the dominant role of the almshouse in the lives of the old. Yet even for those who never set foot within the asylum, the threat of poorhouse residency had a potency that could not be ignored. Reports from almshouse superintendents repeatedly asserted that even the most provident of elderly persons could not escape ending their lives in the institution; the old and their families were warned that they had to take radical steps if they wished to save themselves from this ignominious fate.

In the debate over Social Security, the almshouse became a most pervasive and emotional symbol of the need to guarantee the old freedom from institutionalization. Moreover, the asylum not only served as a moral imperative for the passing of national welfare measures, but dramatically affected the form of the legislation. In their attempt to close the ominous institution, policy makers mandated that no federal relief could be given to a resident of a public institution. As a result, even in its decline, the almshouse came to have a lasting effect on old age through its impact on the growth and shape of the private nursing home industry. Although great distance separated the rhetoric of almshouse residency from its actual reality, both the institution itself and popular perceptions of the asylum combined to leave their mark on the elderly's institutional history.

Since the late seventeenth century, welfare authorities had relied on almshouses to shelter the city's most debilitated and impoverished. Erected first in Boston in 1664, and by 1713 in New York City, Charleston, and Philadelphia, poorhouses served as the last resort for the poor and sick who lacked an appropriate family. While most needy people were placed with their kin or allotted the necessary outdoor relief, a few individuals—largely the orphaned, the insane, the diseased, and the elderly—spent their days confined to an almshouse. Within the walls of the institution, little attempt was made to classify the inmates or reform their ways. Few welfare authorities took particular notice of the fact that a high proportion of the residents were elderly. The aged individuals' lack of family members, and their generally debilitated condition, rather than their advanced age, seemed to justify their placement. In the eyes of the city fathers, they simply represented the most debilitated and isolated of the community's needy population.

Beginning in the mid-nineteenth century, however, the almshouse came to assume an increasingly important role in the care of the dependent old and in the discussion of their assumed needs and capabilities. In Philadelphia, for example, the completion of a large public almshouse in 1835 led city officials to declare that all persons seeking support had to enter the almshouse, rather than receive outdoor relief. Although some outdoor aid was reinstated in 1840, the proportion receiving such assistance was quite small. In contrast to the 798 individuals who attained outdoor relief before the establishment of the poorhouse, only 123 were supplied with such aid. The great majority of applicants were forced to forego such relief or agree to institutionalization. This change reflected both the growing reliance of welfare officials on institutions as the proper form of relief, and their often simultaneous attempt to classify paupers within asylums according to their needs and abilities (Clement, 1985).

The two strands of welfare policy were not unrelated. As waves of immigrants increased the number and heterogeneity of individuals applying for community assistance, charity "experts" began to reassess their seemingly "lax" distribution of aid. They broadly adopted the theory that "alms pauperized" the poor by making them lazy and dependent. As a result civil leaders strenuously opposed all forms of outdoor relief and encouraged civic leaders to build forbidding almshouses and workhouses. Punitive institutions, they argued, would discourage the indolent and vicious from seeking charity, and might "reform" those incarcerated under a strict code of conduct. Through their enforced discipline, they would warn the idle poor that hard work and a harsh regimen awaited all alms-seeking applicants (Rothman, 1971).

Although the old were seen as deserving of public assistance, in the formation of stringent welfare policies, they became victim of the authorities' antagonism about the idle young, foreign poor, and "vicious." Like other, although far less "worthy" individuals, they too were often prohibited from receiving support in their own homes. With the widespread establishment of almshouses, welfare administrators gave them a choice: They could either forego applying for relief or agree to enter the purposefully punitive and noxious almshouse.

For those who then entered the almshouse, mid-nineteenth-century welfare officials then attempted to enact the second component of institutional policy. Within asylums, and among institutions, they separated the inmates according to age, need, and character. Previously, the almshouse had mixed individuals of all ages and backgrounds. In the colonial asylum, the orphan had slept alongside the hardened criminal; the able-bodied immigrant had lodged beside the debilitated elder. By the mid-nineteenth century, however, welfare authorities deplored the lack of "strict" classification. Without proper separation of the needy, they argued, the vagrant would never be reformed into an industrious worker nor would the child be shaped into a self-sufficient adult. Indeed, the "indiscriminate" institution was a school for vice rather than a place for eliminating such wickedness (Katz, 1986).

Given such beliefs, charity experts and municipal leaders hoped both to discourage the lazy from applying for relief, and to institutionalize and control all truly needy paupers through a system tied to their specific needs and capabilities. This categorization went beyond the separation of inmates that occurred in large urban asylums of the early nineteenth century. Not only did reformers attempt to separate the worthy from the indolent, but they erected special institutions based on the perceived disabilities and handicaps of the inmates. Beginning cautiously with homes for the deaf, dumb, and blind in the 1830s, authorities established a variety of institutions that removed large numbers of the dependent, although assumed reformable, individuals from the almshouse. Children were placed in orphanages or dispatched to the countryside, "juvenile delinquents" were assigned to reformatories, the acutely ill were transferred to hospitals, and "lunatics" were confined to asylums for the insane. In some cities, even able-bodied paupers were removed from the poorhouse and placed in work-houses designed to punish and reform. Here, city officials believed, they would find no more warm winters or free meals. Young and middle-aged adults would either learn to work or would suffer for their indolence (Rothman, 1971).

The creation of the new institutions had a dramatic effect on the demographic composition of the almshouse. Without large numbers of children or young adults, the number of inmates within the asylum declined while the proportion of elderly inmates rose significantly. Immediately after the Civil War, for example, children made up 29% of inmates at the Charleston, South Carolina almshouse. In 1867, the great majority were removed to newly created orphanages. With the able bodied already confined to a "Bettering House," and the insane placed in the state insane asylum, the poorhouse became filled primarily by the dependent old (Haber & Gratton, 1987; City of Charleston, 1867). Similarly, in late nineteenth-century San Francisco, the average age of poorhouse residents rose from 37 in 1870 to 59 in 1894 (Smith, 1895).

Such statistics clearly reflected the tendency of welfare officials to remove other groups from the almshouse while allowing the old to remain as residents. To some degree, this policy reflected the pessimistic, mid nineteenth century view of the abilities of the old. Although the young were seen as reformable, and the recently insane of regaining their sanity, the old were viewed as having already lived beyond their time. It made little sense, as the New York Association to Improve the Condition of the Poor (NYAICP) wrote, to expend resources on persons "who, from infirmity, imbecility, old age, or any other cause are likely to continue unable to earn their own support, and consequently to be permanently dependent" (New York Association to Improve the Condition of the Poor, 1853, p. 36). The best that could be given the old was a shelter for their remaining years.

The placement of the old in almshouses was also dictated by economic considerations. Throughout the late nineteenth century, welfare officials looked to send their aged charges to the least costly institution. In 1883, the State of California allocated one hundred dollars for each pauper over

60. Local officials immediately transferred the poverty-stricken elderly to country almshouses in which the yearly cost of sustenance fell well under the appropriated sum. It was hardly surprising, then, that California almshouses, such as the one in San Francisco, rapidly filled with the old. The confinement of the dependent elderly actually served to increase the coffers of each of the state's municipalities (Smith, 1895).

Thus, while new asylums welcomed the insane, the sick, and the reformable, the needy old were greatly underrepresented at these institutions. In insane asylums that advertised quick cures for the recently afflicted, superintendents agreed that it was pointless to spend countless hours or great expense on patients who had little chance for recovery or a productive life (Grob, 1986; Rosenkrantz & Vinovskis, 1978). Similarly, in the late nineteenth century, hospitals managers who had traditionally made room for large numbers of poverty-stricken elderly patients began to alter their policies. In an attempt to convince the public that the modern hospital had evolved into scientific centers for acutely ill, curable, and paying patients, they advised the elderly to seek other shelter. In the 1890s, for example, Carney Hospital of Boston radically altered their long-standing admissions policy. Although they had once reserved an entire floor of the institution for elderly persons, they now rejected all "permanently chronic patients . . ." The new hospital, they declared, was no longer the proper place for such impoverished, and hopeless, individuals (Vogel, 1974; Vogel, 1980).

By the early twentieth century, then, the transformation of the almshouse was well underway. In initially reorganizing the almshouse, welfare authorities had assumed the greatest impact would be felt by the young and able bodied who would either decline relief or come under their control. Although on an individual basis almshouse relief was far more expensive than outdoor assistance, reformers imagined that their costs would be drastically cut; few, they assumed would voluntarily chose the intentionally ominous almshouse. At the same time, reformers removed individuals from the institution who, they believed, needed reform, rather than punishment. Placing children in orphanages, the insane in mental asylums, and acutely ill in short-term hospitals, they hoped to established asylums that promised neither uplift nor comfort, but simply the most horrendous of existences.

In designing this system, welfare advocates hardly directed their wrath toward the old. Yet more than any other group the debilitated elderly experienced the harsh consequences of the redesigned almshouse. Unlike the young, they were rarely judged to be capable of reform; unlike the able bodied, they were hardly able to struggle on their own. Thus, as other individuals were placed in more attractive asylums, or attempted to remain outside the institution, the impoverished elderly became the institution's most prominent residents. Although in 1880 the percentage of almshouse inmates above the age of 60 had been 33%, it grew to 53% in 1904 and 67% in 1923 (Hoffman, 1909; Gratton, 1986; Grob, 1986).

The transformation in the demographic composition of the almshouse was well noted and publicized. Numerous social scientists and welfare reformers studied the population as a microcosm of poverty in America. Although they also chartered national unemployment rates and levels of poverty, the almshouse served as the most tangible and heart-rending symbol of the elderly's plight. Through the wards of the almshouse, they hoped to discover and publicize the impact of late nineteenth-century industrialization. Given the harsh conditions of the almshouse, they asked, and the worthy status of the old, why were the aged incarcerated at all?

In the search for answers, social analysts repeatedly made two critical and erroneous assumptions. First, seeing that the aged had become a majority of the American almshouse population, they assumed that poverty and dependency among the aged had also increased rapidly. In their charts and surveys of individuals *within* the institution, they emphasized the difficulties that awaited even the most providential aged worker. In contrast to past experts who had linked poverty to drink or laziness, they pronounced old age itself to be cause of dependency. The social reformers concluded—without much in-depth study of the self-sufficient old—that even those who struggled outside the asylum were, in time, likely to be institutionalized (Pennsylvania Commission on Old Age Pensions, 1919).

The first assumption of Progressive analysts, however, appears to have had little real merit. The number of elderly individuals in American almshouses was hardly proof that a sudden rise in poverty among the aged ever occurred. Nor did almshouse figures reveal that most elderly individuals would eventually come to depend on some form of public relief. Although the poorhouse population was increasingly composed of aged individuals, the proportion of the American aged who were incarcerated between 1880 and 1920 remained virtually unchanged. As we have seen, the shift in the demographic composition of poorhouses was the result of specific bureaucratic and financial decisions made by politicians and welfare administrators, rather than rising dependency among the nation's aged population.

Yet the first error led to a second, and equally erroneous, supposition. Contemplating the assumed rising dependency among the old, and observing the coincident ascendancy of an industrial economy, Progressive analysts charged that industrialization and urbanization were the sources of the elderly's new vulnerability. Edward T. Devine, Abraham Epstein, Isaac Rubinow, Lee Welling Squier, Arthur J. Todd, Amos Warner, joined by a legion of other critics, asserted that as long as America had been a rural and agricultural land, the old had been greatly respected (Devine, 1898, 1904, 1909; Epstein, 1922, 1929; Rubinow, 1913, 1934; Squier, 1912; Todd, 1915; Warner, 1894; Dahlin, 1983). The elderly's memory of the past was indispensible; their knowledge and skills had great value. In the modern world, however, the aged were left with few significant roles. "The socio-economic problem of the old man or woman. . . ," wrote Isaac Rubinow, "is specifically a problem of modern society, a result of the rapid industrialization within the last century" (Rubinow, 1913, p. 302). Relegated to "the industrial scrap heap," the old, not surprisingly, were forced to end their lives confined to the nation's almshouses (Rubinow, 1913; Todd, 1915).

In reality, however, this assumption was as inaccurate as the belief in the elderly's ever-growing dependency (Haber & Gratton, in press). The perception, though, was clearly in line with late nineteenth-century beliefs about aging that emphasized the elderly's inability to remain vital or independent in modern society. Sociological studies, such as the ground-breaking surveys of the Englishman Charles Booth, and subsequent work by Lee Welling Squier, Abraham Epstein, and other American reformers, seemed to demonstrate that old age and pauperism were inherently related. According to Booth, at least a third of all almshouse admissions were due not to individual failures or misfortunes but simply to the vicissitudes of aging. Moreover, both Booth and Epstein stressed that a startling high percentage of the non-institutionalized old lived in or near poverty. "Old age and dependency," Epstein concluded, "are indeed inter-related and too closely associated" (Booth, 1892, 1894; Simey & Simey, 1960; Squier, 1912; Epstein, 1929, p. 35).

The source of this relationship, all agreed, was industrialization. It denied the older worker an opportunity to make a decent living, provided the young with a wage insufficient to support old age, and tore apart the old systems of family support that had sustained older people for centuries. It was hardly surprising, then, that elderly individuals found themselves both abandoned and impoverished in their old age.

For such experts, the large number of impoverished and incapacitated elderly persons confined to public institutions simply confirmed their expectations. The rise in aged inmates, these critics argued, was a sure sign of the irreversibly expanding dependency of the elderly in industrial society. With time, they assumed, all aged individuals, whether presently institutionalized or not, would face impoverishment and isolation. Subject to incurable illness, likely to experience a diminished capacity for work, and often partly dependent on the earnings of children or Civil War annuities, they could not escape their increasing weaknesses and ultimate obsolescence. "[F]or the great mass of wage-earners," Epstein explained, "inability to maintain their regular employment makes dependency in old age inescapable and inevitable" (Epstein, 1929, p. 60). Many of the aged would share the inevitable fate of tottering "over the hill" to the poorhouse.

Although the rhetoric of almshouse residency clearly did not reflect reality, its impact was enormous. The errors of the reformers did not limit the effectiveness of their arguments or the dominant role their assumptions played in calls for social reform. While patently mistaken, these ideas had striking effects on both the political and social history of old age in America. By the early twentieth century, the inquiries into the causes of old age dependency began to produce consequences far beyond the limited number of inmates who were confined to the asylums' wards. The institution, in fact, had not just become an object of horror for the extremely poor; it had also evolved into a symbol of the supposedly inevitable fate of all older Americans.

Analysts argued, in fact, that their investigations into almshouse conditions had important ramifications: Long lists of individuals waiting to be placed in private institutions, worthy persons still forced to reside in almshouses, and thousands of aged individuals who existed on the edge of poverty all proved the increasing dependency of the elderly in the industrial world. Confusing growing absolute numbers with unchanging proportions, they argued that almshouse residency had become a threat even to the hardworking middle class. In 1925, in her influential study *Aged Clients of Boston's Social Agencies*, Lucille Eaves asserted that "the risks of being left without means of meeting [the needs] of old age are not confined to the workers with low earning capacity but are shared by persons in all ranks of society" (Eaves, 1925, p. 3). Despite the fact that the great majority of aged persons continued to lead self-sufficient lives, the lesson from those within the public asylum seemed clear: Poverty in old age was not limited to the traditionally poor; it had become the dominant threat, and prevailing fear, among America's older population.

Throughout the early twentieth century, public welfare advocates fraternal groups, and state labor federations all exploited this fear, and the horror of the ever encroaching almshouse. In their campaign for new welfare programs, they repeatedly addressed the widespread anxiety that, without the intervention of broad social programs, ill chance or bad health could force even the most industrious individuals "over the hill" to the poorhouse. As a pervasive image, the almshouse needed little explanation. "The poorhouse," wrote Epstein, "stands as a threatening symbol of the deepest humiliation and degradation before all wage-earners after the prime of life" (Epstein, 1929, p. 128). Given this fear, welfare authorities argued that the harsh almshouse should no longer play a central role in the care of the dependent elderly. The aged, they argued, needed care and support, not punitive measures to discourage application of charity.

The reformers' attack on the ominous almshouse then took a number of forms. First, welfare authorities attempted to restructure the almshouse itself. By the early twentieth century they argued that the public institutions no longer housed diverse groups of inmates and should be adapted to their transformed purpose. "The institution as a whole," the visiting medical staff of the Long Island Almshouse and Hospital of Massachusetts wrote in 1904, "because of the infirm character of its inmates, is gradually and inevitably assuming the general character of a hospital" (Long Island Hospital, 1905, p. 15). Homer Folks, Commissioner of New York City's charities, agreed. Campaigning to change the public image of the almshouse, he argued that it had assumed a new function in society. In the past it had served to punish the criminal and discipline the indolent; now its primary role was to provide medical care for the aged and impoverished. "The fact," he declared, "the inmates of our almshouses . . . are definitely removed by physical disability from the possibility of self-support . . . seems to me to be extremely important." Was it not time, he asked, "when the inmates of our almshouse should be considered as more nearly related to hospital patients than paupers?" (Folks, 1903b, p. 298).

In redesigning their institutions, city leaders increasingly acknowledged that the large number of elderly inmates had a permanent influence upon the operation of their asylum. In contrast to the past, Charleston's officials explained, the inmates were now expected to do little real labor as most were "old and infirm, utterly destitute, and unable to take care of themselves" (*Charleston City Year Book*, 1887, p. 193). In such institutions, attempts to dissuade individuals from entering the asylum, or to reform their characters once they arrived, seemed useless. According to the asylums' superintendents, after years of struggle, the old had earned the right to call the almshouse "Home" (*Charities and the Commons*, 1900; *Charleston City Year Book*, 1925, pp. 163–64).

Welfare officials attempted to recognize this transformation and eradicate the notion of a punitive institution. In 1903, the Charity Board of New York City renamed its public almshouse the Home for the Aged and Infirm. In 1913, Charleston, South Carolina officials transformed their asylum into the "Charleston Home" (Folks, 1903a; *Charleston City Year Book*, 1914). In their annual reports they argued that the institutions were no longer punitive places that dispensed only the barest necessities along with the harshest discipline. From New York to South Carolina they reported of the improved conditions within the "home." Aged New York paupers, the managers explained in 1900, would find, "a warm room and clean comfortable beds to sleep in—good wholesome and varied food to eat, a church to go to, plenty of papers, magazines, and books to read." An elderly white South Carolinian, according to the city's authorities, would be treated to steam heat, good food, and plenty of appropriate reading matter (*Charities and the Commons*, 1900, p. 133; *Charleston City Year Book*, 1925, pp. 163–64).

Despite such rosy descriptions, the campaign to reform the almshouse had extreme limitations. Advocates for the old remained largely unconvinced that the institution now served as an adequate shelter. The addition of flowering plants, the distribution of newspapers, or even the alteration of the asylum's name did little to alter the fact that elderly inmates ended their lives in the most demeaning of institutions. Early twentieth-century inquiries into almshouse conditions continued to argue that the elderly unjustly crowded into institutions originally designed to be both repugnant and punitive. Despite the best intentions of superintendents and the efforts of charitable organizations, social reformers asserted that, ultimately, almshouses were nothing more than "concentration camps for the aged" (Rubinow, 1930, p. 178).

The widespread antagonism to the almshouse was then apparent in a second form of institution reform. Since the nineteenth century, benevolent groups had established old age homes as preferred alternatives to the almshouse. To a large extent, these groups were motivated by the belief that some aged individuals—especially if they were native born and female—were too worthy and upstanding to be consigned to such a terrible fate. Their past lives had not been filled with depravity or wickedness; they did not deserve to end their lives amidst the squalor of immigrant-filled almshouses. The solution, many reformers and church groups agreed, was to select the most worthy of the old and house them in newly established old age homes.

The development of these private institutions was, then, intricately linked to the existence of the public almshouse. In Boston, the same elites who espoused harsh principles of public relief and built punitive institutions, contributed to the establishment of private old age homes. Their actions were hardly paradoxical. In their endeavors they demonstrated the persistent belief that the old were deserving of compassionate assistance—although such superior care was limited to individuals of appropriate caste and nativity. For them the problem of worthy, though impoverished, elderly individuals could be remedied simply by placing specific individuals into more pleasant institutional surroundings (Gratton, 1986; Haber, 1983).

Continuously throughout the nineteenth and into the twentieth centuries, the development of old age homes was motivated by the pervasive fear that worthy individuals—generally of an appropriate ethnic or religious background—would end their days confined to an almshouse. Founders of old age homes described their institutions as the only true means of "sav[ing] from the almshouse those whose previous life has been upright and respectable, and for whom almshouse association is cruelty" (*Charities*, 1898a, 1898b, 1898c, 1898d, 1898e). Even the earliest old age home justified its establishment as an alternative to the institution. The organizers of Philadelphia's Indigent Widows' and Single Women's Society explained the need for charitable institutions through what was to become almost the archetypal story. Upon visiting the almshouse, its members discovered two respectable, aged women forced by poverty to end their days confined to undifferentiated wards in the poorhouse. The horror of it was overwhelming; here was tangible proof that individuals of their own class could be reduced to shame and impoverishment. For the Society, the discovery of such humiliated females became a clear call to action. "We feel grateful," the members explained, "that through the indulgence of Divine Providence, our efforts have, in some degree, been successful, and have preserved many who once lived respectfully from becoming residents in the Alms House" (Home for Aged Women, 1880, pp. 5–6). A similar sentiment motivated the founders of Boston's first old age home in 1849. Like the Philadelphia home, the goal of the Association for the Relief of Indigent Females was to rescue worthy elderly women who had "a natural repugnance . . . to be herded with paupers of every character, condition, and clime" (Gratton, 1986, pp. 100–101).

In their establishment of old age homes, organizers, therefore, stressed that they selected only "proper" candidates, rejecting or removing those who failed to live up to their high standards. In contrast to the almshouse, they were not intended for the most impoverished immigrants. According to Henry B. Rogers, President of Boston's Home for Aged Women, the mass influx of immigrants into the city had a dramatic effect upon the almshouse and poor relief. Foreigners, he declared, "have taken possession of the public charities . . . as they have of the houses where our less privileged class formerly resided." Abandoning the almshouse to the immigrant poor, Rogers dedicated the new Boston home as a haven for those who were "bone of our bone, and flesh of our flesh" (Rogers, 1850, pp. 7–8). For numerous founders such as Rogers, the existence of the almshouse was simple proof of the need for such institutions. In their annual reports and fund raising campaigns, they required little more than the image of the ominous almshouse to justify their existence (Haber, 1983; Carleton-Laney, 1988).

While reforming the almshouse and providing institutional alternatives remained central themes of welfare advocates, the symbolic use of the almshouse was not limited to the already incarcerated. By arguing that most aged persons were threatened with institutionalization, advocates for the old extended their appeals well beyond the asylum walls. Through their repeated assertion that even the hardworking old faced dependency, reformers radically changed the impact of the almshouse. In contrast to the past, it no longer stood as an ominous institution, to be avoided through hard work and planning. Rather, its reach had become enormous; reformers argued that most aged individuals were possible candidates for its wards. The most effective solution to the problem of the almshouse, then, was to provide state support to *all* old persons.

In the movement for the establishment of state and national pensions, in fact, the almshouse assumed its greatest impact. In arguing for pensions, welfare advocates used their rhetoric about almshouse residency as a central part of three distinctive, although clearly related, appeals. In each of these arguments, the almshouse reached beyond the few who were actually institutionalized. Instead, for the pension movement, the almshouse had become a symbol far larger than its inmate population.

First, as part of an emotional plea for legislation, the almshouse was evoked to symbolize the callous treatment industrial society awarded the elderly. According to pension advocates, the institution openly violated the long-standing American belief that the elderly deserved respectful treatment. Even in the late nineteenth century, in their successful agitation for a more generous Civil War pension system, annuity advocates had consistently drawn on the indignity of compelling good American citizens to enter the almshouse (Glasson, 1900). By the twentieth century, according to one social analyst, "almshouse," had become "a word of hate and loathing, for it includes the composite horrors of poverty, disgrace, loneliness, humiliation, abandonment and degradation" (Epstein, 1929, p. 128). An early twentieth-century illustration in the magazine of the fraternal group, the Eagles, depicted what was to become a commonly accepted image. In the sketch, an aged couple received notification that the man's services were "no longer required" as today "young men only need apply." The announcement was emblazoned with the words: "Passport to the Poorhouse." Notwithstanding their apparently middle-class surroundings (complete with a needlepoint reading "Bless Our Home"), little question remained as to the fate that awaited them (*The Eagle Magazine*, cited in Quadagno, 1988).

Even almshouse administrators began to argue that the almshouse represented an undeserved and heartless fate for its aged residents. In 1897, Ernest C. Marshall, in his *Annual Report of the Institutions Commissioners to the City of Boston*, strongly opposed placing elderly individuals into the city's institutions. Few of the elderly, he argued, had led unworthy lives or demonstrated vices deserving of such treatment. Although their only crime was to have experienced the loss of their children or the depletion of their savings, the city's laws mandated their incarceration. Arguing that "the placing of these unfortunate poor in the almshouse is not the kind, humane or even just way of treating them," he called on his superiors to insure that "it be no longer said that Massachusetts brings shame to old age, the blush to wrinkled faces, by classing them under the shameful name of paupers" (Marshall, 1898).

The almshouse also served a second symbolic function in the campaign for old age pensions: It was evoked as overwhelming economic proof of the need to reform the welfare system. Such institutions, analysts contended, were fiscally irresponsible because they required inordinate public expenditure. According to a 1923 Department of Labor study of 2183 almshouses, each institutionalized person required $440 annually in public expenditure. More than half of these institutions, the study noted, were patently inefficient. Housing fewer than 25 inmates, they incurred high fixed costs simply for upkeep and maintenance (U.S. Bureau of the Census, 1925). With such a large portion of the budget given to building expenses, the inmates had little hope of receiving adequate daily care. Such economic arguments were not entirely novel. Two decades before, a 1903 investigation of Boston's Long Island Almshouse had found that large budgetary requirements did not result in happy conditions for the aged inmates. Sufficient clothing, comfortable quarters, and ample food were often neglected (*Majority and Minority Reports*, 1903).

But the fiscal irresponsibility of the institutions went beyond their high budgets and meager provisions. Critics had long charged that the elderly could be more efficiently supported in their own homes. By the 1920s, private social workers maintained that $500 per year would support an elderly couple living in the community. Commissions considering public support of the aged set $1 per day, per recipient, or $365 per year as the maximum allotment to be distributed. Both these sums were far less than the cost of supporting individuals in the almshouse (Massachusetts Commission on Pensions, 1925).

This economic perspective served to buttress traditional uneasiness about incarcerating elderly people, and justified replacing the traditional system with old age pensions. "It is well known," wrote the Illinois State Federation of Labor in 1923, "that the cost of maintaining an aged person in a public institution is far in excess of the amount it is proposed to pay such person in the form of a pension" (Illinois State Federation of Labor, cited in Quadagno, 1988, pp. 70–71). In the 1920s, the economic benefits of old age pensions became a central theme in the movement for state annuities. The Fraternal Order of Eagles, instrumental in the campaign's success, asserted that not only did the almshouse represent moral weakness on the part of society, but economic failure as well. Incarceration of the old in an almshouse, they argued, actually cost the taxpayer more than an economically sound old age pension system (Quadagno, 1988).

In the call for the establishment of pensions, the almshouse then served a third symbolic purpose: Its existence, critics charged, not only affected the old but had grave implications for younger persons as well. The dread of almshouse residency was so great, social advocates declared, that individuals would take any step to avoid incarceration. According to Reverend George B. O'Conor, Director of Catholic Charities in the Archdiocese of Boston, the good parishioners of his city's working districts "would rather starve to death" than enter the poorhouse (*Boston Globe*, 1923). As a result, relatives made great sacrifices to save their elders from this ignominious fate, as well as to prevent the entire family from sharing in the individual's shame. Reformers asserted that, faced with a choice of allowing old relatives to enter the poorhouse, or keeping necessary funds for themselves, adult children generally relinquished their own economic security and well-being (Epstein, 1929; Roosevelt, 1929). Such individuals even sacrificed the next generation by placing their own children in the labor market, at the expense of their future skills and education. Consider the dilemma, wrote Mabel Nassau in her 1915 study, *Old Age Poverty in Greenwich Village*, "of the middle generation trying to decide whether to support the aged parents and thus have less to eat for themselves and for their children . . . or to put the old people in an institution!" (Nassau in Lubove, 1968, p. 133).

Social advocates for the aged were not alone in the utilization of the almshouse as a metaphor for strained generational relations. Leading liberal economists presented similar briefs. "Because of the necessity of supporting the aged," wrote the editors of *The Worker in Industrial Society* in 1923, "the children are frequently doomed to under-nourishment; and to a life in the midst of crowded and unsanitary quarters; to leave school early in life and in their turn to join the ranks of the unskilled" (Douglas, Hitchcock, & Atkins, 1923, p. 465). Even politicians argued that the threat of the almshouse insured that resources needed by the young would be spent on the support of increasingly dependent and unproductive aged individuals. "Many married sons and daughters," wrote Massachusetts Senator David I. Walsh in 1927, "in order to spare their aged parents the disgrace of bitterness and pauperism, assume burdens which cannot be borne except at the cost of depriving their children of the rights of childhood and the opportunities of success, and of dooming themselves in turn to an old age of helpless dependence" (*American Legislative Labor Review*, 1927, p. 224).

The assumptions inherent in the multifaceted symbolic use of the almshouse were not, however, universally accepted. Critics of state pensions challenged the inevitability of the almshouse for the old and tried to convince Americans that they could save for old age. "It is difficult to understand," wrote Frederick L. Hoffman in 1908:

> *why those who are so profoundly interested in this subject of old age pensions and the more or less deplorable condition of the poor in old age do not take steps to secure by direct inquiry and careful analysis the fact which will go to explain why three-fourths or more of the population in old age are not in the poorhouses, not public charges, and not economically dependent in any sense whatever (Hoffman, 1909, pp. 383-84).*

Other critics charged that pensions would not "empty the poorhouse, or lessen public relief" (Morse, 1908, p. 257). Yet even conservatives recognized that the almshouse was a most compelling symbol of old age poverty; ultimately, it could not be ignored. The popular perception of the horrible condition in the institution, declared P. Tecumseh Sherman of the National Civic Federation in 1929, was a major factor in the "growing demand for public old age pension laws" (Sherman, 1929, p. 40). The anti-pension group's arguments about the importance of saving and thrift did little to quell the popular fear of eventual institutionalization.

Politicians of the 1920s were quick to grasp the importance of this widely shared anxiety. In his campaign and tenure as Governor of New York, Franklin Delano Roosevelt intensified a theme of his predecessor Alfred E. Smith, and focused upon the seemingly inevitable impoverishment of the aged worker. In his speeches and legislative messages, Roosevelt described old age in terms well known to welfare advocates. The destitution of the elderly, he declared, was an inevitable "by-product of modern industrial life." With urban and industrial growth, the old could do little to escape institutionalization. Age discrimination against older men, Roosevelt stated, meant that the "aged, worn-out worker . . . after a life of ceaseless effort and useful productivity must look forward for his declining years to a poorhouse" (Roosevelt, 1928, 1929).

As Governor, Roosevelt echoed the charge of charity reformers: The existence of the almshouse clearly illustrated the overwhelming need for a broad reaching program of state pensions. The incarceration of the impoverished old, he asserted, was both economically and morally wrong. It represented a "wasteful system" that deprived individuals of their hope and dignity. In both his acceptance speech and subsequent legislative initiatives, Roosevelt used the existence of the almshouse to justify state action. "We can no longer be satisfied," he declared in 1929, "with the old method of putting [the elderly] away in dismal institutions with the loss of self-respect, personality, and interest in life." With the adoption of an old age pension, Roosevelt argued, the old institutional poor law might be abandoned altogether and the elderly allowed to retain their esteem (Roosevelt, 1929; Howe, 1930).

By the late 1920s, Roosevelt, the New York Democratic Party, and politicians around the country had become convinced that broadly based popular support existed for old age pensions. Roosevelt did not hesitate to warn recalcitrant legislators that the fear of dependency in old age was widespread. "Judging by the number of letters I am receiving, there is a more widespread popular interest . . . than most of us people in public life had realized" (Roosevelt, 1928 box 16). Failure to realize the depth of concern was not only emotionally insensitive and economically wasteful, but could result in their own political suicide. Nor was Roosevelt alone in his political use of the almshouse as a salient issue. In the 1930 New York Assembly elections, Democratic candidates seized on the reluctance of Republicans to agree to pension legislation, arguing that "the poorhouse does not belong in this age of progress," since it "costs the State, or rather the taxpayer of each County, more than a proper system of pensions. So it is not only right but economical to wipe the poorhouse out of existence" (Howe, 1930 box 46).

In the critical debate over the Social Security Act in the 1930s, the poorhouse as a symbol reached its broadest audience. The Committee on Economic Security, commissioned by President Roosevelt to examine the conditions of the aged and to recommend legislation, used almshouse statistics to advance the case for a social insurance program. In their 1934 publication, *The Need for Economic Security in the United States*, the committee displayed silhouette figures of older men with canes to represent the rising proportion of elderly in public institutions. "The predominance of the aged in almshouses," they concluded, "is a sign of their increasing dependency." According to the commission, significant measures needed to be adopted to rectify what appeared to be an inevitable, and widespread trend (Committee on Economic Security, 1934).

By the 1930s, business, state, and federal old age pension programs addressed themselves directly to the seemingly widespread threat of incarceration. In part, their plans were designed to save the hardworking and industrious (although now unemployed) elderly from the ignominious fate of poorhouse residency. Pension advocates often took direct aim at the almshouse, declaring that monthly payments to the old would finally cause the demise of the long-hated institution (Epstein, 1922, 1929; Rubinow, 1913, 1934; Squier, 1912). Even the Supreme Court employed the symbol of the ominous almshouse when asserting the constitutionality of the Social Security Act. Writing for the majority in 1937, Justice Cardozo proclaimed that "the hope behind this statute is to save men and women from the rigors of the poorhouse as well as from the haunting fear that such a lot awaits them when journey's end is near" (*Helvering v. Davis*, 1937).

Justice Cardozo's characterization of the reformers' intention was apt indeed. The provisions of the Social Security Act of 1935 clearly reflected the New Dealers' attempt to destroy the long-standing institution. "We were," recalled Pennsylvania's Deputy Secretary of Public Assistance, "rather enthusiastic to empty the poorhouses" (Thomas, 1963, p. 97). Thus, in the federal legislation, residents of public institutions were categorized as totally ineligible for any form of Old Age Assistance; all others, whether residing in private asylums, alone, or with families, could receive state and federal assistance.

Not surprisingly, the legislation did have a significant impact upon the composition of the almshouse. States and counties chose to support the elderly in the most cost-efficient manner. The Old Age Assistance title in the Social Security Act carried a sizable federal subsidy for assistance in the recipients' homes or private quarters, but prohibited such aid in public institutions. It was obviously far more economical for state and local officials to provide federally supported Old Age Assistance than to pay the full cost in a public institution. In Kansas, officials rapidly transferred county homes to "private" control, although the supervisors usually remained the same (Fischer, 1943). In Charleston, South Carolina, New Deal legislation assured that most impoverished elderly individuals in the city and county would receive support through pensions rather than institution shelter; by 1938, 1,360 persons were granted Old Age Assistance (*Charleston City Year Book*, 1939). Sharing in a national trend, Charleston's almshouse population declined. In 1949 the city ruled that the public almshouses fulfilled little function. Most of the 27 inmates, municipal officials declared, could be better treated by receiving relief within their own households (*Charleston City Year Book*, 1949).

Not all the destitute, however, could be returned to their own homes. Charleston's authorities conceded that some aged individuals were in need of extensive medical care; these would be placed in local sanitariums. Similar actions were taken by city and county officials throughout the country. As public almshouses closed their doors for lack of federal assistance, the infirm elderly were placed in private boarding houses and asylums. Many of these establishments had already existed as informal nursing homes. Among the "most dramatic changes" induced by the Social Security Act was the encouragement it gave to a formal nursing home industry. With federal support, proprietors transformed what once had been boarding and rooming houses into more formal homes for the aged (Manard, et al., 1975).

Despite pension advocate assertions that state annuities would eliminate all such homes, the continued need for institutional care for a small proportion of the elderly had not been completely unforeseen. In the early 1930s welfare authorities such as Homer Folks argued that the government needed to recognize the dual function of the almshouse. The great majority of elderly residents, he stressed, were placed in public institutions not only because they were poor but also because they required extensive medical care. According to Folks, only about 15% of the institutionalized old were able to live independently on a pension. "The others," he declared, "are physically infirm and sick, and have various kinds of ailments and conditions that require personal attention of the kind that you could not get in an individual home; [they] require nursing or medical attention . . . in some sort of institution." Testifying before the New York Commission on Old Age Security, Folks argued that the government should not only consider the allocation of pensions but also the creation of an institutional provision for the support of the sick and ailing (Folks, cited by Thomas, 1969, p. 40).

Neither the federal nor state governments took action on Folks' recommendation. In the course of America's welfare history, the almshouse had become a symbol of failure and shameful treatment of the aged, far too pernicious to be granted broad federal support. Despite its relatively small inmate population, it stood as a symbol of an outdated and ruthless welfare system. Moreover, welfare officials did not want their recipients to be classified simply as needy paupers who needed to be rescued from poverty. Instead, they wanted old age pensioners to be seen as hardworking men and women who had earned their pensions through long years of labor. Not surprisingly, then, New Dealers excluded almshouse residents from Social Security and limited the ability of public institutions to provide for the debilitated elderly. As a result, the infirm elderly turned to newly created and largely unregulated private facilities (Snider, 1956). Displaced from the poorhouse and unable to receive support in any public medical institution, the debilitated old became the prime subjects of the burgeoning private nursing home industry of the late 1930s and 1940s (Moss & Halamandaris, 1977).

By 1950 it had become clear that the attack on the almshouse had served its purpose. Fulfilling neither a charitable nor a medical function, the two-hundred-year-old institution had finally lost its central role in the welfare system and could be treated more generously. This assessment, as well as the lobbying of public hospital associations, convinced Congress to amend

Social Security to allow federal support to individuals within both public and private medical institutions. The 1950 legislation, along with the Medical Facilities Survey and Construction Act of 1954, cemented the role Folks had foreseen for public nursing homes. While the old almshouse had become obsolete, federal support of public and private institutions made the nursing home the new shelter for society's most dependent and debilitated old (Thomas, 1969).

The greatest incentive to the private industry, however, came with the passage of Medicare in 1965. According to the legislation, aged individuals were eligible for support for up to 100 days of nursing home residency, following a three-day hospital stay. As a consequence, the nursing home industry, which had grown steadily in the years following Social Security, increased dramatically. Between 1960 and 1976, the number of homes grew by 140%, the nursing beds increased 302%, and, most significantly, the revenues received by the industry rose 2000% (Moss & Halamandaris, 1977).

To a great degree, the current debate over care for the old reflects the history in which it was shaped. For over 300 years, beliefs about the worthiness of the impoverished elderly have remained virtually unchanged. Since pre-industrial times, authorities have judged the aged pauper to be deserving of community relief. In dispensing charity, they generally linked the impoverishment of the old to their declining abilities, rather than to controllable vices or indolence. Yet, despite this persistent belief, the aged poor have been dramatically affected by changes in welfare systems directed to other groups of indigent persons. In the nineteenth century, hoping to limit relief and control the poor, welfare reformers forced recipients of public assistance into noxious poorhouses. Grouped along with the alcoholic, the orphan, and the vagrant, the elderly in need of assistance were threatened with institutionalization. By the late nineteenth and early twentieth centuries their incarceration assumed additional significance. The isolation of the aged in almshouses and private old age homes became a broadly accepted symbol of the declining status of the old. Rather than simply being the result of bureaucratic decisions, their dominant presence in the asylums seemed visible proof of their inevitable debilitation and dependency. In a modern, industrial society, most aged people, it was assumed, would ultimately require some form of public care.

By the 1930s, the attack on the almshouse had gained great momentum. Critics expressed great bewilderment as to how the institution could have come into existence. It seemed to play no ethical role; its costs far outweighed any possible benefits. Yet, in their arguments for state pensions, both welfare advocates and politicians displayed little historic memory. Their characterization of the fiscal irresponsibility of the institution, the immoral treatment of its inmates, and its effect on future generations bore little similarity to earlier expectations or assumptions. Nineteenth-century proponents of the public asylum had always known of the great expense of incarceration. They had been well aware that, on an individual basis, outdoor assistance was less costly. In their opinion, however, the almshouse was not only supposed to support the poor but was also intended to limit the numbers on public relief. By erecting a harsh, forbidding institution, charity officials believed they would discourage individuals from seeking relief and supply assistance to only the most debilitated and desperate.

The criticisms of welfare reformers, however, revealed that their perception of the institution and its inmate population had dramatically changed. According to surveys of charity officials, aged almshouse residents had little hope of avoiding institutionalization. The great majority of individuals within the asylums were there, according to Roosevelt, not as "a result of lack of thrift or energy," but "as a mere by-product of modern industrial life" (Roosevelt, 1929). The evolving nature of industrial society and their own unavoidable physical degeneration doomed them, in ever growing numbers, to the shame of incarceration. In the call for national pensions to replace the institutions, therefore, welfare advocates no longer believed that the almshouse served as a deterrent to indolent members of the lower class. Rather, in the opinion of a broad spectrum of Americans, it had become the inevitable—and the extremely unjust—final "home" for large numbers of elderly individuals who deserved far better treatment.

Although almshouses no longer exist, such institutional anxiety still concerns the nation. The elderly's long-standing fear that their days would end in the almshouse has a clear parallel in the contemporary belief that the nursing home might be their fate (Moss & Halamandaris, 1977). This widely shared fear aptly demonstrates a significant fallacy in the arguments of early pension advocates. In their desire to eliminate the almshouse, such reformers overestimated the effects of Social Security. Misreading the almshouse evidence, they predicted that the distribution of monthly annuities would eliminate the need for long-term institutions. As recent history reveals, however, a considerable minority of older people continued to require such care, and fear its effects, regardless of government stipends. By the 1970s, in fact, the outcry against nursing homes rivaled the late nineteenth and early twentieth century attack on the almshouse. According to consumer groups, it appeared little had changed. While some institutions offered high quality care, many simply warehoused the old and provided waiting rooms for death (Townsend, 1971). As the recent debate over catastrophic illness revealed, long-term care and institutionalization remain major economic and social concerns of old age.

Yet the impact of the pension advocates cannot be dismissed. The movement for old age pensions served to alter radically the condition and concerns of the nation's elderly. Social Security helped the most impoverished of the poor, especially of immigrant origins, avoid the horrors of the poorhouse. For millions of others it removed the desperate—if somewhat unfounded—fear that they might be thrust into a demeaning institutional environment. And for still more Americans, the children and grandchildren of the elderly, the New Deal measure created the assurance that they would not have to choose between providing for their own needs or rescuing their elders from the threat of almshouse residency. In shutting the poorhouse door, Social Security removed the dread of an institution that had cast its shadow over the elderly for more than two hundred years.

## REFERENCES

Achenbaum, W. A. (1978). *Old age in the new land.* Baltimore: The Johns Hopkins Press.
*American Labor Legislative Review.* (1927) *18*: 224.
Booth, C. (1892). *Pauperism and the endowment of old age.* London: Macmillan Company.
Booth, C. (1894). *The aged poor in England and Wales.* London: Macmillan Company.
*Boston Globe.* November 9, 1923.
Braham, D., & Catlin, G. (1874). Over the Hill to the Poor House, in *America's families: A documentary history,* D. Scott and B. Wishy, (Eds.). New York: Harper & Row 1975.
Carleton, W. (1871). Over the Hill to the Poorhouse. In *Growing old,* by G. Moss and W. Moss, (Eds). New York: Harper and Row 1982.
Carleton-Laney, I. (1988). Old folks homes for blacks during the progressive era. *Journal of Sociology and Social Welfare, 16,* 43–60.
*Charities.* (1898a). Charitable needs in New York. Vol. 1, no. 7, 1.
*Charities.* (1898b). Charitable needs in New York. Vol. 1, no. 8, 1.
*Charities.* (1898c). Charitable needs in New York. Vol. 1, no. 9, 9.
*Charities.* (1898d). Charitable needs in New York. Vol, 1, no. 10, 10.
*Charities.* (1898e). Charitable needs in New York. Vol. 1, no. 11, 8.
*Charities and the commons.* (1900). New York City Homes. Vol. no. 17, 133.
*Charleston City Year Book for 1886.* (1887). SC: City of Charleston.
*Charleston City Year Book for 1913.* (1914). SC: City of Charleston.
*Charleston City Year Book for 1924.* (1925). SC: City of Charleston.
*Charleston City Year Book for 1938.* (1939). SC: City of Charleston.
*Charleston City Year Book for 1948.* (1949). SC: City of Charleston.
City of Charleston. (15 May, 1867). *Poor House Journal.* Charleston City Archives. Charleston, SC.
Clement, P. (1985). *Welfare and the poor in the nineteenth-century city.* Rutherford, NJ: Farleigh Dickinson University Press.
Committee on Economic Security. (1934). *The need for economic security in the United States.* Washington, DC: U.S. Government Printing Office.
Dahlin, M. (1983). *From poorhouse to pension,* PhD. dissertation, Stanford University.
Devine, E. T. (1898). *Economics.* New York: Macmillan Company.

Devine, E. T. (1904). *The principles of relief.* New York: Macmillan Company.

Devine, E. T. (1909). *Misery and its causes.* New York: Macmillan Company.

Douglas, P. H., Hitchcock, C. N., & Atkins, W. E. (1923). *The worker in industrial society.* Chicago: University of Chicago Press.

Eaves, L. (1925). *Aged clients of Boston's social agencies.* Boston: Women's Educational and Industrial Union.

Epstein, A. (1922). *Facing old age.* New York: Alfred A. Knopf.

Epstein, A. (1929). *The problem of old age pensions in industry.* Harrisburg, PA: Pennsylvania Old Age Commission.

Fischer, V. (1943). Kansas county homes after the Social Security Administration. *Social Service Review, 17,* 442–65.

Folks, H. (1903a). Disease and dependence. *Charities, 10,* 499–500.

Folks, H. (1903b). Disease and dependence. *Charities, 11,* 297–300.

Glasson, W. H. (1900). *History of military pension legislation in the United States.* New York: Columbia University Press.

Gratton, B. (1986). *Urban elders.* Philadelphia: Temple University Press.

Grob, G. (1986). Explaining old age history. In *Old age in a bureaucratic society,* D. Van Tassel and P. N. Stearns (Eds.). Westport, CN: Greenwood Press.

Haber, C. (1983). *Beyond sixty-five.* New York: Cambridge University Press.

Haber, C., & Gratton, B. (1987). Old age, public welfare and race. *Journal of Social History, 21,* 263–279.

Haber, C., & Gratton, B. (1993). *Old age and the search for security: An American social history.* Bloomington, IN: Indiana University Press.

*Helvering v. Davis.* 1937. WO 0-301, U.S. 619, Fall Term, United States Supreme Court.

Hoffman, F. L. (1909). State pensions and annuities in old age. *Journal of the American Statistical Association, 11,* 363–408.

Home for Aged Women. (1880). *Thirtieth annual report.* Boston: Home for Aged Women.

Howe Papers. (1930). State Campaign 1930: Campaign Strategy. Box 46. FDR Library, Hyde Park, NY.

Katz, M. (1986). *In the shadow of the poorhouse.* New York: Basic Books.

Long Island Hospital. (1905). *Report of the Visiting Medical Staff, Long Island Hospital.* Seventh Annual Report of the Pauper Institutions Department for the Year ending 1904. Boston: City of Boston.

Lubove, Roy. (1968). *The struggle for Social Security 1900–1935.* Cambridge, MA: Harvard University Press.

Majority and minority reports of an investigation of Boston almshouse and hospitals of Long Island. (1904). Boston: Boston Municipal Printing Office.

Manard, B. B., Kent, C. S., Van Gils, D. W. L. (1975). *Old-age welfare institutions.* Lexington, MA: Lexington Books.

Marshall, E. (1898). *Annual report of the Institutions Commissioners to the City of Boston for 1897.* Documents of the City of Boston, number 14. Boston: City of Boston.

Massachusetts Commission on Pensions. (1925). *Report of old-age pensions.* Boston: Commonwealth of Massachusetts.

Morse, F. R. (1908). "Old Age Pensions in Great Britain and Ireland." *Charities and the Commons, 21,* 356–59.

Moss, F. E., & Halamandaris, V. J. (1977). *Too old, too sick, too bad.* Germantown, MD: Aspen Systems.

New York Association to Improve the Condition of the Poor. (1853). *Tenth Annual Report*. New York: NYAICP.

Pennsylvania Commission on Old Age Pensions. (1919). *Report*. Harrisburg, PA: Kuhn Publishing.

Quadagno, J. (1988). *The transformation of old age security*. Chicago: University of Chicago Press.

Rogers, H. B. (1850). *Remarks before the Association for Aged Indigent Females at the opening of their homes*. Boston: Association for Aged Indigent Females.

Roosevelt, F. D. (1928). Campaign speeches. Papers of FDR, Box 16. FDR Library, Hyde Park, NY.

Roosevelt, F. D. (1929). Legislation: Old age pensions. Papers. New York State Archives and Record Administration.

Rosenkrantz, B., & Vinovskis, M. (1978). The invisible lunatics. In *Aging and the elderly*, S. Spicker, K. Woodward, and D. Van Tassell, (Eds.). Atlantic Highlands, NJ: Humanities Press.

Rothman, D. (1971). *The discovery of the asylum*. Boston: Little, Brown and Company.

Rubinow, I. M. (1913). *Social insurance*. New York: Henry Holt & Company.

Rubinow, I. M. (1930). The modern problem of the care of the aged. *Social Service Review, 4*, 178.

Rubinow, I. M. (1934). *The quest for security*. New York: Henry Holt & Company.

Sherman, P. T. (1929). Address at the Annual Meeting of the National Association of Manufacturers. *The older worker in industry*. New York: National Association of Manufacturers.

Simey, T. S., & Simey, M. B. (1960). *Charles Booth: Social scientist*. London: Oxford University Press.

Smith, M. R. (1895). Almshouse women. *American Statistical Association, 4*, 219–62.

Snider, C. F. (1956). The fading almshouse. *National municipal review*, 60–65.

Squier, L. W. (1912). *Old age dependency in the United States*. New York: Macmillan Company.

Thomas, W. Jr. (1969). *Nursing homes and public policy*. Ithaca, NY: Cornell University Press.

Todd, A. J. (1915). Old age and the industrial scrap heap, *American Statistical Association, 14*, 550–57.

Townsend, C. (1971). *Old age: the last segregation*. New York: Grossman.

U.S. Bureau of the Census. (1925). *Paupers in the almshouse: 1923*. Washington, DC: U.S. Government Printing Office.

Vogel, M. (1974). *Boston's hospitals*. PhD. Dissertation, University of Chicago.

Vogel, M. (1980). *The invention of the modern hospital*. Chicago: University of Chicago Press.

Warner, A. (1894). The causes of poverty further considered. *American Statistical Association, 4*, 49–68.

# The Elderly and
# the Almshouses:
# Some Further Reflections

## Maris A. Vinovskis

Carole Haber has written a thoughtful and useful analysis of the relationship between rhetoric and reality in the care of the elderly in almshouses in the nineteenth and twentieth centuries. She points out that although welfare reformers and the popular media often portrayed poorhouses as the inevitable and ominous residences for most of the elderly, in fact only a small percentage of older Americans ever lived in one of these institutions. Moreover, Haber demonstrates how fears of the poorhouse spurred legislation for pensions for the elderly and eventually led to the demise of this institution in the twentieth century.

Although they did not necessarily disagree or challenge her overall interpretation of the role of almshouses in the development of alternative forms of assistance for the elderly, let me suggest a few refinements for her analysis as well as raise some questions that may stimulate further research in this interesting area.

Perhaps it might be useful to look more closely at the changing images of almshouses and how our perceptions of them may vary, depending on who is describing them. For example, Haber discusses in considerable detail the very stark and negative view of poorhouses by welfare reformers and old age assistance advocates. She recognizes that many of their portrayals were inaccurate and deliberately exaggerated, especially in regard to the likelihood of someone being sent there, but argues persuasively that their distortions had a powerful impact on policy makers and the general public.

Yet Haber also reminds us that by the late nineteenth and early twentieth century, not all welfare reformers agreed among themselves on the function or the image of almshouses. She cites the efforts of welfare authorities to restructure almshouses into facilities for medical care and the attempts by reformers like Homer Folks to change their public image. Similarly, in Michigan, the state Board of Corrections and Charities (BCC) suggested in the early twentieth century that all county almshouses should become asylums for the indigent sick—although most local welfare officials resisted efforts at expanding the medical care at those facilities (Whitaker, 1986). Therefore, it would be very useful to know more about the nature and extent of disagreements over the rhetoric about almshouses in the early twentieth century and why the opponents of poorhouses seemed to win so decisively. Did the disagreements among experts over the portrayal of poorhouses affect how policy makers or the public reacted to these institutions? Did the professionals who had a more sanguine view of the possibilities for almshouses also share their opponents' views that most elderly were likely to spend their last days in one of these homes?

One of the difficulties in evaluating the impact of the rhetoric of reformers is that we often do not have comparable information from their opponents. Therefore, I wonder what were images of poorhouses and the likelihood of an elderly person being there, according to the opponents of old age pension programs? When Haber quotes the views about the elderly and almshouses of Massachusetts' Senator David Walsh or New York gubernatorial candidate Franklin Delano Roosevelt in their efforts to help the aged, how did their political opponents respond? Indeed, she mentions Frederick Hoffman, who opposed state pensions and who questioned the inevitability of most elderly going to an almshouse. Too often historians have written about reform efforts from the perspective of the advocates without adequate attention being devoted to those who did not favor those reforms.

If the images of the relationship between almshouses and the elderly may have been somewhat contested among policy makers and welfare reformers and administrators, what about the images in the popular media? Haber seems to imply that the images of the poorhouse in journals, popular music, and early movies were strongly negative and cites the poem in *Harper's Weekly* about "Over the Hill and to the Poor House" as well as D. W. Griffith's 1911 film, *What Should We Do With Our Old?* But were such depictions of almshouses common in the popular media and therefore likely to continually remind the public of the horrors of these institutions? There is always a danger, as we have already seen in our debates about the images of the elderly in the nineteenth century, that we may unintentionally distort portrayals in the popular media by focusing on a few isolated, but provocative discussions of older Americans. What we need is a more systematic content analysis of the images of the relationship between almshouses and the elderly in the mass media.

Haber suggests that the mid-nineteenth-century almshouses played "an increasingly important role in the care of the dependent old and in the discussion of their assumed needs and capabilities." Therefore, we might expect that in popular portrayals of the elderly, especially fictionalized accounts, we may find dramatic instances of the elderly being sent to almshouse or dying alone in poorhouses. Yet a brief, and admittedly limited, examination suggests that we may need further work on these issues.

Jane Range and I did a content analysis of short stories in a popular monthly magazine, *Littell's Living Age*, from 1845 to 1882 (Range & Vinovskis, 1981). Altogether we drew a sample of 293 short stories (about 10% of the total number) and asked a series of questions about the images of the elderly characters in them. Overall our conclusion was that the elderly characters in the fiction published in *Littell's Living Age* were surprisingly healthy and independent. Contrary to the work of David Fischer (1978) on the elderly, we found them portrayed in a much more favorable light.

For each of the elderly characters in the stories, we inquired whether or not the person was in an asylum or an old folks home. It is interesting that only one of the 206 elderly characters in our sample was portrayed as ever being in a poorhouse. In other words, less than 1% of the elderly characters in these short stories were depicted as being in a poorhouse. Unfortunately, we did not attempt to code whether or not a poorhouse was ever mentioned in those stories, but if we had, I would be surprised if poorhouses would have been mentioned frequently.

Perhaps there would be more of a linkage between almshouses and the elderly in mid-nineteenth-century popular literature if we examined other sources of information in the magazines, such as editorials or news accounts. Or maybe the results might be different if we looked at more working-class publications rather than magazines intended for the middle class. Nevertheless, until we produce more detailed, content analyses of popular literature, music, and movies it will be difficult for us to assess how frequently the concern about the elderly and almshouses that Haber cites actually occurred in the media.

Naturally the final logical step in my argument is that we will need to look carefully at the writings of contemporaries to examine the extent of anxiety they had about spending the last years of their lives in a poorhouse. Though any studies based on private diaries and letters are limited by the nature of these sources, they may help us to assess Haber's statement that "[t]he continual and widespread fear of asylum residency had a dramatic impact upon . . . public perceptions of the old. . . ." Although I have no reason or evidence to doubt her statement, I will feel more reassured when additional studies of the private writings of more ordinary Americans are completed.

When we do investigate the views of contemporaries about their likelihood of being in a poorhouse in their old age, let me suggest some useful, possible variations to keep in mind. First, are there economic differences? Naturally we would expect that members of the working class and poor might be the most anxious about ending up in a poorhouse because their economic resources are already somewhat limited. But what about individuals from more affluent, white-collar occupations? John Modell (1978) and others have shown how precarious and sometimes short-lived economic prosperity was in nineteenth-century America—even for members of the middle class. When these more fortunate individuals thought about their old age, was the possibility of residence in an almshouse a real source of anxiety for them as well?

What about ethnic or racial differences? Did African-Americans, for instance, fear ending up in a poorhouse as much as comparable foreign-born or native-born citizens? Indeed, did African-Americans even have an opportunity to obtain the meager help offered in most poorhouses or did they also face discrimination in admittance there as they did in many other areas of public welfare assistance?

Did gender play a role in concern about going to an almshouse in old age? Although the life expectancy of men and women in mid-nineteenth-century America was nearly identical, widowers were more likely to remarry than widows and, therefore, elderly women might be more likely to be alone in facing the prospect of going to a poorhouse (Vinovskis, 1981, 1990b). Moreover, widowers probably were more able to earn enough money to support themselves than widows. On the other hand, several scholars have noted that older widows were more likely to live with their children than elderly widowers. Therefore, were elderly men or women more likely to be in an almshouse?

Andrew Achenbaum (1978) has found, using the 1910 U.S. Bureau of the Census data on almshouse paupers, that elderly men considerably outnumber elderly women in those institutions. Similarly, a study of Michigan county almshouses in the early twentieth century revealed that the majority of elderly inmates were men (Whitaker, 1986). Therefore, were there gender differences, after controlling for other factors, in the degree of anxiety among elderly males and females about being sent to a poorhouse?

In addition to variations in concern about going to a poorhouse based on wealth, ethnicity or race, and gender, what about other life-course factors such as age or the availability of children? Did Americans dread the possibility of going to a poorhouse throughout their lives, or was this particularly troublesome as one approached old age? Because a sizable minority of poor Americans probably experienced going to an almshouse at some point in their younger days, did a previous stay there increase or decrease their fears of returning to such an institution in their old age? Did older Americans who had an ample supply of adult daughters and sons worry less about being sent to a poorhouse than those who had few or no adult children? And when an elderly person entered the almshouse, did that really mean they would stay there until they died? Michael Katz's (1983) analysis of the Erie County poorhouse in New York State between 1829 and 1886 found that among the elderly, approximately two-thirds stayed less than a year.

Another question worth exploring further is whether all or most almshouses were always or usually negatively perceived by the mid-nineteenth century. Scholars such as David Rothman (1971) have shown that antebellum Americans had very contradictory and ambivalent feelings about almshouses. On the one hand, contemporaries viewed them as punitive institutions necessary to discourage idle, able-bodied paupers from taking advantage of the welfare resources of the local community. On the other hand, these same institutions were seen as reforming the poor and helping those deemed incapable of surviving by themselves such as the infirm elderly. While most scholars have emphasized the growing negative attitude toward all institutions by the eve of the Civil War, there was considerable variation and the changes did not take place overnight. Indeed, it now appears that in some states, such as Michigan, there continued to be considerable optimism in some insane asylums after the Civil War that those afflicted could be cured and improved even though most physicians in other states, such as Massachusetts, were more pessimistic (Whitaker, 1986). Therefore, it will be useful to look for local and regional variations in how nineteenth-century Americans viewed almshouses.

Moreover, there was also considerable variation in how much money local almshouses spent on their inmates. In trying to analyze the comparative cost of sending someone to one of the antebellum Massachusetts public mental asylums, as opposed to keeping them in the local poorhouse, Barbara Rosenkrantz and I looked at the average weekly costs for each pauper in Massachusetts almshouses in 1855 (Rosenkrantz & Vinovskis, 1978). We found that the variation was quite large. Although 12.2% of the almshouses spent less than one dollar a week on their inmates, 20.6% spent over two dollars per week. Although some of this may have simply been due to local differences in the cost-of-living, some of it also may have reflected variations in the type of provisions and clothing provided to the poor.

Catherine Whitaker's (1986) study of the Michigan county almshouses also found considerable variation in their quality. According to the state Board of Corrections and Charities (BCC), in the early twentieth century about half of the county almshouses were evaluated favorably, while the rest were described as defective and inadequate. Private citizen groups in Michigan overall tended to have a less favorable impression of some of these county almshouses than state officials. But the important point may be that both state officials and reform-minded citizens saw considerable variation in the quality of local almshouses rather than seeing them uniformly bad.

Probably few, if any, people ever looked forward to going to a poorhouse. Yet for those who were destitute and in dire need of assistance, was the almshouse seen as a desirable option under those circumstances? Susan Kleinberg's (1989) study of aging in late nineteenth-century Pittsburgh maintains that although the City Poor Home sheltered approximately 300 people in the 1870s, it could not accommodate all those who needed its services. Many of the existing studies of almshouses suggest that the elderly were often regarded as more worthy than others, such as able-bodied, single males, and therefore were more likely to be admitted (Grigg, 1984). For these desperate and unfortunate poor, did life in an almshouse appear as totally tragic and frightening or did it seem in part a welcome relief from the hardships they faced without that assistance?

Similarly, we might consider also whether or not the elderly were treated any differently in the poorhouse than others. Despite the growing hostility toward the elderly insane in mid-nineteenth century Massachusetts, Barbara Rosenkrantz and I found that once patients were admitted to one of the asylums, they appeared to have received the same type of treatment that was accorded to others (Rosenkrantz & Vinovskis, 1978). David Juchau (1991) analyzed the case records of patients in the Pennsylvania Hospital from 1873 to 1922 and found that elderly patients did receive less aggressive medical attention than younger ones. However, he also found that while the physicians revealed an increasingly negative view of the elderly in the case records, their treatment of older patients did not seem to change over time. Given the relatively positive view of the elderly in the almshouses compared to younger, able-bodied adults, one wonders if the elderly did not actually receive preferential treatment there. Indeed, while the Pittsburgh City Poor Home resisted allowing young couples to cohabit there together, it did not have similar objections to older couples living together (Kleinberg, 1989).

One might also consider whether or not being sent to an almshouse was the worst possible ending for the poor in nineteenth-century America. Certainly, for many, the fears of a pauper burial seem to have been as strong, or stronger, than the fears of going to the poorhouse. It is interesting to observe that most nineteenth-century insurance policies were primarily intended to cover the costs of a decent burial rather than to provide for the survivors so that they might escape being sent to an almshouse (Zelizer, 1979). Similarly, while many mutual societies and fraternal orders did try to provide some limited assistance to widows, much, if not most, of their funds went to providing a proper burial for their members (Vinovskis, 1990b).

All of this is not to deny that poorhouses were an undesirable and dreaded institution for most nineteenth-century Americans. Being forced to go to such an institution meant that one had experienced great economic hardships as well as considerable emotional embarrassment. Yet there may have been significant local variations in how nineteenth-century almshouses were perceived and operated; and for the those elderly who were poor and destitute, these institutions may have appeared to be the best alternative left in an otherwise seemingly difficult, if not hopeless, life.

Finally, I want to explore further an interesting comment Haber made in regard to Civil War pensions. She observed that pension advocates used the image of Union veterans being sent to almshouses to garner support for increased annuities. I would like to ask whether the very success of those efforts to expand Union pension benefits ironically may have helped to postpone efforts to provide comparable old age pensions for the general population.

Federal pensions to Union veterans were both widespread and generous. The provisions for receiving one became broad enough so that by 1890 the program, in essence, became an old age pension program for Union veterans and their survivors. For certain age-cohorts, these pensions provided substantial assistance and thereby greatly reduced the likelihood of those individuals going to a poorhouse. For example, in 1900 an estimated 30% of all white males aged 55 to 59 and 18% of those aged 60 to 64 were receiving a federal veteran's pension of about $139 annually (the average annual earnings of all employees that year was $375). Similar benefits were available to Union widows who represented a sizable minority of all widows in the late nineteenth century. In 1890 it is estimated that approximately one out of six American widows between the ages of 45 and 54, and one in eight between the ages of 35 and 44, were Union widows (Holmes & Vinovskis, 1992; Vinovskis, 1990a).

Therefore, perhaps for a significant number of aging Union veterans or their survivors at the end of the nineteenth century, federal pensions reduced their likelihood of going to an almshouse and reinforced the idea that public pension assistance could help ease the transition into old age for many Americans. As the possibility of federal veteran's pensions for the next age-cohorts did not exist, perhaps this contributed to the movements for state or federal assistance for the elderly in order to avoid the almshouse alternative.

In closing, I would like to again congratulate Carole Haber on writing such a stimulating and comprehensive essay on the relationship between rhetoric and reality in the provision of almshouses for older Americans. While my comments and suggestions are intended to refine and broaden her analysis, they are not intended as a challenge to her call for carefully reexamining the changing image and role of these institutions in providing assistance for the elderly in the past.

## REFERENCES

Achenbaum, W. A. (1978). *Old age in the new land: The American experience since 1790.* Baltimore: Johns Hopkins University Press.

Fischer, D. H. (1978). *Growing old in America.* (Rev. ed.) New York: Oxford University Press.

Grigg, S. (1984). *The dependent poor of Newburyport: Studies in social history, 1800–1830.* Ann Arbor, MI: UMI Research Press.

Holmes, A., & Vinovskis, M. A. (1992). Impact of the Civil War on American widowhood. In S. J. South & E. S. Tolnay (Eds.), *The changing American family: Sociological and demographic perspectives.* Boulder, CO: Westview Press.

Juchau, D. (1991, November). The Pennsylvania Hospital: Trends in medical practice with a focus on patient age, 1873–1922. Paper presented at the Social Science History Association Meeting, New Orleans.

Katz, M. B. (1983). *Poverty and policy in American history.* New York: Academic Press.

Kleinberg, S. J. (1989). *The shadow of the mills: Working-class families in Pittsburgh, 1870–1907.* Pittsburgh: University of Pittsburgh Press.

Modell, J. (1978). Patterns of consumption, acculturation, and family income strategies in late nineteenth-century America. In T. K. Hareven & M. A. Vinovskis (Eds.), *Family and population in nineteenth-century America.* Princeton, NJ: Princeton University Press.

Range, J., & Vinovskis, M. A. (1981). Images of elderly in popular literature: A content analysis of Littell's living age, 1845–1882. *Social Science History,* 5, pp. 123–170.

Rosenkrantz, B. G. & Vinovskis, M. A. (1978). The invisible lunatics: Old age and insanity in mid-nineteenth-century Massachusetts. In S. F. Spicker et al. (Eds.), *Aging and the elderly: Humanistic perspectives in gerontology.* Atlantic Highlands, NJ: Humanities Press.

Rothman, D. (1971). *The discovery of the asylum.* Boston: Little, Brown, and Company.

Vinovskis, M. A. (1981). *Fertility in Massachusetts from the revolution to the Civil War*. New York: Academic Press.

Vinovskis, M. A. (1990a). Have social historians lost the Civil War? Some preliminary demographic speculations. In M. A. Vinovskis (Eds.), *Toward a social history of the American Civil War: Exploratory essays*. New York: Cambridge University Press.

Vinovskis, M. A. (1990b). Death and family life in the past. *Human Nature, 1*, pp. 109–122.

Whitaker, C. J. (1986). Almshouses and mental institutions in Michigan, 1871–1930. Unpublished PhD thesis. University of Michigan.

Zelizer, V. (1979). *Morals and markets: The development of life insurance in the United States*. New York: Columbia University Press.

# Symbols of the Old Age Pension Movement: The Poorhouse, the Family, and the "Childlike" Elderly

## Michel R. Dahlin

In her fine chapter on the rhetoric and reality of the poorhouse, Carole Haber shows us how a symbol used in public debate—a symbol carefully cultivated by reformers and promoted to the public—could develop a momentum and a life of its own. The symbol of the poorhouse, as it developed, shaped the formation of public policy in ways its promoters had neither imagined nor intended.

Haber's essay explains three important developments: first, how almshouses came to play a central role in the history of old age, beginning in the nineteenth century; second, how the poorhouse was subsequently employed as a powerful negative symbol in the debate over old age pensions; and third, how this negative view of poorhouses shaped Social Security legislation.

Almshouses, Haber reminds us, were designed as punitive institutions to encourage the idle and vicious to seek honest labor. Society feared those individuals who were unemployed and lacked a propertied stake in the orderly functioning of the community. The aged poor were never the focus of this public concern, and the fact that they came to dominate the poorhouse population was the unintended consequence of piecemeal reform whereby other needy groups were removed to specialized institutions designed for their care and rehabilitation. Dread of the almshouse was not the result of a successful negative public relations campaign. Instead, it was the *reality* of the poorhouse life—hopeless, monotonous, skimpy and mean-spirited—that made the symbol of the poorhouse so effective. Jane Addams's Hull House memoirs provide an example which illustrates graphically how the impoverished residents of her neighborhood viewed the almshouse:

> *some frightened women had bidden me to come quickly to the house of an old German woman, whom two men from the county agent's office were attempting to remove to the County Infirmary (poorhouse). The poor old creature had thrown herself bodily upon the small and battered chest of drawers and clung there, clutching it so firmly that it would have been impossible to remove her without also taking the piece of furniture. She did not weep nor moan nor indeed make any human sound, but between her broken gasps for breath she squealed shrilly like a frightened animal caught in a trap. . . . The poor creature who clung so desperately to her chest of drawers was really clinging to the last remnant of normal living—a symbol of all she was asked to renounce (Addams, 1910, pp. 118–119)*

As Haber explains, there were efforts to provide benevolent old age homes so that worthy elders need not suffer the "shame of the poorhouse." In late nineteenth-century cities, for example, ethnic and religious groups built homes for their countrymen. Unlike the native born, who viewed elderly impoverished immigrants as suitable candidates for the poorhouse, members of immigrant groups felt compassion for those whose struggle to get ahead in America had not produced a prosperous old age. They sought to provide the solace of familiar foods, languages, religious holidays, and customs in a benevolent home for their elderly compatriots (Butners, 1980, p. 345). Without the menacing reality of the poorhouse, they probably would have invested less effort and fewer collective resources in building homes for needy members of their group.

The fear of the poorhouse had a real impact on the whole working class, not just on immigrants. While the almshouse was designed to discourage the young, able-bodied poor from avoiding labor, it had a direct impact on the elderly and their families. It encouraged adult children to make great sacrifices to keep aging parents out of the almshouse. The elderly were added to already crowded homes and apartments, and soups were watered down a bit more to fill the extra bowl now set at the kitchen table. Some families even endured the disruption of garrulous, quarrelsome, incontinent, and demented aged relatives, or bore the constant burden of nursing the bedridden elderly, or the wearisome task of minding the senile. If the reality of the poorhouse had been less grim and its stigma less severe, struggling adult children of destitute old parents would have been less reluctant to allow or encourage their dependent elders to turn to the almshouse for assistance. In the case of needy old people who had no children or close kin to turn to, the reality and the symbol of the poorhouse similarly led them to endure truly miserable living conditions rather than turn to public assistance, which could mean exile to a poorfarm or almshouse.

The most compelling evidence for the power of the poorhouse is found in the lengths to which the working class elderly and their families would go in order to avoid having to turn to this dread institution. It is easy to overlook this reality; it was so deeply embedded in the consciousness of the time that its influence on individual decisions and family strategies went unremarked. But for the elderly, the poorhouse represented less the last resort before doom than doom itself. And for this reason they and their families did their utmost to avoid it.

Carole Haber's chapter stimulated my thinking about other symbols relating to the elderly, symbols that inhabit the sphere of public consciousness and popular debate. She presents the poorhouse as the central symbol around which concerns about the aged were focused in the early part of this century—an eminently reasonable assessment—but I would add two other themes that were also influential at the time. Like the poorhouse, these symbols were employed to sell the idea of public old age pensions and, like the poorhouse, they came to shape public policy in unintended ways. These two themes are the failure of the family and the supposedly childlike qualities of the old.

The failure of the family was an important theme in the campaign for old age pensions. The family was supposed to be the primary source of aid for the dependent elderly; but reformers argued that the family, especially the working-class family, was no longer able to perform this role as a result of industrialization, at least not without making sacrifices that middle-class reformers considered unacceptable, such as sending children to work at a young age or destroying privacy in the family by adding aged relatives to already over-crowded homes. Moreover, reformers thought that the new urban ethic of consumer spending and entertainment was making the younger generation less willing to bear its customary burden. There was a growing emphasis, again primarily in the middle class, on putting the needs of the nuclear family ahead of extended family obligations. This conflict of duties seemed to indicate that the family could not continue to bear the burden of the aged unassisted. Reformers argued that the old age pension would give the elderly resources which would enable them to contribute to the family rather than drain its resources (Dahlin, 1983, pp. 198–202). The failure of the family became an integral part of the argument for old age pensions (and several other Progressive reforms as well).

Haber has pointed out that the elimination of the poorhouse through Social Security legislation produced unanticipated results, such as the stimulation of construction of private nursing homes. Likewise, the provision of Social Security pensions to the elderly also affected the family in ways that had not been predicted. It freed the old from financial dependence on children and led, not to happy and conflict-free co-residence, but to a sharp decrease in co-residence of the elderly with their children in the years following its adoption (Kobrin, 1976). This change in residence patterns shaped subsequent policies and programs for the elderly in ways that Progressive Era advocates of the old age pensions had never imagined.

Another image much used in the early twentieth-century debate over the plight of the aged was the idea of the old as childlike. For example, an editorial in the *Independent* ("Old Age Pension," 1906) complained: "In no country has old age received anything like the consideration that has been bestowed upon the children, and yet both extremes of life are equally helpless," (p. 705). And pension advocate Alexander Johnson (1925, p. 339) wrote, "The irremedial helplessness of old people makes their problems, like those of children, peculiarly a field for social action." State pension promoters emphasized these similarities because of the apparent strength of public sympathy and tenderness toward children, a feeling which seemed to be on the verge of achieving reforms for children, such as child labor laws (Chambers, 1967, p. 29; Rapson, 1971, p. 34).

Reformers of the Progressive period had a special interest in children, whom they regarded as keys to the future (Trattner, 1974, pp. 96–97). The old were clearly unlike children in this sense: They were not keys to the future. Molding or rehabilitating them was not only difficult, but largely profitless; they would not be alive long enough to justify the effort. Nonetheless, reformers continued to press the analogy of youth to old age upon the public. Because everyone seemed to agree that children deserved the best, linking the old to children was a means of spreading the child's cloak of deserving innocence over the old as well. Reformers argued that the elderly were entitled to the same non-judgmental care as children because they were as helpless as young children. Homer Folks (1903, p. 338), well-known child welfare worker and public health advocate, wrote of the elderly, "As in caring for children, we take little account of their good or ill desserts but only of their needs, may we not follow a similar course in caring for those in their second childhood." Linking children and old people as helpless and calling old age "second childhood" reflected more than the conscious efforts of reformers to improve the lives of the elderly. It also reflected an unconsciously but unmistakably paternalistic attitude toward the old.

Dependent old people shared with all other dependent groups a loss of self-determination. But the elderly, like the young, were to be granted freedom from moral responsibility for their dependence. And this brought them not only public sympathy but also the loss of any say in their fate. The old were not treated as adults, but as children. The sympathy they gained in being viewed, like children, as innocently helpless was offset by their loss of responsible adult status. The analogy between children and old people did not *cause* the elderly to lose power and responsibility; rather it reflected their powerlessness. The reformers' continued use of the child analogy, however, did nothing to enhance the dignity of the old (Dahlin, 1983, p. 81). Again a symbol, used to sell the old age pension, had unintended consequences. Ironically, in recent years welfare reformers have brought back this analogy to the public policy arena, this time arguing that children are as worthy and needy as the old and should thus be assisted as generously as are the old.

Having discussed two other symbols besides the one introduced by Haber —the poorhouse—I need to turn now to an area of disagreement in our understanding of the history of old age. Carole Haber writes that when reformers of the Progressive Era investigated the problems of the elderly, they made two critical errors: first, they concluded that rates of poverty and dependence among the elderly were rising and, second, that industrialization and urbanization were the root causes of the elderly's increased economic vulnerability. Instead, Haber argues, it was the changing demographic profile of the poorhouse which led reformers to a miscalculation of the economic status of the old. She points out, very correctly, that the development of specialized alternative institutions for other needy groups actually explains the transformation of the almshouse into a home for the pauperized elderly. The rising proportion of elderly among the inmates of poorhouses is not in itself evidence of their immiseration; it is a reflection of increasing specialization in charity work.

Highlighting this demographic fallacy is not enough, however, to dismiss the Progressives' *perception* of increased poverty among the aged. Ignoring the almshouse population, it would still have been possible for reformers to argue for a significant, and possibly even worsening, poverty among the elderly. For example, national employment figures for men 65 and older fell by one fifth between 1890 and 1930, an actual decline from 68.3% to 53.9% (Gratton, 1986, p. 66). Overall property ownership, a traditional source of security among the elderly, was also declining slightly (Dahlin, 1983, pp. 11–13). (Today some historians and economists dismiss these figures as inflated or misleading, but early twentieth-century reformers took them at face value.) Also, perceptions of sharply reduced work opportunities for the aged—actually the result of the cohort effect in the occupational structure and of the appearance of rationalized hiring policies in large industries based on age rather than other measures of physical qualification—lent credence to the scenario of a steadily worsening economic situation.

In general a new sense of scientific possibilities for the remedy of ancient social evils—unemployment, accident, destitution, and death—made early twentieth-century social activists less willing to accept these risks stoically. They sought to regularize the rules of the game of life. They believed it could be done, and so they saw old social problems with new eyes. They were less tolerant of human suffering. One example of the new ethic of controlling risks can be seen in the rise of life insurance coverage among middle-class breadwinners. According to Viviana Zelizer (1979), by the late nineteenth century it had become the middle-class husband's obligation to provide some economic security for his family in the event of his untimely death. Expectations of appropriate standards of living were rising and old strategies for coping were no longer acceptable. For these reasons I believe the focus on poverty in old age sprang from much more than a misunderstanding of poorhouse demographics. People believed in the possibility of eliminating the destitution which the poorhouse represented.

Haber points out that in 1935, when the Social Security Act was adopted, Social Security legislation deliberately brought about the demise of the despised poorhouse by specifying that its funds could not be paid to almshouse residents. She further points out that many contemporaries expected that Social Security pensions would make poorhouses totally unnecessary.

Certainly the destruction of the poorhouse was deliberate and intentional; it reflected deep public revulsion against the institution. But the exclusion of poorhouse residents from eligibility for Social Security benefits served a second and equally important purpose. This eligibility restriction was designed to avoid tainting Social Security recipients with the stigma of the unworthy poor. Social Security's proponents did not want the program to be considered just another welfare measure. Instead it was to be a program for the deserving, who earned the assistance they got by contributing to the fund throughout their working lives. True, the Old Age Assistance (welfare) part of the Social Security Act would cover the needy aged, but the focus of the program was on the Old Age Security (pension) part. The plan was that Old Age Assistance would be nearly phased out as subsequent generations of workers paid into the system long enough to qualify for Old Age Security. The poorhouse's association with the idle, vicious, and undeserving poor threatened the image of Social Security that policy makers were promoting; so poorhouse inmates had to be excluded. (In reality, some county welfare agents helped ambulatory aged almshouse inmates move out and into private boarding homes or residence hotels in order to become eligible for Social Security.)

Toward the end of her paper, Carole Haber concludes that, by destroying the poorhouse, legislators unwittingly laid the groundwork for the rapid development of the private nursing home industry. It is possible that, had Social Security funds been allowed to support almshouse inmates, poorhouses might have evolved into publicly funded nursing homes. Control of nursing homes then would have lodged in the public sector rather than in the private sector, and this would undoubtedly have made some difference in the historical evolution of nursing homes.

Providing income for the dependent old through Social Security not only led to the demise of the poorhouse and, indirectly, to the rise of the nursing home, it also reduced the economic dependence of the old on their children and changed the nature of intergenerational obligations. Early in this century, the elderly were seen to stand in the ominous shadow of the poorhouse. Today, even though the poorhouse is long gone and its shadow no longer darkens the outlook of the elderly, its legacy can be found in contemporary social welfare policies for the aged. Similarly, the ideas of family failure and "childlike" old age also still influence programs and policies for the elderly.

## REFERENCES

Addams, J. (1910, reprinted 1960). *Twenty years at Hull House*. New York: New American Library.

Butners, A. I. (1980). Institutionalized altruism and the aged: Charitable provisions for the aged in New York City, 1865–1930. *Dissertation Abstracts International, 41,* O9A. (University Microfilms No. 81-04915).

Chambers, C. (1967). *Seedtime of reform*. Ann Arbor, MI: University of Michigan Press.

Dahlin, M. (1983). From poorhouse to pension: The changing view of old age in America, 1890–1929. *Dissertation Abstracts International, 43,* 11A. (University Microfilms No. 83-07142).

Folks, H. (1903). Disease and dependence. *National Conference of Charities and Corrections*, p. 338.

Gratton, B. (1986). *Urban elders: Family, work, and welfare among Boston's aged, 1890–1950*. Philadelphia: Temple University Press.

Johnson, A. (1925). At the end of the road. *Survey, 54*, p. 339.

Kobrin, F. E. (1976). The fall in household size and the rise of the primary individual in the United States. In M. Gordon (Ed.), *The American family in social-historical perspective*, (2nd ed., pp. 69–81). New York: St. Martin's Press.

Old Age Pension. (Editorial). (1906, September 20). *The Independent, 61*, p. 705.

Rapson, R. (1971). *The cult of youth in middle-class America*. Lexington, MA: D. C. Heath and Co.

Trattner, W. (1974). *From poor law to welfare state: A history of social welfare in America*. New York: Free Press.

Zelizer, V. R. (1979). *Morals and markets: The development of life insurance in the United States*. New York: Columbia University Press.

# CHAPTER 4

# The State, the Elderly, and the Intergenerational Contract

## Toward a New Political Economy of Aging

**Debra Street**
**Jill Quadagno**

Until about the mid-1960's, most research in social gerontology focused on the individual experiences of aging people. As such, much emphasis was placed upon psychologistic and microsocial aspects of the aging process. In the past two decades, however, the transformation of the position of the elderly within the Western industrialized democracies has given increasing salience to an approach that locates the understandings and realities of aging within political and economic institutions. Adherents of this new political economy of aging believe that the "social and economic status of elderly people is defined not by biological age but by the institutions organized wholly or partly on production" (Walker, 1986, p. 149). Many experiences affecting older people, they argue, are "a product of a particular division of labour and structure of inequality rather than a natural concomitant of the ageing process" (Fennel, Phillipson, & Ever, 1988, p. 53). They also claim that understanding the relationship between the state and the elderly means understanding the operations of the modern welfare state, for as Myles (1989, p. 2) notes, the modern welfare state is, first and foremost "a welfare state for the elderly."

Implicit in the political economy perspective is the notion that the welfare state represents an intergenerational contract, a bargain between the working and retired over the quality of life in old age. Theorists differ, however, on how this intergenerational contract is constituted and on what impact it has on independence in old age. Broadly speaking, the relationship between the elderly and the state has been characterized in two dominant ways. One thesis defines the intergenerational contract as a mechanism of labor market management, in which social policies result from the needs of capital to control the labor supply. Implicit in this argument is the view that, by restricting their access to the labor market, social welfare policies have increased the dependence of older people upon the state. A second perspective defines the intergenerational contract as a product of class struggle, which has resulted in a citizen's wage. Implicit in this latter view is that, by deferring wages that are recouped during retirement, the citizen's wage has made older people autonomous from the coercion of the market.

In this chapter we first examine these two dominant views of the intergenerational contract derived from a political economy perspective. We then demonstrate the limitations of both approaches for understanding contemporary debates about public provision for older people which have centered around issues drawn from demographic and generational equity perspectives. Finally, we argue that such either/or approaches misrepresent the issues facing mature welfare states today. Instead we reconstitute the concept of the intergenerational contract to include the dynamics of age, gender, and race, within a political and economic context.

## THE POLITICAL ECONOMY
## OF THE INTERGENERATIONAL CONTRACT

### Labor Market Management—Contextual Dependency

The thesis that public pensions are a mechanism of labor market management is predicated on the idea that the state intervenes in labor-capital relations to protect the needs of the capitalist economy. As Walker explains:

> *. . . the structural dependency that superannuation creates rests on the predomi-*
> *nance of wage-labour and distribution through the market. The existence of welfare*
> *state provision . . . does not challenge the prevailing system of distribution, but*
> *supports it and therefore institutionalizes economic dependency through pension*
> *rules and regulations (Walker, 1986, p. 154).*

Pensions perform several functions for capital: They stabilize labor markets, maximize productivity, and increase capital formation. To suggest that the state serves only the needs of capital oversimplifies the case, to be sure, for pensions also ameliorate conditions for older workers displaced by industrial capitalism. But the support provided to workers also serves a legitimation function for the state (O'Connor, 1973).

With the institutionalization of retirement, older people become marginalized and dependent, at least in part, because of restricted access to the labor market (Estes, 1986, pp. 122–124; Hardy, 1988, p.312; Walker, 1980, p. 49). Dependency is also increased because individual autonomy is compromised. According to Walker (1991):

> *Of course the social contract on which these transfers is based is not like any nor-*
> *mal contract in that it is imposed by the state on those in employment rather than*
> *being freely negotiated and is heavily sanctioned by the work ethic, or what should*
> *more correctly be called the paid employment ethic. (Walker, 1991, pp. 1–2)*

It is therefore the social relationship between age and the labor market that conditions dependency (Walker, 1980, p. 49).

Neither retirement policies regulated by the state, nor "old age," nor financial and economic dependency are static over space and time (Jacobs & Rein, 1991). Rather, they vary across nations and within a given nation in different periods. In the United States, the first pensions were in private industry. Because the private pension was a "gratuity" offered to workers by employers, pensioners had no legal right to the pension. Private pensions were often used by employers to guarantee a loyal and cooperative workforce; separation from the job under any condition not sanctioned by the employer often entailed the loss of pension rights (Graebner, 1980). This "carrot and stick" approach was used frequently by private industry as a means of labor market control: By discouraging turnover, pensions could guarantee a stable workforce; by defining pensions as a deferred wage, workers could be forced to accept lower wages (Quadagno, 1984, p. 637).

The Social Security Act of 1935, born in an era of working-class agitation and economic depression, sought to reconcile the apparently disparate interests of capital and labor. In an era of massive unemployment, one aspect of the intergenerational contract intrinsic to the act was that of "retirement as a form of unemployment relief; older workers [were] retired to create places for younger ones" (Graebner, 1980, p. 264). By tying benefits to labor force, the Social Security Act also linked the social welfare system to the private labor market (Quadagno, 1988).

Chris Phillipson argues that the British system of public provision has been even more closely linked to labor market needs. During the postwar manpower shortage immediately following World War II, the British government encouraged older workers to delay retirement. In the late 1950s and 1960s, however, technological changes, combined with decreasing international competitiveness of British industries, led to high unemployment. To create a smaller and more efficient work force, government policy was reversed. Such mechanisms as job release schemes now encouraged rather than discouraged retirement (Phillipson, 1986, pp. 132–134). Phillipson (1986) concludes that the institutionalization of retirement may be viewed "as a concession by capitalism, one which may be partially withdrawn (in times of labour shortage), extended (in times of mass unemployment), and be subjected to cuts or increases in expenditure, depending on political elections and/or the need for social harmony" (1986, p. 135).

Access to sufficient resources to meet basic needs is a prerequisite for "successful" retirement for elderly people, if success is equated with independence. In Britain, over 60% of retired people live at or close to the poverty level (Phillipson, 1986, p. 136); in the United States just over 25% of those over 65 are categorized as poor or "near" poor (U.S. Senate, Special Committee on Aging, 1990, p. 27). Have public pensions compromised their independence?

Those who view retirement as a mechanism of labor market management argue that economic insecurity in old age results from separation from the labor market, which increases the economic dependency of elderly people. But such an argument obscures differences between high and low income earners in terms of the penalty retirement creates, and ignores considerable historical evidence suggesting that economic insecurity has often accompanied old age. It also ignores the fact that public pensions have been the vehicle for financial independence for many elderly people, especially when supplemented with other forms of income. Additionally, the labor market management theory has only a limited capacity to take life course dynamics into account.

Recognition of these flaws in the labor market management perspective led to a new thesis about the nature of the intergenerational contract. While not denying the coercive aspects of public pensions, power resource theorists saw this component as only the first phase in an historical progression toward a citizen's wage.

## The Citizen's Wage—Potential for Autonomy

The concept of the "citizen's wage," derived from power resource theory, portrays the intergenerational contract as an opportunity for increased individual autonomy. Power resource theorists believe that under certain conditions the working class can use the state as a vehicle to counteract the inequities of the market. Power mobilization occurs when collectivities that are relatively weak in terms of market resources use political resources to affect the outcome of market conflicts (Korpi, 1989, pp. 309-328). The ability of wage earners to initiate social programs that modify market forces depends on the degree to which working-class parties make effective use of the franchise. Thus, independence means autonomy from the coercion of the market.

Not all social programs are constituted to maximize autonomy. When wage earners are successful in organizing labor parties to represent their interests, they create "social democratic" welfare states. Social democratic welfare states are characterized by universal benefits that are granted as civil rights earned through worklife participation (Korpi, 1989, p. 310). They emerge from strong labor movements, which create welfare states that decommodify wage workers by endowing "individuals with a relative independence of the cash nexus and work compulsion" (Esping-Anderson, 1989, p. 224). The outcome is a more egalitarian society in which resources are redistributed more equitably and individuals gain strength for communal action.

When wage earners are unable to effectively mobilize political resources (generally because they fail to create a labor party), a "liberal" welfare state results. Liberal welfare states are dominated by "social assistance" policies characterized by strict entitlement rules, social stigma, and modest benefits. Social assistance supports the market by decreasing the security of the poor, forcing them to rely on their labor power (Esping-Anderson, 1989, p. 25). The outcome is a class-political dualism with stratification based on the fragmentation of workers into universal and nonuniversal benefit recipients. In the first instance, autonomy and independence for the elderly person are maximized; in the second, inequities inherent to the marketplace are reproduced in retirement policies that increase dependence, at least for non-privileged former workers.

The degree of autonomy granted the elderly through social provision varies not only across nations but also across historical time within a nation. The historical perspective highlights the fact that the two concepts of public provision—as a mechanism of labor market management and as a citizen's wage—are not necessarily competing views but rather complementary parts of a transformative sequence. The historical process involves the transition from a "social assistance" model to a "social security" model consisting of the twin attributes necessary for social security—universality and a substitutive retirement wage sufficient to allow maintenance of pre-retirement living standards (Myles, 1989, p. 267). In the United States, this historical transition occurred between 1969 and 1972 when a series of benefit increases and program enhancements culminated in a new intergenerational contract. Guaranteed cost-of-living increases improved the "social wage" by insulating the working class from downward pressure on wages during rises in unemployment; more significantly "an ever-growing and increasingly important portion of the national wage bill [was] removed from the market and made subject to a democratic political process" (Myles, 1989, p. 280). In terms of individual economic security, the large real increases in Social Security represented an avenue to increased individual autonomy for elderly people. The institutionalization of the "citizen's" wage was a triumph for the individual arising from the income security guaranteed by the state— "the right to cease working before wearing out" (Myles, 1989, p. 280).

Implicit in this model of the intergenerational contract is a life course perspective, the idea that the deferred wage represents a transfer of wages from one's working life to one's old age. The right to pensions with replacement rates adequate to maintain a previous standard of living adheres in this lifetime transfer concept. Pensions are not a transfer between generations per se (although power resource theorists do not deny that tax transfers are involved) but rather a transfer of credited labor toward autonomy in later life.

Increasingly, this view has been challenged by those who argue that pensions represent nothing more than a transfer of resources from the working population to the aged. Adherents of the political economy perspective have been hampered in responding to this reconstruction of the intergenerational contract, because they analyze the political process primarily as a form of state intervention in the conflict between capital and labor and because their model is unable to take demographic arguments into account. This demographic perspective vastly oversimplifies current debates regarding the nature of dependency and the extent of the societal obligation to alleviate it.

## FROM LIFE COURSE TO INTERGENERATIONAL TRANSFERS

### The Demographic Perspective—Dependency Ratios

Demographers frequently use "dependency" ratios to describe the demands likely to affect the political and economic arrangements of the market and state as a result of population aging. The societal dependency ratio represents a combination of the gerontic dependency ratio (number of persons 65 and older per 100 persons of "prime working age" of 20 to 26 years) and the neontic dependency ratio (individuals under the age of 20). Thus, dependency ratios "indicate the contribution of the age composition of a population to society's problem of economic dependency" (Siegel & Tauber, 1986, p. 83).

Using U.S. Census Bureau data, demographers establish past patterns of the societal dependency ratio and use various levels of immigration, fertility, and mortality to make future projections. Based upon these projections, it is estimated that by 2050, increases in the gerontic dependency ratio accompanied by only small declines in the neontic dependency ratio, will result in a substantial rise in total dependency (Siegel & Tauber, 1986, p. 105). Siegel and Tauber (1986, pp. 113–114), for example, argue that these demographic conditions will have "profound social and economic consequences," including oppressively high tax rates to support older nonworkers, a shrinkage of the productive capacity of the economy, and "vast expenditures . . . to be made for the 'maintenance' of the burgeoning number of elderly persons."

There are a number of characteristics implicit in the foregoing discussion of societal dependency ratios that carry an ideological message. For instance, by what criteria is it justifiable to use "age" as a kind of shorthand for "dependency"? What theoretical concept places individuals under 20 years of age and over 65 in a category classified as "dependent"? Apparently, the answer resides in lack of attachment to the labor force. Yet the extent of labor force participation varies across the entire life course and by race and gender. Labor force participation is not solely, nor even primarily, a function of age. In 1987, for example, approximately one-third of women with children between the ages of 6 and 17 were not in the labor force nor were nearly half of those with children under age 6. (U.S. Bureau of the Census, 1987). Should all women caring for children be considered dependent? Should dependency ratios then be reconstituted by gender? Similarly, not all individuals over the age of 65 are truly dependent by this criterion. More than 16% of older men in 1987 received income from wages (U.S. Bureau of the Census, 1987). Undeniably, many elderly men, and especially women, depend for economic security upon an intergenerational transfer of funds from workers to retirees through Social Security taxes. It is equally true, however, that others possess sufficient wealth that they are in no way "dependent" upon working Americans.

By using the societal dependency ratio, demographers have selected chronological age as an easily quantifiable measurement amenable to current methodological techniques to infer a future causality, without attending to the implicit assumptions contained within the model. Age is used out of context, outside of the realities of a historical social world, and thus robbed of much of its meaning. Inadequate theorizing about social policy/age/class/dependency used in this model robs it of both interest and persuasive explanatory power. For the model to be rich, useful, and more complete, it must include the complex of structural arrangements within which such a dependency ratio is to be understood. Yet the dependency ratio concept, flawed as it is, has been combined with a simplistic notion of democratic political processes and has become a central construct underlying contemporary debates about Social Security. Although this chapter is concerned primarily with economic and financial dependency, this is but one dimension of dependence (see Walker [1982] for a taxonomy detailing other dimensions of dependency).

### Views of Dependency and the Generational Equity Debate

Challenges to the intergenerational contract as currently constituted have figured prominently in academic circles and the press in the United States over the past ten years. Implicit in this literature is "a relatively uncritical acceptance of both the conflict hypothesis and the link between demographics and policy change in the realm of welfare" (Walker, 1991). The assumptions are (1) that there is a finite amount of resources available for social spending; (2) that conflict between the generations will inevitably increase as competition for scarce economic resources increases; and, (3) unless present levels of entitlements for the elderly (public pensions, medical care) are substantially reduced, the demographic imperative of the aging population will place an intolerable economic burden on the state.

In the United States these issues have been framed in terms of "generational equity." The generational equity debate is based upon three premises: (1) that in recent years the elderly as a group have benefited disproportionately in terms of social spending when compared to other age groups; (2) that these gains have come at the expense of other age groups; and (3) that the elderly have had the power to make the decisions (and deliberately set out to do so) that permit this advantage to continue.

The generational equity debate derives from the reconstruction of the nature of the intergenerational contract from a vision of a citizen's wage as a life course transfer to a dependency ratio framework reconstituted around the idea of intergenerational transfers. Yet the debate highlights the inadequacy of the "citizen's wage" construct, based as it is on labor-capital relations, to respond to a core contention of the critique: that the elderly, as a group, have had the political power to control policy decisions and have made the choices that have resulted in the impoverishment of children. Seriously addressing the issues in this debate means reconstructing the concept of the citizen's wage around a model that recognizes the elderly as active participants in the political process, not merely passive recipients of a deferred wage.

Until the late 1970s, the "compassionate" stereotype of the aged as frail and in need of assistance, as "deserving" poor, predominated in discussions about elderly people in American political circles (Binstock, 1984). By 1978, however, this stereotype had undergone a transformation. No longer were the elderly universally perceived as poor, frail, and deserving help. A new stereotype was emerging—that of relatively well-off, politically powerful, and self-interested voters. As Binstock (1984) notes, the media, political speeches, public policy studies, and scholarly writings converged to create a new image of elderly people:

> *Because of demographic changes, the aged are becoming more numerous and politically powerful, and will be entitled to even more benefits and substantially larger proportions of the Federal budget. They are already costing too much, and in the future will pose an undeserved, unwarranted, and unsustainable burden on the American economy (Binstock, 1984, p. 157).*

Initially, attention was focused primarily on the fact that Social Security was becoming too costly because of increasing numbers of elderly people. As an article in *Forbes* magazine declared, "The myth is that they're sunk in poverty. The reality is that they're living well. The trouble is there are too many of them—God bless 'em" (Flint, 1980, p. 51). Thus, generational rhetoric—that the elderly were likely to overtax the system due to their sheer increase in number—paralleled closely the demographic approach to the intergenerational contract.

By the early 1980s, however, generational rhetoric shifted from concerns about the burden of population aging to a theme of a self-centered elderly population usurping more than their fair share of the nation's resources. To the demographic "imperative" was added the contention that elderly people had set out to command a political agenda of self-interest.

Opponents of increased Social Security benefits organized and institutionalized their opposition under the aegis of Americans for Generational Equity (AGE) founded by Senator Dave Durenberger in 1984 (Quadagno, 1991, p. 16). A dramatic opening salvo occurred when Governor Richard Lamm of Colorado appeared on ABC's Nightline (April 4, 1984) asserting that "too much technology and money was being spent on the elderly population during their last years in comparison to the young, who have their entire lives ahead of them" (Wisensale, 1988, p. 773). Such viewpoints, however, were not restricted to politicians. Demographer Samuel Preston lent scholarly credence to the attack, arguing that there is direct competition between the young and old for society's resources: "let's be clear that the transfers from the working-age population to the elderly are also transfers away from children" (Preston, 1984, pp. 451–452).

Biomedical ethicist Daniel Callahan agreed that money spent on health care for the elderly "deprived younger generations of circumstances, goods, and wealth they need to realize their full potential" (Callahan, 1986, p. 336). He advocated three aspirations for an aging society: (1) to stop pursuing medical goals that combine the features of high costs, marginal gains, and primarily elderly benefit; (2) that the old shift their priorities from their own welfare to that of younger generations; and (3) that the elderly should accept death as a condition of life, at least for the sake of others (Callahan, 1986, pp. 333–334). As the generational equity theme was aired more widely, its contentions entered into the writings of the popular media (Binstock, 1983, p. 136) until even traditionally liberal voices echoed the core thesis (Quadagno, 1991).

The idea that expenditures on older people represent a loss of resources represents a reconstruction of the intergenerational contract. It presents age cohorts as locked in conflict over scarce resources and, most importantly, denies the legitimacy of the deferred wage as an earned right. Instead of defining elderly people as rightful beneficiaries of a societal collective bargaining agreement, it defines them as an age-based interest group whose benefits represent a bad investment.

## FALLACIES OF THE GENERATIONAL EQUITY ARGUMENT

The generational equity debate has been built on the assumption that there is an elderly voting bloc with sufficient power to determine political decisions on specific issues. This assumption can be attacked on three fronts: first, that there are explicit contests promoting elderly interests at the expense of other segments of the population; second, that given choices that would benefit groups other than elderly people, the elderly would vote against such measures; and, third, that the elderly constitute a voting bloc with the capacity to determine outcomes within the American political process.

### Age versus Youth as Explicit Contests

For it to be true that there are explicit contests pitting elderly interests against those of other age groups, American voters would have to be capable of making choices about the relative value of social programs. For example, they might be faced with decisions about cutting expenditures in social welfare programs for the poor, such as Aid for Dependent Children or Medicaid, in order to preserve or increase benefits in programs primarily directed towards the elderly, such as Medicare and Social Security. One of the major problems with this assumption is that federal spending does not come out of one pot. The two major programs that directly benefit the elderly, Medicare and Social Security, are largely self-financed through payroll taxes and employer contributions (Hess, 1985, p. 16). These taxes are specifically earmarked for Social Security and Medicare and kept separate from general revenues. By contrast, programs designed to meet the needs of other groups, such as AFDC and Medicaid, come out of general tax revenues. Questions about whether Social Security or Medicare spending levels should be maintained or raised are predicated on decisions about the perceived solvency or political possibility of raising taxes specifically earmarked for those two programs, and separate from raising general revenues. So decisions regarding Social Security and Medicare (except for a small portion of Medicare funded out of general revenues) are reached independent of any direct connection with political decisions made regarding the distribution of general funds for such things as education, poverty relief, medical care for the poor, low-cost housing, and the like.

The locus of decision making must also be considered when examining whether elderly people are "winning" explicit contests over the allocation of social spending. Decisions about social spending are not made by referendum; there is no mechanism by which any age group, young or old, directly makes such decisions, at least in terms of federal programs. Rather, in the American form of representational government, such legislative decisions about the disposition of federal spending are made by votes cast in the Senate, and in the House by representatives elected by people comprising all age groups of eligible voters. Thus, to the extent that the elderly wield political power, it is indirect.

### Elderly Voting Behavior as Self-Interested

One can also challenge the notion that there exists a powerful self-interested motivation for elderly voters. Most recent research has found little substantive evidence that elderly voters would act to defeat measures that would benefit other age cohorts of the population. By 1979 in Florida, for example, elderly voters constituted approximately 25% of the total electorate (Matura, 1982, p. 24). Because of the high proportion of older people in Florida, the state became the natural site for studies of elderly voting behavior. These studies were based on the premise that if there really were an age-conscious voting bloc that acted in its own self-interest, such behavior would likely be manifested in a state like Florida, where proportions of elderly in the population exceeded the national average.

One study of Florida political behavior, funded by the Administration on Aging, found no evidence that the elderly constituted a voting bloc or that they voted in a self-interested manner. Among the findings of the study were the following: (1) there was greater disparity in partisan affiliations among seniors than among younger citizens; (2) there was little evidence of political involvement of seniors strictly in terms of self-interest; and, (3) there was no evidence of a movement among seniors to develop and adopt policies that solely benefited them (Dobson & St. Angelo, 1982, p. 83).

Further analysis of the survey results from the foregoing study found consistently high levels of citizen support for government intervention on behalf of seniors across age groups—23.5% for the youngest age group (18–25) and 26.1% for the oldest age group (76+) (Dobson & St. Angelo, 1982, p. 104). These results show the strength of support for the elderly across generational boundaries; differences in support were far more likely to occur along party lines and by socioeconomic status than by age (Dobson & St. Angelo, 1982, p. 105).

Another Florida study, this one based on socioeconomic and demographic information from the United States Census and county-level taxing and spending data, examined whether communities having a large population of older residents would lend support to a "grey peril" hypothesis. The "grey peril" hypothesis predicts that elderly people will resist local taxing and spending for programs "lacking immediate benefit for the aging while promoting services appealing to older persons" (Button & Rosenbaum, 1990, p. 27). Based on the analysis of their data, the authors found no evidence that the elderly exerted a positive influence on spending for the services that they were "presumed to value," such as health care, transportation, and housing and that an aged population appeared to have a "benign" influence upon local tax revenues (Button & Rosenbaum, 1990, pp. 34–35).

A national study, using data from the 1973 and 1986 General Social Surveys, tested the hypothesis that elderly individuals favored public spending patterns that supported their own interests as opposed to those which supported the interests of children. The authors found "no support whatsoever for the 'cohort' view in the self-interest hypothesis that predicts that the elderly favor redistributive transfers away from low-income families with children and toward low-income members of their own age group" (Ponza, Duncan, Corcoran, & Groskind, 1988, p. 462). In fact, elderly respondents were slightly more supportive than average of transfers to low-income families with children. Resistance to income transfers to low-income recipients was related to high-income in all age classes (Ponza et al., 1988, p. 462). These studies provide strong evidence that the notion that the elderly behave in an exclusively self-interested manner is at odds with what is actually happening in the U.S. political arena.

The evidence that elderly political behavior is not exclusively self-interested is not unequivocal, however. Several studies show that older Americans are less likely to support tax expenditures on education (a social program of presumably no direct benefit to them) than are younger age groups (Button & Rosenbaum, 1990; Ponza et al., 1988; Vinovskis, 1991). In a study based on the analysis of the *American National Study, 1988: Pre- and Post-Election Survey*, Vinovskis concluded that age was the best predictor of support for more federal funding for education, with oldest respondents least likely to support additional funding.

These studies highlight one of the problems facing those interested in determining whether the political behavior of older people is primarily based on self-interest. Social spending programs in the United States are funded at several levels. Taxes for Social Security, a federal program, are levied on working Americans. Medicare, another federal program, is funded both through payroll tax contributions and premiums from beneficiaries. AFDC and Medicaid, on the other hand, draw revenues from both state and federal coffers, whereas public schools receive funds from federal, state, and local taxes. Looking at these programs from the perspective of elderly voters, it would appear that they would be most likely to support additional taxing and spending for Social Security and Medicare. Not only do these programs benefit them directly, but they also cost them the least, because their funds come mainly from working Americans. Similarly, one would expect older people to oppose state and local taxes that fund AFDC and education, since they would derive little direct benefit from these programs. However, elderly people generally are less supportive of increased federal spending for any reason than are younger age groups (Vinovskis, 1991). And despite attitude surveys (Ponza et al., 1988; Vinovskis, 1991) and a county level funding study showing that age related variables are related to lower levels of public school funding (Button & Rosenbaum, 1990), there is no consistent evidence that older people behave politically in a way that benefits them and deprives other age groups.

To suggest that attitudes are a suitable proxy for behavior is risky business; to infer that having a large older population causes decreased public school funding is to risk the "ecological fallacy." One cannot conclude that simply because there is a correlation between decreased school funding and increasing older population that it is older people who "cause" the decrease. As Rosenbaum and Button point out in a study of local government officials' perceptions of the impact of older people in local politics, their data "provided little support for the notion that large retiree populations in Florida's cities and counties share an anti-tax or anti-growth mentality as sometimes predicted . . . attitudes towards public issues often vary among older persons, like younger ones, according to socio-economic, political, and other characteristics" (Rosenbaum & Button, 1989, p. 305).

## The Elderly as a Voting Bloc

Finally, the premise that elderly people constitute a voting bloc can be challenged on a number of fronts. In terms of the generational equity view, elderly self-interest has been assumed, and has been characterized as being "abetted by the strong political power of the elderly as a group" (Callahan, 1986, p. 329) which needs to be addressed by a willingness on the part of the aged to "forgo the use of their political power for their own improved health care and to shift their energies to the needs of the young" (Callahan, 1986, p. 335). But are the elderly a voting bloc? Evidence suggests they are not.

It is true that elderly people vote in greater proportions than do other age cohorts. In 1988, 19% of all Americans who reported voting in that year's elections were 65 years of age and older (U.S. Senate, Special Committee on Aging, 1990, p. 119). Yet the fact that elderly people vote in greater proportions than do other age groups does not necessarily mean they wield greater power. Although they hold potentially decisive margins in elections, there is scant evidence to date that they vote as a bloc. As Jacobs (1990, p. 350) concludes in a review of the literature on the political behavior of elderly people, "the bulk of the evidence shows more similarities than differences in the political beliefs of older and younger citizens. Put another way, there is no substantial evidence of any fundamental political cleavage in the United States based on age."

The elderly in the United States are a heterogeneous group, and to suggest that they do now, or will soon, form a single voting and influence bloc merely because of age, contradicts the evidence. Elderly people have divergent interests—some are wealthy, others are poor—and as one writer puts it, they have different priorities in terms of such things as "more or less taxes, low-cost housing or life-care condos, more primary care, or job protection. It is hard to see a central rallying cry for these elderly groups" (Morris, 1989, p. 496). It seems no more likely for the elderly to coalesce into a homogeneous voting entity in the future than it has been in the past.

Elderly people, like most other Americans, vote along lines of party affiliations and the interests of their socioeconomic class.

Generational equity proponents also claim that because population aging will increase the proportion of elderly voters in the United States, it will significantly increase their political power. This may be so, but simply being a larger proportion of the population does not necessarily translate into political power. Women currently comprise more than 50% of the population, yet there is little evidence to suggest that numerical strength has been translated into political power in terms of gaining elective office and agenda setting. Additionally, other segments of the population who may self-identify as voting blocs, such as Hispanics and African-Americans, will also increase in terms of percentage of the population—and may prove to be countervailing influences to any potential increase in elderly power (Torres-Gil, 1986, pp. 291–242). And finally, for any of the foregoing to have an important impact on the U.S. political scene, the groups in question, whether based upon gender, age, or race/ethnicity, will be influential to the extent that group members see themselves as having homogeneous interests and vote as blocs based on those interests. It is precisely this contextual understanding that is missing from strictly demographic models and generational equity arguments.

Not only have the proponents of generational equity resorted to a core thesis of demographic determinism, they have also combined this perspective with a naive analysis of the potential capacity of elderly voters to determine political outcomes in questions of social spending. It is not through individual exercise of the franchise that the elderly wield their political influence, but rather through activities of old age interest groups.

### The Power of the Elderly Lobby

The political power of older people has been manifested through senior citizen organizations, which grew rapidly in the 1970s. These organizations have engaged in advocacy efforts and have been active in bringing issues to light as well as lobbying and monitoring the behavior of politicians and reporting it to their constituents.

The American Association of Retired Persons (AARP) is the largest voluntary organization in the United States. Founded in 1958, mainly to provide insurance to retirees, it had 28 million members by 1988. Although AARP maintains a nonpartisan stance in terms of politics, it lobbies on behalf of issues relevant to older people. It has a paid staff of 1300, an annual budget of approximately a quarter of a billion dollars, and its magazine, *Modern Maturity,* has the highest circulation of any magazine in the United

States (Day, 1989). *Modern Maturity* publishes voter's guides on candidates' positions on relevant issues for older people, runs a wire service that provides newspaper reports on elderly issues, and sponsors a weekly television series.

The National Council of Senior Citizens was founded by the AFL-CIO in 1962 to lobby for Medicare. It has approximately four-and-a-half million members, primarily blue-collar workers and union members, and retains a liberal Democratic bias. Organized around 4000 active local clubs, NCSC has access to the full lobbying power of the AFL-CIO. Moreover, its smaller size and shared background of its members (trade unionists), make it more capable of taking a stance on particular issues than the unwieldy AARP.

The National Committee to Preserve Social Security and Medicare was founded in 1982 and has more than five million members, a budget of $40 million and a well-funded political action committee. Finally, the National Association of Retired Federal Employees has a membership of approximately half a million and is concerned primarily with issues of interest to retired federal employees. It has an annual budget of five million dollars and a large political action committee. These do not exhaust the extent of the old age lobby, but merely illustrate the more powerful organizations.

The lobbying ability of these senior organizations has been most effective in protecting Social Security. During the 1988 presidential election, in New Hampshire alone, AARP mailed out 250,000 pieces of literature detailing the candidate's positions on Social Security, long-term health care, and other issues of relevance to older people. Yet because it is so large and its membership so diverse, AARP cannot take a position on most issues. Its political neutrality constrains its political power, even as politicians overestimate its impact.

What is most significant about the senior citizen lobby is not its sponsorship of particular candidates, for its size and cross-class nature make agreement on issues other than Social Security unlikely, but rather its impact on the political agenda. Even though there is little evidence that older people use their voting strength politically, politicians are fearful of their political potential. Even when the 1987 stock market crash put every social program under scrutiny, Social Security remained off the bargaining table.

Yet the success of the elderly lobby in protecting resources must not be misconstrued as an ability to initiate new programs. A program of national long-term care separate from poverty-based Medicaid, a priority of most senior organizations, has made no headway. The political power of the elderly is limited and fragmented except in the most narrow sense of maintaining the existing contract.

## Implications of the Generational Equity Debate

On the face of it, the impact of the generational equity debate may appear insignificant. Social Security and Medicare remain intact, and no dismantling of those popular programs has occurred. Still, the reconstruction of the ideology surrounding the intergenerational contract has complicated the issues surrounding old age policy in the United States.

The generational equity issue clouds understanding of the dynamics of support for elderly programs by suggesting that it is an elderly power bloc that pushes them through Congress and sustains them. Historically, it simply has not been the case that the organized demands of older persons have been responsible for enacting or amending Social Security and Medicare (Binstock, 1991, p. 333). The generational equity argument also obscures other important issues about social spending, such as the disproportionately high number of children, older women, and minorities who live below poverty level. It ignores the fact that there is a larger proportion of elderly who are "near poor" than in any other age segment of the population: 15.2% of persons over 65 are considered "near-poor" as opposed to only 8.2% of those under 65 (U.S. Senate, Special Committee on Aging, 1990, p. 27). In fact, elderly people are nearly twice as likely to live within 125% of the poverty level as is the rest of the U.S. population.

These arguments also cloud our ability to understand why poverty rates among children are skyrocketing. Insofar as trends in income and poverty are concerned, since 1974 it has NOT been increases in elderly incomes that have contributed to the gap between the aged and children, but rather increasing poverty rates in the youngest population (U.S. Senate, Special Committee on Aging, 1990, p. 41). Among these causes are increased general revenue outlays on military expenditures and service of federal debt, which reduces funds for other social programs, the absence of a national health insurance system, the exclusion of women and minorities from high paying jobs, divorce and an attendant lack of child support from noncustodial parents, to name just a few.

Most literature on the politics of aging credits widespread societal support, not just among the elderly, but among other age segments of the population, for the success of elderly entitlement programs. Little evidence of intergenerational conflict exists, because most programs designed to serve the elderly generate substantial support from other age groups as well. There are a number of reasons for this widespread support. Almost everyone is affected by old-age policy. "Younger adults are concerned not only about their own future as retirees, but they are also concerned about their own parents and other elderly family members who would often rely on more economic support from the family were it not for government support" (Myles, 1984, p. 170). Old age programs result in a societal sharing of burdens that previously fell solely on the family members of aged individuals.

## CONCLUSIONS

Although one can argue that a transformation in dependency relations occurred when the modern U.S. welfare state was born with the passage of the Social Security Act in the 1930s, it was a situational transformation rather than a transformation in the conditions of dependency itself. What occurred was a transference of dependency from the family and the private sector to the state. This transformation of the locus of dependence happened neither because of demographic determinism nor elderly people's political power.

It is no longer satisfactory to declare that the relations of the modern welfare state are ordered solely by state intervention in the conflict between capital and labor. Nor is it adequate to argue that the outcomes of these mediations determine the institutional constitution of retirement and old age. Although both labor market management and power research theory provide valuable insights about the impact of class-capital relationships on the intergenerational contract, they by no means provide us with the whole picture.

Demographic changes in the age-constitution of nations and economic realities of recessions have moved "renegotiation" of the intergenerational contract to the main stage of the political arena (Walker, 1991). The outcomes of these negotiations must be understood as more than merely a convergence or divergence of class-capital relations institutionalized by the state. The constitution of the emerging intergenerational contracts represent not only the dynamics of the relationship between class and capital, but the cross-cutting influences of age, gender, and race, as well.

As Myles sees it, the future of the welfare state hinges on the resolution of the debate of "whether an economy built on principles of security or insecurity is more likely to lead to higher standards of living and the well-being of all" (Myles, 1989, p. 137). An analysis of class interests alone is insufficient to answer questions arising from this debate. Effects of age, gender, and race cut across classes, and differentially empower individuals. Life course perspectives encompassing these variations enrich the previous political economy models, which were largely silent on these issues. Incorporating such a life course framework within a political and economic context can address directly theories about the nature of dependency beyond the nexus of capital/labor relations. The failure of previous models to take the full breadth of life course dynamics into account has contributed to the misunderstandings intrinsic to the generational equity debate. Only by recognizing the differential impact of life course trajectories within the political and economic milieux can the relationship between elderly people and the state be fully understood.

## ACKNOWLEDGMENTS

We appreciate the comments of Edward Berkowitz, Dennis Shea, and Alan Walker on an earlier draft of this manuscript.

## REFERENCES

Binstock, R.H. (1983. The aged as scapegoat. *The Gerontologist, 23*(2), 136–143.

Binstock, R.H. (1984). Reframing the agenda of policies on aging. In M. Minkler & C. L. Estes (Eds.), *Readings in the political economy of aging* (pp. 157–167). Policy Politics, Health and Medicine Series. Farmingdale, NY: Baywood Publishing Company.

Binstock, R.H. (1991). Aging, politics, and public policy. In B. B. Hess & E. W. Markson (Eds.), *Growing old in America* (4th ed.) (pp. 325–340). New Brunswick, NJ: Transaction Publishers.

Button, J. & Rosenbaum, W. (1990). Gray power, gray peril or gray myth? The political impact of aging in local sunbelt politics. *Social Science Quarterly, 71*(1), 25–37.

Callahan, D. (1986). Health care in the aging society: A moral dilemma. In A. Pifer & L. Bronte (Eds.), *Our aging society: Paradox and promise* (pp. 319-339). New York: W. W. Norton.

Day, C. L. (1989). *What older Americans think: Interest groups and aging policy*. Princeton, NJ: Princeton University Press.

Dobson, D. & St. Angelo, D. (1982). *Politics and senior citizens: Advocacy and policy formation in a local context*. Grant No. 90-A-1374, U.S. Department of Health, Education, and Welfare, Administration on Aging.

Esping-Anderson, G. (1989). The three political economies of the welfare state. *Canadian Review of Sociology and Anthropology, 26*(1), 10–36.

Estes, C. (1986). The politics of aging in America. *Ageing and Society, 6*, 122–134.

Fennel, G., Phillipson, C., & Ever, H. (Eds.) (1988). *The sociology of old age*. Philadelphia: Open University Press.

Flint, J. (1980, February 18). The old folks. *Forbes*, p. 51.

Graebner, W. (1980). *A history of retirement*. New Haven: Yale University Press.

Hardy, M. A. (1988). Vulnerability in old age: The issue of dependency in American society. *Journal of Aging Studies, 2*(4), 311–320.

Hess, B. (1985). America's elderly: A demographic overview. In B. Hess & E. Markson (Eds.), *Growing old in America* (pp. 3–21). New Brunswick, NJ: Transaction Books.

Jacobs, B. (1990). Aging and politics. In R. H. Binstock & L. K. George (Eds.), *Handbook of aging and the social sciences* (3rd ed.) (pp. 349–359). San Diego: Academic Press.

Jacobs, K. & Rein, M. (1991). The future of early retirement: The Federal Republic of Germany. In J. Myles & J. Quadagno (Eds.), *States, labor markets and the future of old age policy* (pp. 250–261). Philadelphia, PA: Temple University Press.

Korpi, W. (1989). Power, politics and state autonomy in the development of social citizenship: Social rights during sickness in eighteen OECD countries since 1930. *American Sociological Review, 54,* 309–328.

Matura, R. C. (1982). The Politics of aging in Florida: A case study of the Silver-Haired Legislature. Doctoral dissertation. University of Florida.

Morris, R. (1989). Challenges of aging in tomorrow's world: Will gerontology grow, stagnate, or change? *The Gerontologist, 29*(4), 494–501.

Myles, J. F. (1984). Conflict, crisis and the future of old age security. In M. Minkler & C. L. Estes (Eds.), *Readings in the political economy of aging* (pp. 168–176). Farmingdale, NY: Baywood.

Myles, J. (1989). *Old age in the welfare state: The political economy of pensions* (rev. ed.). Lawrence, KS: University of Kansas Press.

O'Connor, J. (1973). *The fiscal crisis of the state.* New York: St. Martin's Press.

Phillipson, C. (1986). The state, the economy and retirement. In A. Guillemard (Ed.), *Old age and the welfare state: Studies in international sociology, Vol. 28* (pp. 127–139). London: Sage.

Ponza, M., Duncan, G. J., Corcoran, M., & Groskind, F. (1988). The guns of autumn: Age differences in support for income transfers to the young and old. *Public Opinion Quarterly, 52,* 441–466.

Preston, S. (1984). Children and the elderly: Divergent paths for America's dependents. *Demography, 21*(4), 435–457.

Quadagno, J. S. (1984). Welfare capitalism and the Social Security Act of 1935. *American Sociological Review, 49*(5), 632–647.

Quadagno, J. S. (1988). *The transformation of old age security, class and politics in the American welfare state.* Chicago: The University of Chicago Press.

Quadagno, J. (1991). Interest group politics and the future of Social Security. In J. Myles & J. Quadagno (Eds.), *States, labor markets and the future of old age security* (pp. 36–58). Philadelphia: Temple University Press.

Rosenbaum, W. A. & Button, J. W. (1989). Is there gray peril? Retirement politics in Florida. *The Gerontologist, 29*(3), 300–306.

Siegel, J. S. & Tauber, C. M. (1986). Demographic dimensions of an aging population. In A. Pifer & L. Bronte (Eds.), *Our aging society: Paradox and promise* (pp. 79–110). New York: W. W. Norton.

Torres-Gil, F. (1986). Hispanics: The special challenge. In A. Pifer & L. Bronte (Eds.), *Our aging society: Paradox and promise* (pp. 219–242). New York: W. W. Norton.

U.S. Bureau of the Census. (1987). Money income of households, families and persons in the United States, 1987. *Current Population Reports,* P-60, No. 162. Washington, DC: U.S. Government Printing Office.

U.S. Bureau of the Census. (1987). Trends in child care arrangements for working mothers. *Current Population Reports.* Special Studies Series P-23, No. 117. Washington, DC: U.S. Government Printing Office.

U.S. Senate, Special Committee on Aging (1990). *Aging America: Trends and projections.* Washington, DC: U.S. Government Printing Office.

Vinovskis, M. A. (1991). *An historical perspective on support for schooling by different age cohorts.* Paper presented at the conference The New Contract between Generations: Social Science Perspectives on Cohorts in the 21st Century, University of Southern California, Los Angeles.

Walker, A. (1980). The social creation of poverty and dependency in old age. *Journal of Social Policy, 9,* 49–75.

Walker, A. (1982). Dependency and old age. *Social Policy & Administration, 16*(2), 115–135.

Walker, A. (1986). Social policy and elderly people in Great Britain: The construction of dependent social and economic status in old age. In A. Guillemard (Ed.), *Old age and the welfare state, Studies in International Sociology, Vol. 28* (pp. 143–167). London: Sage.

Walker, A. (1991). *Intergenerational relations and welfare restructuring: The social construction of a generational problem*. Paper presented at the conference The New Contract between Generations: Social Science Perspectives on Cohorts in the 21st Century, University of Southern California, Los Angeles.

Wisensale, S. K. (1988). Generational equity and intergenerational policies. *The Gerontologist, 28*(6), 773–779.

# Intergenerational Equity and Academic Discourse

## Edward D. Berkowitz

One's discipline informs one's reading of the paper by Street and Quadagno, as does one's perspective on the structure and conduct of public policy.

Like all historians, I deal in particulars and indulge in what other social scientists sometimes call "thick description." Macromodels of change tend to make me uncomfortable because they often strike me as simplistic. A phenomenon as complicated as the United States Social Security program cannot be easily encapsulated as a concession of capital to labor or as something that labor wrests from capital. Instead, in my historical view, each phase of the program comes complete with its own story, its own uneasy mix of facts, perceptions, and demographic imperatives. I suspect that social scientists regard most historical narratives as, in effect, too nuanced, so weighted down with facts as to be of little analytic value.

Given these cultural preconceptions, I wonder why anyone would be brave enough to attempt historical sociology, yet the field appears to be flourishing. Jill Quadagno stands as one of the field's most skilled practitioners. As much as anyone, she has managed to speak to both historians and sociologists. On the one hand she has increased our historical understanding of such specific phenomena as pensions for Civil War veterans. On the other hand, she has reinvigorated the Marxist interpretation of the welfare state. Quadagno understands that history tests many of the macro generalizations about the welfare state. Simply put, things that are true in one period of time may not be true in another period of time. As I have said in the context of reviewing one of her books, she allows her macrovariables to have refreshing micro variations.

In this particular case, Debra Street and she demonstrate that some fashionably grand notions of the welfare state do not explain much about the intergenerational equity issue in Social Security. The authors begin with the fundamental fact that we have a large and successful Social Security program. It simply does not do to talk about America as a laggard in the development of retirement pensions for the elderly. Further, current historical research demonstrates that this program, although triumphant, was not an inevitable triumph. Nor can its development easily be ascribed to the self-interested actions of bureaucrats, capitalists, or workers alone.

As both historians and sociologists understand, programs have their own imperatives. In the case of social insurance, we know that such programs are difficult to sustain, much less to begin, during depressions. We know that old-age insurance was a less significant and less politically popular program than old-age assistance for at least 15 years after the passage of the Social Security Act in 1935. We know that organized labor had very little to do with its founding and only became an active partner in its expansion and defense during the 1940s. By virtue of Martha Derthick's perceptive description of the program, we know that its bureaucratic leaders have pursued an agenda that has not always meshed with the desires of either labor or capital (Derthick, 1979). Above all, we know that the very design of the program has changed over time and that generalizations about the program in 1935 no longer were valid in 1939, much less 1950 or 1972 or 1983 (Berkowitz, 1991).

Given their understanding of Social Security's history, Quadagno and Street have little difficulty discrediting the intergenerational equity argument. This argument, simply stated, holds that our present political structure skews tax dollars toward the elderly and, in the process, deprives children of much-needed funds. The argument is correct in noting the imbalance between social insurance and welfare expenditures. Since most of the social insurance money goes to the elderly in the form of annuities or medical services, the elderly receive more of our social welfare expenditures than any other age cohort. Further, our political system tends to shift costs to the future and, in the process, creates inequality. Baby boomers will presumably retire at a later age than do present retirees, because the official retirement age for "full" benefits will be raised. Future generations will presumably pay higher taxes than the present generation of workers.

No one denies these facts and inferences. The question is whether money for Social Security somehow deprives children of money for things like schooling. Here I must shift from my identity as a historian to my role as a policy analyst. Perhaps, as some have suggested, we could dismantle our distribution system to use Social Security taxes for schooling or some other socially uplifting project, yet I find little support for this idea in Washington. I do note that Senator Moynihan wants to lower Social Security taxes and that President Bush and nearly everyone else wants to lower the federal debt. Although I can see Social Security taxes being lowered, I cannot imagine liberated Social Security taxes going to children.

I find it tempting to view the intergenerational equity argument simply as a politically correct way to discredit the Social Security program by turning baby boomers against their elders. The first step in this exercise consists of encouraging members of different age cohorts to view themselves as somehow separated from the members of other cohorts. It becomes possible in this manner to harness the political energy of the large baby boom group and to convince them that their interests are distinct from those of their parents or grandparents. When my mother gets sick, that is her problem, not mine. When my grandfather dies, the care of my grandmother should not be a central concern of mine. This view encourages us to believe that, although I might be vitally concerned with my daughter's education, the quality of my mother's life concerns me less. Social Security's defenders reply, with considerable justification, that, as one advocate puts it, "we are all in this together." Social Security's detractors note that one can hold this organic view of society only if one believes that the system will continue to benefit the elderly in the future. If slow economic growth or pure greed causes the system to break down, then it will be every generation for itself.

The second step in the intergenerational equity argument consists of blurring the boundaries of Social Security and transforming it into a program that only benefits the elderly. Such a view, although commonly held, is flat-out wrong. Social Security provides current protection against the risks of disability and death. Baby boomers will soon be the chief beneficiaries of these forms of protection. Further, one's family stands to gain far more in disability or survivors' benefits than the average elderly couple receives from old-age benefits. Indeed, disparities in the average benefit size between disability and old-age have accounted for many of the political battles over Social Security in the last 15 years (Berkowitz, 1987).

The third step in the intergenerational equity argument consists of promoting a view of public policy as a zero sum game with negative societal consequences. In this view, a transfer of money to the elderly reduces the amount of money going to young people by the exact amount of the transfer. Further, the transfer diminishes societal productivity because money that goes to the young represents an investment in America's future, whereas money that reaches the elderly is a form of current consumption. Such a view, although not inaccurate, leads to the conclusion that we should aid the young, rather than maintaining the old.

Here is where proponents of the intergenerational equity argument shade the truth. They use the intergenerational equity argument to undermine Social Security, but they fail to mention that they have other arguments to cast doubt on the effectiveness of programs aimed at the young. Charles Murray reserves his most devastating arguments to show how Aid to Families with Dependent Children lowers the labor force participation rate, compromises the morality of women, and consigns people to lives of poverty. Nor does he think highly of the Elementary and Secondary Education Act of 1965 or other recent efforts to bring federal aid to education (Murray, 1984). Still other arguments get trotted out to criticize our system of health insurance for the indigent. Proponents of the intergenerational equity argument do not want to increase federal aid to the young so much as they want to discredit federal social spending in general. It is not only Social Security, but the entire welfare state that they oppose. They cynically play on people's perceptions and on the balkanized nature of policy discourse to achieve their objectives.

Social Security remains the primary target of the intergenerational equity argument, yet Medicare presents the most tempting target for criticism. Although Street and Quadagno do not dwell on the differences between Medicare and Social Security, such differences are significant. The elderly can be mobilized on Medicare issues, as the recent flap over catastrophic health care coverage illustrated, yet they do not respond as vehemently to changes that appear to be technical in nature, such as the installation of the Diagnosis Related Group system of hospital reimbursement, as they do to perceived cuts in old-age insurance. Medicare remains a much more vulnerable program than Old-Age and Survivors Insurance. The reasons, which concern Medicare's inherent design and current costs, have little to do with the citizen's wage or some other nuance of academic discourse. Here, as elsewhere, the particulars of social policy matter more than do academic slogans.

The intergenerational equity argument also gives liberals a bum rap, as if they were unconcerned about the fate of the young in their desperate effort to curry favor with the elderly. Such thinking confuses the reform program of the New Deal with the reform program of the Great Society. Ever since the 1950s, after all, the liberal agenda has highlighted social welfare spending as an investment in America's future, rather than as an ameliorative measure for the poor.

I have noticed this fact in my research on the life of Wilbur J. Cohen, an important proponent of the Social Security program. Cohen regarded prosperity as the central reality of the 1950s and urged policymakers to adjust to it. "For a long period of time," he noted in a talk before an academic audience during the 1950s, "the bitter memory of the depression in the minds of millions of people, and the fear of another depression in the minds of countless others, was a significant factor affecting attitudes and pressures with respect to many different kinds of programs. . . . Rather than justify changes or improvements in social programs on the basis of a crusade against the threat of unemployment or depression," he urged that changes "be justified on a high level of economic literacy which assumes a continued increase in productivity and wages and the ability of the country to finance improvements in social welfare out of a growing national income" (Cohen, 1957).

Cohen, in common with Democratic liberals in Congress, wanted to replace the depression agenda of the New Deal with a growth agenda. If the government funded necessary public goods, the argument went, its actions would reap dividends in the form of greater productivity and an increased national product. "We need more schools, more roads, more hospital beds, and more housing. We want more teachers, more doctors, nurses, social workers," he told his 1957 audience, invoking the familiar liberal boilerplate of the era (Cohen, 1957).

Indeed, education, aimed at the young, became the main social service promoted by the Great Society. It served as the least common denominator of social policy, involving none of the conflicts that marred workfare for welfare mothers or civil rights. Its mandatory status and its efficacy went unquestioned. It appeared to confirm a central lesson of Wilbur Cohen's life and the lives of other members of Cohen's generation: that education paid dividends. As if to underscore this fact, a Michigan study on poverty, in which Cohen participated in the late 1950s (which stated unambiguously that poverty could be abolished "easily and simply by a stroke of the pen") concluded that education had the most impact on earnings and a "powerful effect on occupational advancement, job security, and income stability as well." The study quoted with approval a 1960 article by a conservative economist who had written, "the cost of . . . education is an investment that will earn more than its cost" (Morgan, David, Cohen, & Brazer, 1962, pp. 9, 11).

Not surprisingly, education became one of the key tests of Cohen's political ability to secure the items on the growth agenda. Along with Medicare and workfare, Cohen made education legislation a priority, and he played a key role in the passage of the Elementary and Secondary Education Act. Nothing better defined the differences between the New Deal and the Great Society than the contrast between Social Security, on the one hand, and aid to education, on the other.

For our purposes, we should underscore the fact that the same people who developed Social Security and brought us Medicare also tried to pass programs in aid of younger people. Further, they enjoyed almost as much success in their campaign on behalf of the young as in their campaign on behalf of the old.

All of which reinforces the points made by Street and Quadagno: history matters. As we ponder old age as a social construct, we must continue to highlight the process of change over time. We must also scrutinize carefully the way that various actors in the policy arena construct the truth for fear that rational academicians may become pawns in other people's games. In this manner, matching the sociologists' macro social models and the historians' thick descriptions may come to pay dividends, rather than serving only as a sterile form of current intellectual consumption.

## REFERENCES

Berkowitz, E. (1987). *Disabled policy: America's programs for the handicapped.* New York: Oxford University Press.

Berkowitz, E. (1991). *America's welfare state: From Roosevelt to Reagan.* Baltimore: Johns Hopkins Press.

Cohen, W. J. (1957, March). *The Future of Social Security,* An Address in Honor of Professor Edwin E. Witte, University of Wisconsin, Symposium on Labor and Government, Madison, Wisconsin, in Wilbur Cohen Papers, State Historical Society, Madison Wisconsin.

Derthick, M. (1979). *Policymaking for Social Security.* Washington, DC: Brookings Institution.

Morgan, J. N., David, M. H., Cohen, W. J., & Brazer, H. E. (1962). *Income and welfare in the United States.* New York: McGraw-Hill Company.

Murray, C. (1984). Losing *ground.* New York: Basic Books.

# Elderly Persons and the State: Distribution Across and Within Generations

## Dennis G. Shea

The role of the state in developing pensions and health services for the elderly and the future of the welfare state are assuredly worthy of more attention than can be given them in such a short space. The main focus in this comment will be the potential effects of a life course framework on the current and future ability of the state to address the problems of income support and health care coverage for the young and old.

Incorporating a life course approach may not be successful in creating a political economy of aging which can capture the debate on the future of the welfare state. Proponents of the life course framework underestimate the political task necessary to counter those who raise the issue of generational equity. Those who wish to address the remaining areas of need among the elderly or among the young using the life course as a theoretical foundation, must be able to convince Americans that redistribution of well-being is a fundamental role of the state, especially when there is a lack of adequate economic growth.

The first section below briefly reviews the system of income support and health care coverage that characterizes the role of the state towards the elderly, introducing three rationales for government involvement. The second segment turns to the current state of well-being among the elderly, arguing that proponents of a life course framework underestimate the import of distributional issues within the elderly population. The final section focuses on the future role of the state towards elderly persons.

## THE ROLE OF THE STATE IN DEVELOPING PENSIONS AND HEALTH SERVICES FOR THE ELDERLY

The development of pensions and health services for the elderly, like most developments in the United States, was a combination of public and private measures. It is too easy to ignore the complexity of how public policy is established and attribute the development of the role of the state to an attempt by the state to intervene to protect the needs of capital. It is also misleading to attribute the development of the role of the state simply to attempts by workers to establish a "citizen's wage." While both of these views have elements of truth, neither completely captures the efforts of both public and private groups to create a system of support for elderly persons.

Pensions were developed simultaneously by both private employers and the emerging trade unions. The period from 1875 to 1930 saw more than 400 pension plans established by employers covering more than 10 percent of the nonagricultural labor force. In addition, by the time of the Great Depression, more than one-third of trade union members belonged to unions which provided various types of retirement and disability benefits (Greenough & King, 1976; Munnell, 1982).

This private system of pension support, and the private savings of many retirees, however, were decimated by the events of the 1930s. The establishment of Social Security and subsequent actions by the government set the stage not for the removal of the private pension system, but for its expansion. Various agencies of the government played an active role in furthering the development of a private pension system. Wartime price controls, which allowed for increases in fringe benefits, and corporate and personal tax deductions for contributions to pension plans led to rapid growth in the 1940s. The 1948 decision by the National Labor Relations Board, which made fringe benefits subject to collective bargaining, set the stage for continued growth in the 1950s. The Employment Retirement Income Security Act (ERISA) in 1974 confirmed the government's commitment to a stable system of private pension support (Munnell, 1982).

This combination of public and private programs is similar to the development of the system of health care coverage for elderly persons. The use of established private insurers to administrate the program, and the adoption of deductibles and co-payments all demonstrated the intent of Medicare to supplement, not replace a private system, which by 1963 provided 56 percent of the elderly with coverage of hospital care (Cohen, 1985; Gornick, Greenberg, Eggers, & Dobson, 1985). The subsequent history has, as in pensions, been a history of growth, not decline of the private system. By 1989 more than three-quarters of the elderly had private health insurance (HIAA, 1991).

The continued growth of the private systems of income support and health care coverage after the introduction of a public system has raised the question of why we have a public system at all. The success of the private systems at providing income and health care security for a growing minority of the elderly population naturally led to discussion of whether government intervention was needed. Many have argued, perhaps most vehemently with respect to Social Security, that the public system merely supplants and does not supplement the private system (Feldstein, 1974, 1980, 1982; Munnell, 1974).

Lesnoy and Leimer (1985, p. 17) suggested two rationales for Social Security, which can apply equally to public health insurance. They write, "one possible rationale is the political judgment that the private voluntary system is too small." Thus, the argument can be made that individual myopia or market failure in a private system requires public intervention. With respect to health care, Arrow (1963) has argued that the importance of uncertainty in medical care leads to the development of non-market social institutions which attempt to bridge the gaps in the private market. As the private system of pensions and health insurance grew during the 1970s and 1980s, this rationale appeared to become less valid.

The second rationale provided by Lesnoy and Leimer (1985, p. 17) ". . . is that the public system has a element of insurance not possible in the private system." As Quadagno (1990, p. 635) noted, one of the basic metaphors used in the creation of Social Security was that "the program was analogous to private insurance."

The analogy is even more applicable to Medicare. Public and private systems of risk pooling reduce risk. In fact, the larger the risk pool, other things equal, the greater the risk reduction. Public systems, in this rationale, are superior to private systems because they pool risks across a larger group, thus increasing the amount of risk reduction.

In addition, as evidenced by the administrative costs of the U.S. health care system, private systems of risk reduction, because of their smaller size and their lack of standardization, can lead to an overall level of higher costs, which must be balanced against the advantages of freedom of choice which they can provide (Woolhandler & Himmelstein, 1991). As Quadagno (1990) noted, the insurance rationale, especially with respect to Social Security, suffered great criticism in recent years, primarily from proponents of generational equity.

A third argument, not mentioned by Lesnoy and Leimer (1985), is that public intervention, in both Social Security and public health care or health insurance, can be justified in terms of redistribution and equity. Undeniably, the intent of Social Security was to redistribute income. In fact, the redistribution planned was primarily within, rather than between generations. In any case, redistribution of both types now occurs.

Boskin, Kotlikoff, Puffert, and Shoven (1987) found early cohorts in Social Security received rates of return on contributions which exceeded 6%, while current cohorts will receive rates of return between 1 and 3%. More notable, however, are the distributional effects within a single cohort. When persons are stratified by income and family status, rates of return within the 1945 cohort varied from –0.53% to 3.9%. The largest dollar transfers are received by low-income single-earner couples and single females.

The distributional impact of Medicare is much more clearly across generations, with general revenues being used to finance health care for the elderly. Its effects within the elderly population have certainly narrowed the differences in access to medical care. Link, Long, and Settle (1982) showed the significant narrowing of differences between rural and urban elderly persons and white and black elderly persons.

The recent lack of economic growth has, however, raised the issue of distribution of benefits and costs within the elderly population. Smeeding and Straub (1987) demonstrated that the current system of health care coverage for the elderly puts a significant burden on the group too well-off for Medicaid, but too poor to be covered by the private system. Feder, Moon, and Scanlon (1987) showed that the current system of universal benefits with common premiums and coinsurance places a larger burden on the low-income elderly population.

Each of these programs, in part, recognizes an implicit intergenerational contract that links children with their parents. Both are funded through taxes that redistribute well-being from the young workers to the older retirees. In addition, both redistribute well-being within a given generation as well. In the past two decades the first two rationales for public intervention have been weakened. Furthermore, the distributional effects of the public systems of income and health care support for the elderly population are less controversial when incomes of workers are increasing, when the population is growing, and when age is identified with need. In the next section, I consider the current state of well-being among the elderly, arguing that proponents of a life course framework underestimate the import of distributional issues within the elderly population.

## THE CURRENT STATE AND DYNAMIC
## OF WELL-BEING OF THE ELDERLY

When economic growth occurs, a society can redistribute income simultaneously with a general increase in economic well-being. The root of the current conflict between the generations lies in the combination of slowed economic growth for the nation, rising well-being of elderly persons, and redistributive social policies. The explicit redistribution across generations and the tacit redistribution within generations that characterized the role of the state with respect to elderly persons conflicted with the slow economic growth and the rising well-being of the average elderly person in the 1970s and 1980s.

Generational equity muddies the issue of the role of the state because it does not adequately recognize the conflicts within generations that impact policy towards elderly persons. The conflict over who benefits and who pays for income support and health care programs for elderly persons is not simply a question of generational equity, because the distributive effects of the programs are not confined to taking from the young and giving to the old. In this regard, there exists a need for greater understanding of the roles of race, gender, and other factors. Recognition of the life course as an important theme, however, may do little to muster political support for a change in the definition of the role of the state which can aid in solving the remaining problems of need in America. An examination of the static level of well-being and the dynamic paths to well-being of elderly persons reveals the considerable diversity which may prevent the life course from being a unifying concept.

It has been shown in many studies that the economic problems that slowed income growth for most Americans did not impact the elderly to nearly the same degree. Median income of elderly families rose by 50% from 1970 to 1986, two-and-one-half times the rate for all families (Congressional Budget Office, 1988). With only minor adjustments to data reported to the Census Bureau, the average elderly individual was just as well-off as the average individual under age 65. In comparison to the household income of young children, the household income of the average elderly person is quite substantially higher (Crystal & Shea, 1990a). Whether public policy actively created this situation or quietly stood by while the private market created a new reality of well-being may well be a moot point. In either case, the future role of the state must be adjusted to the current reality of well-being among older persons.

The failure of the generational equity argument is not its interpretation of why the elderly are so well-off while children are so poor, but their conclusion that the elderly are well-off and that children are poor. The reality of well-being in both age groups is much more complicated.

While the income of the average elderly person compares quite favorably to that of the average non-elderly person, the level of inequality in both older and younger age groups is much higher than among persons in the middle of life's ages. The bottom 40% of the population of persons over age 75 receive 14.9% of the total income (adjusted for wealth) in that age group. The bottom 40% of the population of persons under age 6 receive 16.0% of total income. The bottom 40% of the population age 35 to 44 receives 18.4% of total income (Crystal & Shea 1990a). Despite a substantial drop in inequality from 1967 to 1983, inequality was still higher among family units headed by someone age 65 and older, and was highest among family units with a head over age 85 (Radner, 1986).

Furthermore, this static diversity among the elderly understates the actual diversity that exists. There are multiple paths to the various combinations of income, wealth, health, and health insurance that characterize elderly persons. Some may be characterized by a path of cumulative advantage as success breeds success. Others may face cumulative disadvantage with initial minor failures translating into lack of access to private pensions or private insurance and poor earnings histories resulting in lower income from Social Security (Crystal & Shea, 1990b).

As a result, even if elderly persons could agree on how public or private proposals could solve their current needs, they may not agree on how policy could have prevented them from becoming dependent in the first place. Adopting a life course framework may clarify the role of the state vis-á-vis elderly persons. This clarification, however, may not solve the practical problem of adjusting policy to the new reality of need and dependence in America.

## THE FUTURE ROLE OF THE STATE AND THE FUTURE ELDERLY

The heterogeneity of elderly persons, both in a static and a dynamic sense, requires an explicit confrontation in America of the question of what defines dependence and what response is necessary to dependence. The political conflicts within the current elderly population over how to modify policy reveal the difficulty faced by those who wish to counter arguments of generational equity. The original structures of Social Security and Medicare were erected on the assumption that dependence and age were nearly equivalent. If age is not isomorphic with dependence, then those who wish to make policy must first develop a new definition of dependence.

Incorporating a notion of the life course in a new definition of dependence will, in all likelihood, result in a more explicit recognition of the distributional effects of changes in policy. More importantly the life course framework will focus increased attention on the current redistribution within generations that occurs as a result of Social Security and Medicare. Thus, advancing the idea of the life course may, in fact, lead to an erosion of support for current programs.

The solution is not to deny the relevance of the life course for the understanding of the role of the state and elderly persons. Those who wish to incorporate a life course perspective, however, must recognize the enormous obstacles to be overcome. Most Americans believe that active redistribution by the government is unacceptable public policy (Kluegel & Smith, 1986). In the absence of economic growth, a change in public policy which can address the remaining needs of both young and old in America must recognize and confront the aversion of Americans towards distributional policies.

I would argue that any incorporation of the life course perspective must be accompanied with an emphasis on the false dichotomy in American policy between insurance and redistribution. Public and private insurance systems act to redistribute and equalize losses. Similarly, many programs which redistribute well-being act to insure individuals against unpredictable events (Arrow, 1963). The distinction between the two is more semantic than real.

Thus, the task is not simply to convince Americans that security is better than insecurity, but that redistribution is a necessary element of security and a fundamental role of government. More than a half-century ago, John Maynard Keynes (1936, p. 374) commented.

> For my own part, I believe that there is social and psychological justification for significant inequalities of incomes and wealth. . . . But it is not necessary . . . that the game should be played for such high stakes as at present.

The current debate on the role of the state provides an opportunity for us to consider a better balancing of the stakes of this game between young and old, rich and poor, male and female, black and white. The resolution of this debate hinges on changing American attitudes about the role of government and redistribution, which is a much more difficult task than proponents of the life course have previously considered.

## REFERENCES

Arrow, K. (1963). Uncertainty and the welfare economics of medical care. *American Economic Review, 53*(5), 941–973.

Boskin, M., Kotlikoff, L., Puffert, D., & Shoven, J. (1987). Social Security: A financial appraisal across and within generations. *National Tax Journal, 40*(1), 19–34.

Cohen, W. (1985). Reflections on the enactment of Medicare and Medicaid. *Health Care Financing Review,* (Supplement), 3–11.

Congressional Budget Office. (1988). *Trends in family income: 1970–1986.* Washington, DC: U.S. Government Printing Office.

Crystal, S., & Shea, D. (1990a). The economic well-being of the elderly. *Review of Income and Wealth, 36*(3), 227–247.

Crystal, S., & Shea, D. (1990b). Cumulative advantage, cumulative disadvantage, and inequality among elderly people. *The Gerontologist, 30*(4), 437–443.

Feder, J., Moon, M., & Scanlon, W. (1987). Medicare reform: Nibbling at catastrophic costs. *Health Affairs. 6*(1), 5–14.

Feldstein, M. (1974). Social Security, induced retirement, and aggregate capital accumulation. *Journal of Political Economy, 82*(5), 905–926.

Feldstein, M. (1980). International differences in Social Security and savings. *Journal of Public Economics, 33*(1), 225–244.

Feldstein, M. (1982). Social Security and private saving: Reply. *Journal of Political Economy, 90*(4), 630–642.

Gornick, M., Greenberg, J., Eggers, P., & Dobson, A. (1985). Twenty years of Medicare and Medicaid: Covered populations, use of benefits, and program expenditures. *Health Care Financing Review* (Supplement), 13–59.

Greenough, W. C., & Francis, P. K. (1976). *Pension plans and public policy.* New York: Columbia University Press.

Health Insurance Association of America (HIAA). (1991). *Source book of health insurance data.* Washington, DC: Author.

Keynes, J. M. (1936). *The general theory of employment, interest and money.* Cambridge, UK: Royal Economic Society.

Kluegel, J., & Smith, E. (1986). *Beliefs about inequality.* New York: Aldine de Gruyter.

Lesnoy, S., & Leimer, D. (1985). Social Security and private saving: Theory and historical evidence. *Social Security Bulletin, 48*(1), 14–30.

Link, C., Long, S., & Settle, R. (1982). Equity and the utilization of health care services by the Medicare elderly. *Journal of Human Resources, 27*(2), 195–212.

Munnell, A. (1974). The impact of Social Security on personal saving. *National Tax Journal, 27*(4), 553–568.

Munnell, A. (1982). *The economics of private pensions.* Washington, DC: The Brookings Institute.

Quadagno, J. (1990). Generational equity and the politics of the welfare state. *International Journal of Health Services, 20*(4), 631–649.

Radner, D. (1986). Changes in the money income of the aged and nonaged, 1967–1983. *Studies in Income Distribution, 14.* Washington, DC: Social Security Administration.

Smeeding, T., & Straub, L. (1987). Health care financing among the elderly: Who really pays the bills. *Journal of Health Politics, Policy and Law, 12*(1), 35–52.

Woolhandler, S., & Himmelstein, D. (1991). The deteriorating administrative efficiency of the U.S. health care system. New *England Journal of Medicine, 324*(18), 1253–1258.

# The Prophecy of *Senescence*

## G. Stanley Hall and the Reconstruction of Old Age in Twentieth-Century America

**Thomas R. Cole**

> Many of those who attain advanced years are battered, water-logged, leaky derelicts without cargo or crew, chart, rudder, sail, or engine, remaining afloat only because they have struck no fatal rocks or because the storms have not yet swamped them.
>
> *—G. Stanley Hall, 1922*

> Best for old people would be real jobs, real family relationships, real functioning in society. But if they cannot be given real lives, they must have proxy ones.
>
> *—George Lawton, 1943*

In January 1921, an *Atlantic Monthly* article entitled "Old Age" opened ominously: "After well-nigh half a century of almost unbroken devotion to an exacting vocation, I lately retired. . . . Now I am divorced from my world, and there is nothing more to be said of me save the exact date of my death." At 77, G. Stanley Hall, a professional psychologist and Clark University's founding president, found nothing enjoyable about retirement. "I really want, and ought, to do something useful and with unitary purpose. But what, and how shall I find it?" (Hall, 1921b, pp. 23, 24).

Informed by a scientific world view, Hall sought to orient himself not by taking his spiritual bearings but by checking his physical inventory. Visits to several doctors convinced him that physicians knew very little about old age. A bewildering array of advice provided little comfort or security. "Thus, again, I realized that I was alone—indeed, in a new kind of solitude—and must pursue the rest of my way in life by a more or less individual research on how to keep well and in condition. In a word, I must henceforth and for the most part be my own doctor"(Hall, 1921b, p. 25).

After months of "painful renunciation" verging on despair, Hall emerged in a new mood of belligerency, eager to struggle against "ignorance, error, and the sins of greed and lust." The "current idea of old age itself" headed the list of evils he had previously lacked the courage to attack. Hall sought the most authoritative and normative ideas of both life and death in the study of biology. The result was *Senescence, the Last Half of Life* (1922), the first major work in American social gerontology—a book whose tone of decline and vision of old age reveal large debts to Hall's Puritan ancestors and his rural mid-Victorian childhood.

For all its indebtedness to the past, *Senescence* is a prophetic book. At once a personal document, an aging manual, and a call to scientific study and professional service, *Senescence* is a rambling, often frustrating text. Yet its confusions and contradictions are revealing—not only of Hall's personal and intellectual life, but also of broader currents in American culture. The historical timing of Hall's life (1844–1924), his temperament, and his professional interests all prepared him both to experience the crisis of the "civilized" ideal of aging and to search prophetically for a resolution (Cole, 1992, Chapters 4–7).

The alternating moods of despair and belligerency or exhilaration that Hall revealed in his *Atlantic Monthly* article (later included in *Senescence*) did not begin with his retirement from Clark University. Plagued by recurring feelings of worthlessness and isolation since childhood, Hall had suffered a prolonged psychic crisis in the 1890s. Within a few short years, Hall's parents died, his wife and daughter were accidentally asphyxiated, and his dream that Clark would emerge as a great modern university was dashed. In addition, when he reached the age of 50 in 1894, Hall had produced neither a major psychological work nor a coherent world view. Feeling haunted and oppressed by the "Great Fatigue" of death, Hall described the "early psychic symptoms of old age" (Ross, 1972, pp. 252–253).

By age 60 Hall had apparently recovered from this malaise to produce his long-awaited *Adolescence* (1904), a monumental work that put forward his ideals of education, description of adolescent development, and theory of genetic psychology. Hall's work was saturated with the values and tensions of the nineteenth century. In particular, his idealized view of adolescence as the apex of human development—the period "before the decline of the highest powers of the soul in maturity and age" (Hall, 1904, v. 2, p. 361)—reflect values embedded in Victorian ideas about the course of life.

Hall suffered from a sense of exhaustion and confinement that plagued many late nineteenth-century intellectuals who protested the spiritual impoverishment of modern civilization (Lears, 1981). Searching for a source of regeneration and a unified world view, Hall turned to the theory of evolution for a biologically based ideal of human development whose optimum condition was health (Ross, 1972). Echoing nineteenth-century evangelicals, (Cole, 1992) *Adolescence* counterposed the purity and vigor of youth to the fragmented, deadening, and routinized qualities of urban industrial life. "There is really no clue by which we can thread our way through all the mazes of culture and the distractions of modern life save by knowing the true nature and needs of childhood and adolescence. . . . Other oracles may grow dim, but this one will never fail"(Hall, 1900; cited by Ross, 1972, p. 335).

Not surprisingly, this idealized oracle of adolescence did eventually fail. When his retirement in 1920 triggered a familiar cycle of depressive withdrawal followed by intense activity, Hall courageously turned to complete his study (begun earlier during his mid-life crisis) of the last half of life. Confronting both a personal and social crisis of aging, Hall abandoned his earlier celebration of adolescence and struggled to find meaning in old age by deepening his understanding of evolutionary biology.

According to Hall's theory of "genetic" psychology, individual development recapitulated and paralleled the evolutionary development of the species (Ross, 1972). In the years following World War I, Hall painted a gloomy picture of mankind facing conflict and decay on all sides. Deprived of the exhilarating sense of progress that had sustained it for generations, mankind was "drifting perilously close to the wrecking reefs." Here again, Hall's own aging paralleled the decline of classical bourgeois culture, intensifying the search for regeneration. According to Hall, civilization itself had reached the age of senescence, paralleling a crisis of aging that confronted men who now lived longer and retired earlier than their forebears. "We are suffering chiefly from unripeness," he wrote. "The human stock is not maturing as it should" (Hall, 1922, p. 244). Hall summoned science to the evolutionary task of stimulating the full flowering of human maturity. Truly ripe old age (or senectitude) had been a "slow, late, precarious, but precious acquisition of the race, perhaps not only its latest but also its highest product." Its modern representatives were pioneers whose task was to add "a new story to the structure of human life" (Hall, 1922, p. 407).

A veritable prodigy of "well-conserved senectitude," Hall condemned the "antiquated scriptural allotment of three-score and ten years," claiming that the "man of the future" would plan 20 more years of activity. In explicitly patriarchal language, Hall called on older people (presumably men) to become "prophets" who could inspire, castigate, and "convict the world of sin, righteousness, and judgment. Thus, there is a new dispensation which gray-beards alone can usher in. Otherwise, mankind will remain splendid but incomplete" (Hall, 1922, pp. 411, 409).

If Hall's fantasy of veneration resurrected by evolution suggests inner conflicts about his own supercession and death, these personal troubles also reflect broader public issues. *Senescence* poignantly registers the crisis of the civilized ideal of aging and prophetically forecasts a new kind of old age brought forth by scientific professionalism. Within little more than 500 pages, Hall unfolds a complicated program: He urges his readers to prepare wisely for old age while in their 40s, "the dangerous age"; summarizes a large body of international research from biology, physiology, medicine, and social science; calls insistently for the development of gerontology, especially in the areas of physical and mental health; discusses his own research on the psychology of old age and death; and hammers away at his central message—that the aged have a vital yet unrecognized role to play in the modern world, a role requiring greater knowledge of the last stage of life. To appreciate the prophetic import of *Senescence*, we must see that its call for a "new story" atop the "structure of human life" forecasts the creation of old age as an institutionally separate stage of the modern life course.

Throughout the nineteenth century, the separation of work from the household and the expansion of wage labor had quickened the pace of generational replacement in the work force by substituting market competition for the rhythms and conflicts of the family cycle. Victorian morality, the cultural handmaiden of liberal capitalism, weakened older traditions emphasizing the religious, spiritual, and moral significance of the second half of life. Scientific professionalism, closely allied with corporate capitalism (Lasch, 1977) deepened the assault on traditional esteem for the end of life.

By the 1920s the conjunction of shrinking roles in the family and the work force, increasing longevity, and waning existential significance generated an unstable space at the end of the life course. The resulting crisis, whose timing and impact varied considerably depending on class, sex, race, ethnicity, region, and religious perspective, seemed to require the reconstruction of a stage of life increasingly devoid of social purpose, cultural value, or material well-being (Achenbaum, 1978; Dahlin, 1980; Fischer, 1978).

## THE CALL FOR GERONTOLOGY

Hall understood that the crisis was symbolic as well as structural: "the old-age problem is not merely economic, philanthropic, social, or even medical, but also . . . perhaps chiefly psychological" (1922, p. 244). Like the gerontologists who followed him, Hall sought essentially to rationalize and control old age rather than to change the economic structure and cultural milieu that made it so repugnant. "The future welfare of the race depends upon the development of an old age . . . [resulting from] a better knowledge and control of the conditions of this state of life" (Hall, 1922, p. 244). The crisis of aging cast doubt on Hall's belief that evolution, aided by science, would ensure human progress toward harmony and ultimate perfection. Many signs at the turn of the century suggested that old age indicated decay and degeneration rather than survival of the fittest. Perceptions of the uselessness of men after 60 and of growing poverty and chronic disease rates in old age raised the prospect that the aged signaled the decay of Western civilization.

Though he never attempted a careful explanation of the "old-age problem," Hall pointed to the increasing pressure of "the advancing upon the receding generation" and the exhausting speed of an industrial economy. "The intensity of modern life with its industrial and managerial strain compels earlier withdrawal from its strenuosities. We live longer and also begin to retire earlier, so that senescence is lengthening at both ends." Surveying the response to Osler's valedictory address, Hall favored the work of W. A. Newland Dorland, who confined the validity of Osler's fixed period ideas to manual laborers. Both Hall and Dorland considered old age one of evolution's choicest products—indicating survival of the fittest rather than impending extinction. If Osler was right, it was only because mankind had not outgrown the abnormally precocious habits of its "short-lived precursors." In the future, modern man would become more and more "an afternoon and evening worker" (Hall, 1922, pp. 280, 6, 29).

Unfortunately, the "excessive strains" of middle age blighted and dwarfed old age, stunting the higher late-developing powers so badly needed by modern society. The issue, again, became one of health. Hall agreed with Metchnikoff that man's "greatest disharmony" was now the "morbid nature and brevity of old age." In effect, he sought a revival of the positive pole in America's bifurcated imagery of aging: "The highest goal of all endeavor is to overcome the present degeneration of senescence, to cultivate physiological old age" (Hall, 1922, p. 262).

Many contemporary observers, including the Roosevelt Conversation

Committee, also feared a loss of vitality among older Americans. In a Report on National Vitality (1909), economist Irving Fisher summarized data which showed that while death rates below age 40 fell substantially during the second half of the nineteenth century, death rates above age 40 were increasing (Fisher, 1909). Gains in longevity during this period were limited to men and women below age 60; degenerative diseases were on the rise.

"We are witnessing a race between two tendencies," wrote Hall, "the reduction of acute infections, such as typhoid, and increase of the chronic or degenerative disease, such as sclerosis, Bright's disease, etc. . . . We are freer from germs than our ancestors but our vital organs wear out sooner. And this degeneration of our bodies follows that of our habits (Hall, 1922, p. 164). A true Victorian moralist, Hall attributed much of the degeneration of senescence to sexual gratification that sapped vital energy and accelerated bodily decay. Most aging people clung to their fading youth, allowed themselves to indulge in "sexual recrudescences," and soon exhibited traits of senile narcissism. These erotic outbreaks, according to Hall, were dangerous to individual health, domestic happiness, and public morals.

On the other hand, the proper ideal of old age was "complete chastity, psychic and somatic." Hall argued that the old should epitomize purity. Only those "in whom asceticism and sublimation [had] . . . done their perfect work" could enjoy the consummate joys of old age, the "higher ideals of life and mind." Others would drift aimlessly, like "battered water-logged, leaking derelicts . . . remaining afloat only because they have struck no fatal rocks" (Hall, 1922, pp. 426, 377).

Interestingly this concern with sexuality also infused the theories of evolution, microbiology, and physiology upon which Hall drew to explain the aging process (Child, 1915; Loeb, 1919; Mechnikoff, 1908; Pearl, 1921; Steinach, 1927; Voronoff, 1920; Weismann, 1893). With the German biologist August Weismann (1893), Hall believed that aging and death entered the world not through original sin but through evolution. Weismann denied that primordial unicellular organisms grew old or died—instead, they simply divided into two exactly equivalent parts, neither one older than the other. Since these rejuvenating divisions left no corpse behind, Weismann concluded that unicellular organisms were immortal.

The trouble began with the evolution of cell differentiation and specialization. As specialized cells developed higher powers, they lost their rejuvenating capacity and became subject to degeneration and death—all except the sex cells or "germ plasm," which retained the pattern of endless growth and division, thus remaining deathless. According to Hall, senescence in humans began with the waning of reproductive power—the progressive loss of germ plasm or declining hormonal production of the sex glands. Final extinction of the *vita sexualis*, known as the "climacteric," left old age stranded—the only stage of life unable to affect heredity. The aged, Hall wrote, live "completely isolated from the main currents of the life of the race. They have already died racially or to the phylum and await only a second or individual death" (Hall, 1922, p. 257).

Hall, then, explained aging as a consequence of multicellular functioning. With the evolution of higher organisms, not all somatic cells became highly specialized; white blood cells and connective tissue cells, for example, remained quite primitive to accomplish their respective tasks of fighting infection and supporting the various organs. Hall's description of "the aging soma" contains a wonderfully revealing metaphor, associating senescence with the decline of bourgeois self-reliance.

Comparing the "primitive white blood cells and connective tissue cells" to "very robust, fecund proletarians," he charged them with incessantly "waging war upon the nobler, more professional and expert, but less independent cells which have sacrificed most of their cruder, pristine powers for service to the body corporate." Little by little, the higher cells succumbed to the "barbaric but vigorous cells" that made up the connective tissues. "We die because nature tends so strongly to develop the cruder type of cell. . . ." Biological aging, then, had become a kind of cellular class struggle in humans. Perhaps the higher, "more professional" cells could ingeniously develop some new mechanism for extending their domination. Discovery of the thyroid gland, whose secretions apparently checked "this aggression of the lower upon the higher cells," offered hope for an endocrinological solution (Hall, 1922, pp. 307, 308).

Discussing the *fin de siècle* enthusiasm for prolonging and rejuvenating life, Hall expressed cautious optimism that glandular and hormonal research might someday restore old age to the "main currents" of the human race. The work of Steinach and Voronoff suggested that injecting sexual hormones, ligating the *vas deferens* or Fallopian tubes, or implanting young gonads in old people could restore them to active functioning. Hall also experimented in various fads of prolongevity; he tried several dietary and hygienic measures—from Pohl's spermine tablets and vitamins to self-massage, olive oil, and exercises—apparently to no avail.

Hall was especially pleased with Steinach, who argued that "there is a false old age that has been imposed by civilization upon elderly people and given them a role they have more or less passively accepted" (Hall, 1922, p. 302). Foreshadowing the recent gerontological critique of stereotypes and age-segregation, he expressed an angry solidarity with his older readers: "At no stage of life do we want more to be of service than when we are deprived of our most wonted opportunities to do so. We do not take with entire kindness to being set off as a class apart" (Hall, 1922, p. 302).

Despite his emphasis on biology, Hall did not expect biomedical research alone to transcend "false old age" or the "degeneration of senescence." As a genetic psychologist, Hall had long insisted that each stage of life had its "own feelings, thoughts, and wills, as well as its own physiology." The psychological task of senescence was to "construct a new self. . . . We must not only command a masterly retreat along the old front but a no less masterly advance to a new and stronger position, and find compensation for what old age leaves behind in what it brings that is new" (Hall, 1922, pp. 90, 403).

What did old age bring that was new? Certainly not proximity to God, personal immortality, or eternal glory. These, according to Hall, were the necessary fictions of weak souls. Where were the compensations, if not in religion? He rejected the blandishments of rest, retirement, and reminiscence, which he characterized as "senile regression." Hall argued that the normal tendency of old age was not letting go but taking hold of life—synthesizing experience, drawing the "moral of life," giving "integrity to the soul." Here, then, lay the compensatory source of a "new self," the psychological material for creating a new "outlook tower to guide the human race" (Hall, 1922, pp. 427, 133).

But why was humanity suffering from "false" old age? What was stifling the "normal" developmental tendency to bring together life's lessons? In order to explain the psychological degeneration of senescence, Hall resorted to the old bifurcation of old age (Cole, 1992, Chapters 4–6). Just as bad habits explained the physiological degeneration of senescence, Hall invoked failure of will to explain why the "normal" psychic development from maturity to senectitude was generally arrested. Most men and women lacked the courage to confront their aging selves without delusion. After age 40, suffering from "meridional perturbations," they usually exhausted themselves trying to "seem younger . . . remain necessary, and circumvent the looming possibilities of displacement" (Hall, 1922, p. 367; Hall, 1921a). Self-deception and overdrafts of vital energy created physiological and psychological bankruptcy.

Here, in the first academic discussion of the "midlife crisis," Hall depicted the psychological trauma characteristic of a highly competitive, future-oriented society—a society that simultaneously lengthened life and drained it of substance. *Senescence*, after all, was subtitled "The Last Half of Life," which Hall conceived essentially as a falling away from maximum power and efficiency. On page one, Hall compared life to a "binomial curve rising from a base line at birth and sinking into it at death (Hall, 1922, p. 1). Having adopted morale or maximum vitality as the chief goal of humanity, (Hall, 1920) Hall could find little meaning or value in physical and mental decline.

Given this perspective, Hall's vision of wisdom in old age remains hollow and unconvincing. Hall himself apparently derived little satisfaction from it. In the foreword to *Senescence*, he expressed "unique relief" at completing a study which he found increasingly depressing (Hall, 1922). The wisdom that modern society reserves for old age, it seems, lies not in practical guidance or experienced judgment but in acceptance of historicity, contingency, and mortality (Erikson, 1968, pp. 138–141). "Do not let me hear/of the wisdom of old men," writes Eliot in *Four Quartets*,

> *but rather of their folly*
> *Their fear of fear and frenzy, their fear of possession,*
> *Of belonging to another, or to others, or to God.*
> *The only wisdom we can hope to acquire*
> *Is the wisdom of humility: humility is endless.*
> *(Eliot, 1971, pp. 26–27).*

And yet, modern culture—which prizes self-mastery, efficiency, and technical control almost exclusively—provides precious little nourishment for the developmental seeds of such wisdom.

Hall must have sensed the thinness of his rhetoric, for he was not willing to let men and women face old age alone and unassisted. Without "initiators into the last stage of life," most people would never achieve his ideal of fully ripened senectitude. According to Hall, the world had "so far attempted almost nothing that could be called a curriculum for the later years of life—physical, intellectual, moral, social, or even hygienic or religious" (Hall, 1922, pp. 427, 80). This claim, however, was untrue and highly misleading. Throughout Hall's lifetime, ministers and popular writers often served as "initiators" into older, religious "curricula" for the later years.

In fact, the middle-class Protestant "curriculum" for old age was a significant element in the flood of self-help literature that poured into the literary marketplace during the nineteenth century (Douglas, 1977: Haltunen, 1982; Cole, 1992, Chapter 7). Advice about aging occupied a very small but steadily growing place in this genre, which aimed at providing standards of conduct for a newly urban, middle-class readership. Generally written by older ministers or female authors, advice about aging shifted from a Calvinist to an increasingly liberal Protestant perspective during the nineteenth century. Allying itself with middle-class values of individualism and materialism, Protestant advice literature tended to celebrate the goals of the first half of life. By the early twentieth century, advice about aging had lost much of its appreciation for the mysteries of existence; writers and ministers struggled against the waning existential significance of aging and a weakening pattern of socialization to old age.

Hall's position reflects this erosion of Protestantism's vision of life as a spiritual journey. In effect, he was calling for a new "curriculum," based on science rather than religion. Gerontology was a regrettably young field of inquiry, but he believed firmly that future research in the biology, psychology, and medicine of senescence would lay the foundations for a socially useful reconstruction of the self in old age. Scientists and helping professionals would become the new "initiators" into the last stage of life.

## THE RECONSTRUCTION OF OLD AGE AND THE RISE OF THE AGING INDUSTRY

In the late twentieth century we can appreciate the prescience of Hall's remarks. Authoritative understanding of old age is now attributed almost entirely to science—biological, medical, social. We are accustomed to the idea of aging as a problem that has many aspects and requires the intervention of trained professionals. Gerontologists regularly publish handbooks on various aspects of aging and methods of managing them (Schneider & Rowe, 1990; Birren & Schaie, 1990; Binstock & George, 1990; Cole, Van Tassel, & Kastenbaum, 1992). Departments of gerontology offer advanced degrees for those who would make a career in the field.

Geriatrics is a growing part of undergraduate medical education, and several fellowships have been established for post-residency training. The National Institute of Aging and the Administration on Aging attest to federal commitment to research and social service. Aging as an area of professional study and social service has become a major influence on the way Americans conceptualize and experience the final years of life. The scientific study and management of aging has itself become an industry, linked to the regulation of the modern life course.

The creation of old age as the capstone of the institutionalized life course awaited the growth of the welfare state. Following the example of Germany (Kohli, 1987) and other Western industrial democracies (e.g., Great Britain, 1908; Austria, 1909; France, 1910; the Netherlands, 1913), the United States instituted a national pension system in 1935 through the Social Security Act (Quadagno, 1989) for retired workers. Public pensions for retired workers helped prevent old age pauperism (Quadagno, 1982), cleared the labor market for younger workers (Graebner, 1980), and helped forestall more radical programs of social change.

In linking retirement benefits to a specific age, public pension systems provided the economic basis for a chronologically defined phase of life beyond gainful employment. By the mid-twentieth century, this "new" phase of life was becoming a mass phenomenon. Increasing life expectancy, the dramatic growth of the elderly population, the spread of retirement and the expansion of Social Security benefits transformed old age into the final stage of the institutionalized life cycle (Gratton, 1984; Markides & Cooper, 1987).

A fuller understanding of the aging industry—and its role in creating old age as an institutionalized stage of life—awaits much more research, but it is safe to say that Hall would not have been pleased with the results. Psychologists who studied aging in the decade after Hall often documented and legitimated the separation of the old from the rationalized work place of advanced capitalism (Foster & Taylor, 1920: Jones & Conrad, 1933; Miles, 1931, 1932, 1933).

This separation resulted not from any ill intent on the part of the investigators, who generally took firm stands against age discrimination in industry. It followed, rather, from the goals and values inherent in the scientific investigation of mental functioning in later life. Much of this research, like the Stanford Later Maturity Study (funded by the Carnegie Corporation in the late 1920s and early 1930s), originated in the army's wartime methods of classifying and selecting manpower and in industrial management's drive to exact greater quantities of output from smaller quantities of labor time (Baritz, 1960; Noble, 1977).

The new "curriculum" that emerged in the mid-twentieth century was premised not on vital participation in the public world but on virtual exclusion from it. Having helped ease the old out of the work place, psychologists and other helping professionals channeled their needs into the consumption of goods and services. Like George Lawton, spokesmen for the aging industry sometimes acknowledged that old people needed "real jobs, real family relationships, real functioning in society." Lecturing to a class of old age professionals in 1943, Lawton starkly revealed the new "curriculum" for old age: "If they cannot be given real lives, they must have proxy ones," he claimed. "Nine million old people today . . . need schools, recreation centers, arts and crafts centers, sheltered work shops, adult playgrounds, marriage brokers, social clubs. They need bureaus for the exchange of services" (Lawton, 1943, p. 32).

By the 1940s, the outlines of a professional aging industry began to take shape in major urban areas across the country. Both the scientific study of aging and social services for the aged proliferated steadily with the exception of the war years, which temporarily exempted older people from marginality. On the medical front, the U.S. Department of Public Health established a Unit of Gerontology; several state health departments initiated special programs for controlling chronic disease; Cleveland, Pittsburgh, St. Louis, New Haven, New York, Chicago, and Rochester, New York, undertook studies to determine the medical needs of their aged (Shock, 1951).

After the passage of the Social Security Act, social workers, often employed in Old Age Assistance programs, began to define the casework needs of the aged (Smith, 1939). A dozen major cities sponsored community surveys to define the elderly's social and emotional needs and develop facilities for meeting them. By 1950, many had established recreational programs, generally supported by public welfare departments, settlement houses, park districts, and other community agencies. Counseling centers and guidance clinics sprang up in Ann Arbor, Chicago, Minneapolis, and New York. These programs in turn generated a demand for trained personnel to carry out and expand them.

The service wing of the aging industry relied heavily for legitimation and planning on the research findings of its academic counterpart. Accordingly, social science in the 1940s shifted its focus away from old age pensions and employment to problems of personal and social adjustment. The Social Science Research Council sponsored extensive research into these topics, under the direction of Ernest R. Burgess and Robert J. Havighurst of the University of Chicago. (Cavan, Burgess, Havighurst, & Goldhammer, 1949; Pollak, 1948). After the Committee on Human Development was established in Chicago in 1948, interest in lifespan development gradually replaced the focus on adjustment in old age. The Chicago group led the way to the social psychology of aging, which developed quickly in the 1950s, largely through the Committee's massive, decade-long research effort, the "Kansas City Study of Adult Life," funded by the Rockefeller Foundation and the National Institute of Mental Health. Programs in social gerontology also emerged at Duke University and the University of Michigan.

Midway through the 1940s, gerontology and geriatrics societies were formed and began publishing their own journals. Various educational and training programs, both for old age professionals and for lay persons hoping to "grow old successfully," sprang up in Ann Arbor, Berkeley, Chicago, and New York (Shock, 1951). By 1950, the reconstruction of old age was well underway, although its financial foundation—soon to include private pension investment trusts, life insurance benefits in retirement, and increased federal support—had not yet solidified (Myles, 1984). The new shape of old age and the life course was brilliantly satirized in Saul Steinberg's 1954 *Lebenstreppe* cartoon (Habelt, 1983).

The aging industry grew most rapidly after 1965, when Congress passed both Medicare and the Older Americans Act (Achenbaum, 1983). A host of new programs, organizations, and providers sprang up to serve the aged in one way or another. As Carroll Estes has shown, public policy basically defined old age as a problem in need of special services prescribed and provided by professionals. Perceived as dependent and isolated, old people were now subjected to age-segregated "solutions" that often undermined autonomous functioning (Estes, 1980).

Although it would have dismayed him, G. Stanley Hall had anticipated many features of this "new story." He had seen the need to rebuild the unstable social space at the end of the life course generated by the widening gap between length of life and that portion of it spent working and raising a family. He had urged the scientific creation of a "curriculum" for the later years, attacked stereotypical notions of old age, and formulated his version of the tasks of "successful aging." And yet, Hall had not foreseen the dangers to individual autonomy, social justice, and existential integrity that lay in the scientific management of aging.

These dangers were already implicit in Hall's vision of a new old age brought forth by science. *Senescence* never clearly identifies the relationship between those who would initiate old people into the last stage of life and the fully ripened aged who would occupy a vital role in the modern world. Being both a scientist and an old man, Hall apparently did not consider the problem. Yet, as the culture of professionalism (Bledstein, 1976) insinuated itself into new areas of social life, it claimed authority in the name of scientific expertise which found little use for the wisdom of old age, however fully ripened. The very forces, in other words, that Hall summoned to unleash the full maturity of old age expropriated the authority of that maturity.

By attacking religious belief systems that were already compromised in their efforts to nourish and redeem aging and death, Hall unwittingly deepened the cultural void surrounding the end of life. Yet in spite of himself, Hall did not allow the scientific search for explanation and control to suppress his human search for meaning.

Although he scorned those "weak souls" who believed in God and personal immortality, Hall implicitly acknowledged the religious dimension in his own life. He concluded *Senescence* (p. 518) by printing, without comment, two poems: William Cullen Bryant's "Thanatopsis" and Alfred Tennyson's "Crossing the Bar." Tennyson's poem depicts dying with the familiar image of life's journey:

*Crossing the Bar*

*Twilight and evening bell,*
*And after that the dark!*
*And may there be no sadness of farewell,*
*When I embark.*

*For tho' from out our bourne of Time and Place*
*The flood may bear me far,*
*I hope to see my Pilot face to face*
*When I have crost the bar.*

Why did Hall choose the language of poetry to complete a scientific study of senescence? Implicitly, it seems, he understood the limits of his vision of a modern old age brought forth by science. He was affirming unscientific truths he had learned in his Puritan childhood: We are all "weak souls" and growing old is, after all, a spiritual journey.

Seventy years later it is clear that gerontology has been terribly slow to appreciate the spiritual dimension of aging. We are just beginning to do the necessary groundwork: breaking down obsolete Berlin Walls between the sciences and the humanities; grinding new humanistic lenses to investigate the search for meaning in later life; locating personal meanings within their structural and cultural contexts (Cole, 1992). Our own postmodern era again faces the task of reconstructing old age in the wake of the campaign against ageism, the rise of generational equity, and concerns about the cost of an aging population. Unfortunately, we have inherited ideological tendencies and ethnic prejudices that also shaped G. Stanley Hall's thinking. Amid the late nineteenth-century crisis of Victorian morality and the decline of classical liberalism, old age in America came to symbolize an intractable barrier to the American dream of limitless accumulation of individual health and wealth. Middle-class fears of the poorhouse were heightened by the growth of pauperism among older immigrants and the urban working class. Aging mid-Victorian American men raised the specter of "race suicide" as evidence of low birth rates, divorce, and chronic illness among Anglo-Saxon Protestants. These seemed to contrast with the fecundity and hardiness of foreign-born urban masses.

In the late 1970s and 1980s, old age again emerged as a lightning rod for the storms of liberal capitalism and middle-class identity. This time, it was middle-aged baby boomers who were susceptible to neoconservative Cassandras forecasting intergenerational Armageddon and the bankruptcy of the federal government (Longman, 1987). Fears about declining fertility (Wattenberg, 1987), about the growing population of Asian, Arab, and Hispanic Americans, and the burden of an aging population merged with the fiscal and ideological crises of the welfare state. Personal anxieties about growing old were conflated with pessimism about the future. Critics and commentators represented the aging of our institutions with metaphors of decline, exhaustion, and collapse (Moody, 1988).

Like G. Stanley Hall, we are faced with the task of reconstructing old age—

this time a diverse, postmodern old age (or old ages) that envisions the productivity and contributions of some elders and appreciates the coexistence of frailty and wisdom, physical decline and spiritual growth in others. We must do this while extending the accomplishments of the welfare state to those still in need of reasonable levels of income, services, and health care support. In contrast to G. Stanley Hall, we will have to overcome our culture's tendency to split old age into positive and negative poles—a "good" old age (the health culmination of proper middle-class living) and a "bad" old age (punishment for immoral, unhealthy behavior). We can no longer afford this dualism, which feeds both the false pessimism and the superficial optimism in contemporary discussions of our aging society. In rebuilding a moral economy of the extended life course (Kohli, 1987), we must attend to questions of justice within and between different stages of life, and we must also forge new and diverse meanings and purposes for the last half of life. These are exciting, if daunting, tasks, to which historical inquiry has much to contribute.

## REFERENCES

Achenbaum, W. A. (1978). *Old age in the new land.* Baltimore: Johns Hopkins University Press.

Achenbaum, W. A. (1983). *Shades of gray.* Boston: Little, Brown.

Baritz, L. (1960). *Servants of power.* Middletown, CT: Wesleyan University Press.

Binstock, R. H., & George, L. K. (Eds.). (1990). *Handbook of aging and the social sciences.* New York: Academic Press.

Birren, J. E., & Schaie, K. W. (Eds.). (1990). *Handbook of the psychology of aging* (3rd. ed.). New York: Academic Press.

Bledstein, B. (1976). *The culture of professionalism.* New York: Norton.

Cavan, R. S., Burgess, E. W., Havighurst, R. J., & Goldhammer, H. (1949). *Personal adjustment in old age.* Chicago: Science Research.

Child, C. M. (1915). *Senescence and rejuvenescence.* Chicago: University of Chicago Press.

Cole, T. R. (1992). *The journey of life: A cultural history of aging in America.* New York: Cambridge University Press.

Cole, T. R., Van Tassel, D. D., & Kastenbaum, R. (1992). *Handbook of the humanities and aging.* New York: Springer Publishing Co.

Dahlin, M. (1980). *The problem of old age, 1890–1920.* Unpublished doctoral dissertation, Stanford University, Stanford, CA.

Douglas, A. (1977). *The feminization of American culture.* New York: Alfred A. Knopf.

Eliot, T. S. (1971, originally published in 1943). East Coker. In *Four Quartets.* New York: Harcourt, Brace & World, Inc.

Erikson, E. (1968). *Identity: Youth and crisis.* New York: W. W. Norton.

Estes, C. (1980). *The aging enterprise.* San Francisco: Jossey-Bass.

Fischer, D. H. (1978). *Growing old in America* (Expanded ed.). New York: Oxford University Press.

Fisher, I. (1909). *Report on national vitality.* Washington, DC: U.S. Government Printing Office.

Foster, J. C., & Taylor, G. A. (1920). Applicability of mental tests to persons over fifty years of age. *Journal of Applied Psychology, 4,* 39–58.

Gratton, B. (1984). *Urban elders.* Philadelphia: Temple University Press.

Graebner, W. (1980). *A history of retirement.* New Haven, CT: Yale University Press.

Habelt, R. (1983). *Die Lebenstreppe, Bilder der menschlichen Lebensalter.* Bonn: Rheinland-Verlag.

Hall, G. S. (1900). Child study and its relation to education. *Forum, 29,* 700.

Hall, G. S. (1904). *Adolescence* (2 vols.) New York: D. Appleton.

Hall, G. S. (1920). *Morale: The supreme standard of life and conduct.* London: D. Appleton.

Hall, G. S. (1921a). *The dangerous age. Pedagogical seminary, 28,* 275–294.

Hall, G. S. (1921b). Old age. *Atlantic Monthly, 127,* 23–31.

Hall, G. S. (1922). *Senescence, the last half of life.* New York: D. Appleton and Company.

Haltunen, K. (1982). Confidence men and painted women. New Haven, CT: Yale University Press.

Jones, H. E., & Conrad, H. S. (1933). The growth and decline of intelligence. *Genetic Psychology Monoaraphs, 13,* 233–293.

Kohli, M. (1987). Retirement and the moral economy: An historical interpretation of the German case. *Journal of Aging Studies, 1*(2), 125–144.

Lasch, C. (1977). *Haven in a heartless world.* New York: Basic Books.

Lawton, G. (Ed.) (1943). *New goals for old age.* New York: Columbia University Press.

Lears, J. (1981). *No place of grace.* New York: Pantheon.

Loeb, J. (1919). Natural death and duration of life. *Science Monthly, 9,* 578–585.

Longman, P. (1987). *Born to pay: The new politics of aging in America.* Boston: Houghton Mifflin.

Markides, K., & Cooper, C. L. (Eds.) (1987). *Retirement in industrialized societies: Social, psychological and health factors.* London: Wiley.

Metchnikoff, E. (1908). *The prolongation of life.* New York: G. P. Putnam's Sons.

Miles, W. R. (1931). Measures of certain abilities throughout the life span. *Proceeding of the National Academy of Sciences, 17,* 627–633.

Miles, W. R. (1932). The correlation of intelligence scores and chronological age from early to late maturity. *American Journal of Psychology, 44,* 45–78.

Miles, W. R. (1933). Age and human ability. *Psychological Review, 40,* 99–123.

Moody, H. R. (1988). *Abundance of life: Human development policies for an aging society.* New York: Columbia University Press.

Myles, J. (1984). *Old age in the welfare state: The political economy of public pensions.* Boston: Little, Brown.

Noble, D. (1977). *America by design.* New York: Alfred A. Knopf.

Pearl, R. (1921). The biology of death. *Scientific Monthly, 12,* 193–214, 321–335, 444–457, 489–516.

Pollak, O. (1948). *Social adjustment in old age.* New York: Social Science Research Council.

Quadagno, J. (1982). *Aging in early industrial society.* New York: Academic Press.

Quadagno, J. (1989). *The transformation of old age security: Class and politics in the American welfare state.* Chicago: Unviersity of Chicago Press.

Ross, D. G. (1972). *Stanley Hall.* Chicago: University of Chicago Press.

Schneider, E. L., & Rowe, J. W. (1990). *Handbook of the biology of aging.* New York: Academic Press.

Shock, N. (1951). *Trends in gerontology*. Stanford, CA: Stanford University Press.

Smith, G. (1939). *What are the case-work needs of the aged?* Proceedings of the National Conference of Social Work. Sixty-Fifth Annual Session, pp. 587–595.

Steinach, E. (1927). Biological methods against the process of old age. *Medical Journal and Record, 125,* 77–81, 161–164.

Voronoff, S. (1920). *Life: A study of the means of restoring vital energy and prolonging life*. New York: Dutton.

Wattenberg, B. (1987). *The birth dearth*. New York: Pharos Books.

Weismann, A. (1893). *Essays upon heredity and kindred biological problems* (2nd ed.). Oxford: Clarendon Press.

# What Became of the Prophecy of *Senescence?* A View from Life-Span Psychology

**Anna G. Maciel**
**Ursula M. Staudinger**

Thomas Cole presents an intriguing view from the perspective of cultural history on aging in the twentieth century. His "new story" has a dual purpose: it affords insights into the personal struggle of an early twentieth century psychologist (Hall, 1922) to come to terms with his own aging process, and a pioneering vision on the scientific approach to aging, thereby providing all important impetus to the growth of gerontology. At the same time, Cole's is a portrait of the dialectics between social climate and structure, and the rise of the institution of an aging industry in postmodern America. In his conclusion, Cole leaves us with a dilemma: the very forces in "professional science" to which G. Stanley Hall appealed to turn their attention towards the "last stage of life," are proving to undercut their own purpose. In following the prevailing stereotype they are painting a picture of old age which is unduly pessimistic; they neglect the heterogeneity of the aging process, and their optimism does not do sufficient justice to the individual and social potential of old age.

The following comments are directed at this dilemma, and will examine if and in what way life-span psychology has addressed this issue. Without doubt, during the decades following Hall, psychological research and theory have primarily espoused a view of old age which focused on decline of functioning, much in keeping with ideas among the general public that later life is not a period rich in gains (e.g., Butler, 1969). This is not to say that there were no exceptions to this position (e.g., Cowdry, 1939; Demming & Pressey, 1957; Lorge, 1936). Yet, primarily the past two decades have brought forth an increasing body of work which recognized this tendency as a shortcoming, and argued forcefully for a revision of this one-sided position and the development of a more balanced view on aging (e.g., P. B. Baltes, 1987; Labouvie-Vief, 1985; Perlmutter, 1988; Schaie, 1983). What then are some of the major findings from the body of psychological knowledge about old age and the aging process? Presenting these findings, we will take the area of intellectual functioning as a sample case, first give an overview, and then elaborate in more detail on one aspect of the potential of old age.

## AGING IS MORE THAN DECLINE

The first important step away from the conception of aging as decline in juxtaposition to development as growth was the realization that aging is multifaceted, that it is composed of multiple trajectories which relate to different areas of functioning (e.g., P. B. Baltes, 1987). These trajectories may rise, may drop, or may stay stable. In the area of intellectual performance, for example, empirical evidence has demonstrated that there is decline indeed, primarily in speed of cognitive processing (e.g., Salthouse, 1991). However, evidence has also shown that knowledge-related performance can stay stable or even show increases (e.g., Blanchard-Fields, 1986; Cornelius & Caspi, 1987; Perlmutter, Kaplan, & Nyquist, 1990). This seemingly contradictory evidence can be reconciled, for example, in a dual-pronged view of intellectual functioning across the life span, which encompasses growth and stability in the pragmatics or crystallized aspects, and decline in the mechanics or fluid dimension of intelligence (P. B. Baltes, Dittman-Kohli & Dixon, 1984; Horn & Cattell, 1967).

## DIFFERENT INDIVIDUALS AGE DIFFERENTLY

Aging is not a unidimensional process but rather a highly complex system of interdependent processes. The result of this interplay is great inter-individual variability, at least up to a certain age. It may be the case that in the last period before death physiological processes become increasingly important such that variability is reduced, but this hypothesis still awaits empirical corroboration (e.g., P. B. Baltes & M. M. Baltes, 1992; K. F. Riegel & R. M. Riegel, 1972). Similarly, it is not enough to consider the age-related trajectory of one area of functioning, or to study a single aging individual in order to understand the aging process. There are 70-year-olds who, across various tasks, show intellectual performance comparable to that of an average 40-year-old, but there are also 70-year-olds who perform on the level of an average 90-year-old.

## WHO DEFINES WHAT IS A DECLINE?

A life-span psychology view on aging furthermore implies that aging is not studied solely as a process intrinsic to the individual. Rather, aging is conceptualized and studied from a systemic perspective. Society, social structure, individual living conditions, and physiological processes are considered constituent parts of this system (e.g., Lerner, 1986). Sensitivity to a number of factors is therefore necessary. First, it appears that society and the prevailing value-system provide the framework for what are labeled gains and losses. Second, social and cultural structures also afford differential opportunities for gains, such that different life paths provide varying opportunity structures for development (e.g., Staudinger, Cornelius, & P. B. Baltes, 1989).

As to the first factor, the question is whether what is labeled loss or decline is a qualitative change in performance instead, having to do with age-related changes in life tasks, for example (e.g., Havighurst, 1972; Schaie, 1977). Congruent with the prevailing value system in our society, which is primarily oriented towards speed, progress, economic productivity, and youthfulness, a loss in speed, for example, can only be interpreted as decline.

The second factor mentioned above addresses the possibilities which a society provides for old individuals to find meaningful roles (e.g., Riley, 1986). How can an aging person keep active and show his/her potential if society confines them to idleness? It would seem that neither the investigation of one area of functioning, the study of one individual, nor consideration of one society at a given historical time is sufficient to understand aging and its potential.

## IS DECLINE IN PERFORMANCE
## ALSO DECLINE IN COMPETENCE?

An important strand of research has addressed the question whether apparent loss could be disuse instead (e.g., Botwinick, 1967; Denney, 1982). If that assumption were true, performance increases might be gained simply by training the disused functions. And in fact, an increasing body of research now shows that older adults can be trained on some cognitive tasks, evidencing higher performance levels than before training (e.g., P. B. Baltes,

& Lindenberger, 1988; Schaie & Willis, 1986). At the same time, training research also points to age-related limits in plasticity. Training gains are larger for younger than older adults, and older subjects show less reserve capacity than their younger counterparts (e.g., Kliegl & P. B. Baltes, 1987).

## STRATEGIES AND MECHANISMS OF DEALING WITH THE GAINS AND LOSSES OF AGING

Based on the evidence that aging is characterized by loss, stability, and gain at the same time, we might expect gains to help compensate for losses. And in fact, returning to the example of intellectual functioning, research has shown that aging individuals benefit from years of professional experience. For example, Salthouse (1984) was able to show that old expert typists, compared to their younger colleagues, can compensate for loss of speed by reading farther ahead in the text to be typed. More generally, evidence increasingly shows that losses in cognitive mechanics can be offset by strategic compensation in knowledge-based pragmatics (P. B. Baltes, 1987).

Another area where strategies and mechanisms seem to enable the aging individual to maintain levels of functioning is subjective well-being and the sense of self in old age. Aging individuals seem to develop the ability to keep their level of well-being high despite adverse conditions, for example, when facing severe illness or the loss of significant others. Social comparison, transformation of the self-concept, and regulation of the system of goals (e.g., P. B. Baltes & M. M. Baltes, 1990; Brandtstädter & Baltes-Götz, 1990; Brim, 1988; Taylor & Lobel, 1989) seem to be key components in this effort. Apparently, individuals invest energy into areas where they still function well. They may also he able to change and adapt the meaning systems in their lives to the new circumstances. For example, a loss in sensory acuity can be seen as a chance to free oneself from external information overload, and to focus on internal processes instead (e.g., Mergler & Goldstein, 1983).

Taken all together, there is potential for unique gains in old age in the area of cognition as well as in the aging self. This growth potential may not be achieved earlier, because it appears to require experience and life-long processes of adaptation. Perhaps *the* most prototypical area of growth in old age is wisdom; that aspect which G. Stanley Hall attempted to come to terms with, and the prophecy of which Cole has called unconvincing.

## WHY SHOULD WE TALK ABOUT WISDOM IN THIS CONTEXT?

There are three reasons why wisdom seems specifically relevant in this context. First, throughout cultural history wisdom has been associated with the later life stage, and has even been called a "life-cycle philosophy" (Assmann, 1991). In the presence of a prevailing negative stereotype of old age, it appears to be one of the few positive attributes which consistently emerges as late life potentials. As shown in Figure 5.1, Heckhausen, Dixon, and P. B. Baltes (1989) found that among 100 personality attributes, only wise and dignified were rated to be both highly desirable and associated with later life.

Second, the positive aspect of Hall's vision, the "prophecy of old age," and "truly ripe old age" as "highest product of the race," has much in common with the century-old vision of wisdom as an ideal virtue. This vision, however, also suggests ambivalence; ambivalence about whether or not wisdom is something which is humanly achievable, let alone achievable by many. In Aristotle's view, the achievement of what he called "practical wisdom" manifested in skillful insight about the right course of action in a particular situation and could only come about by accumulating life-experience and continued learning from role models (Jeannot, 1987). As P. B.

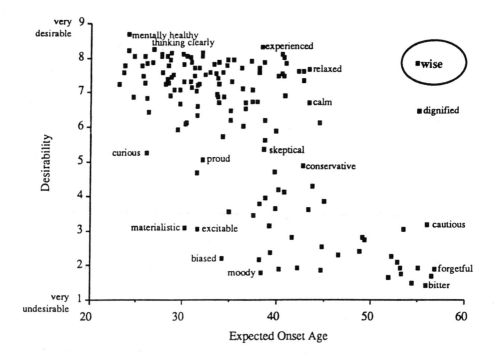

Figure 5.1. Desirable personality attributes associated with later life (adapted from Heckhausen, Dixon, & P. B. Baltes, 1989).

Baltes (1991) points out, the attainment of wisdom is thought to be a life-long task, and embodies the notion of an ideal state of insight and functioning concerning the meaning and conduct of life. The "virtuous" aspect contained in Hall's vision, however, contains vestiges of Victorian morality, and in comparison to both earlier and later views, strikes us as arcane and dogmatic in its suggestion that sexual restraint was a key route to aging successfully.

A third reason why wisdom seems relevant in this context is G. Stanley Hall's own personal struggle during the later phase of his life. This can only be speculative, but his struggle appears reminiscent of the dialectic movement between integration and despair described by E. Erikson (1959), characteristic of the final stage of psychosocial development. Disappointment in humanity, loneliness, and despair are regarded as results of an unsuccessful search for ego integrity, while acceptance of one's one and only life cycle, assuming responsibility for it, and recognizing the value of alternatives to the chosen path, mark the strength of old age in this view and culminate in generativity and wisdom (Rosel, 1988).

Approaching wisdom from a framework of scientific psychology now appears promising because (1) wisdom provides a conceptual reference point for examining culturally shared beliefs about positive aspects of aging, and (2) it may become an empirical reference point for examining the unique characteristics of those individuals who, by observers' consensus, embody this notion.

Empirical research on wisdom is still in its infancy, and perhaps in the end it will prove to be an intractable phenomenon by those means which are espoused by the present scientific paradigm. Yet, in the process, perhaps we may be able to learn about important aspects of life experience, social knowledge, and the meaning system surrounding old age.

Studying wisdom may also be important because it provides a reference point for a systematic search for positive markers and the potential of aging. Although biological models define aging primarily as a loss phenomenon associated with decline in adaptive capacity, a search for progressive and growth-oriented aspects not only demonstrates a new spirit, but it also poses challenges for the design of social policy (P. B. Baltes & M. M. Baltes, 1990). Currently, empirical evidence from the behavioral sciences for positive psychological changes in old age is not overwhelming. A better understanding of wisdom may help us identify the facets of the aging self and mind which harbor opportunities for gains, and also for aging more successfully. Thus, wisdom could serve as a prototype for what might be possible and what one can aspire to achieve.

## WISDOM, CULTURE, AND THE POTENTIAL OF OLD AGE

Wisdom in an absolute sense appears to be universal. Yet how it manifests and is talked about appears to also show culturally and historically specific features. Just as Cole focuses on the interconnections between aging research and the larger socioeconomic context, the currently rising scientific interest in the study of the "wisdom of old age" can be interpreted as an expression of the renewed search for ideals in postmodern society.

The task for elders, as sketched by Erikson, as a strive toward one's own individual integrity in the sense of finding inner peace is very old. The concept of wisdom, as it is discussed in contemporary literature (e.g., Assmann, 1991), contains aspects which may be rather specific to postmodern civilization, while some core existential knowledge involving the *conditio humana* seems to be common to the notion of wisdom in any culture. The value for the preservation and transmission of such knowledge, however, may have had a different status depending on the concerns of the culture. In our present day and age, very few elders are consulted because of their knowledge of existential problems. This may not only be one expression of the prevailing negative aging stereotype, but also a function of present-day technological advances. However, the wise were always few and far between.

Whereas wisdom in this absolute sense could only he expected of the very few, there are other aspects of life knowledge which require accumulated experience and reflection, and seem more attainable (Staudinger & Dittmann-Kohli, 1992). In a definition which is less strict, Assmann (1991) defines wisdom as adaptive knowledge. She points out that in traditional cultures (pre-industrial societies), preservation and transmission of adaptive knowledge was a prime concern. Technical know-how, use of tools, the ways and means of food supply, secrets of healing, the rules of living together, sacred myths, in short, everything that contributed to the survival of the group, was important knowledge to transmit. She further argues that modern civilizations have no counterpart to wisdom defined in that way, that is, no similar body of knowledge cherished by the community as a common treasure. Extending this line of argument, there may be no concomitant need to cherish elders as informants and carriers of that type of knowledge, which at present is transmitted through books and the educational system.

The postmodern wise person appears to be "an expert in problems for which no rules exist" (Welsch, 1989). This is echoed by contemporary views which define wisdom, (cf., Sternberg, 1990) for example, as the reconciliation of contradictory information (Clayton, 1982), the making and accepting of compromise at developmental crisis points rather than seeking complete resolution (Blanchard-Fields, 1986), judgment under uncertainty

(Meacham, 1983), and a post-formal level of reasoning involving the integration of affect and cognition (Labouvie-Vief, 1990).

To be experts in the uncertain appears to involve a different kind of "professionalism" than is marked by a strive for accumulation of health and wealth. The limits implicit in Hall's vision of a scientific approach to old age can be understood to be a function of having as a reference point that aspect of a negative aging stereotype which, at the same time, he is trying to overcome. Approaching the topic via evolutionary biology with its implicit ideal of health, he finds himself in the position to focus on the losses, with a rather unconvincing view of the gains. A certain level of physical health seems to be necessary for the development of potential in old age. But given a baseline of non-pathology, the potential is far greater than the constraints of a solely biological model would allow.

Perhaps present psychological views of successful aging are no different in principle, critics could argue, in that they now apply a standard to old age measured in terms of capitalist efficiency. The counter-argument could be that differences exist because specific attempts are made to apply standards which are not external to the individual (P. B. Baltes & M. M. Baltes, 1990) and because a frame defined in terms of potentials for positive growth is in principle different from one defined in terms of probable limitations.

## THE AGE-OLD VISION OF WISE PERSONAGES

Starting from a positive ideal of aging, in what ways can scientific methods be applied to the study of this ideal? In keeping with Thomas Cole's renewed call for the study of aging in cross-diciplinary fashion, philosophy, the humanities, and religion have, over the centuries, dealt with an ideal view of old age by addressing the question of wisdom. Who then are some of the people who represent these ideals—who are the wise and what are their characteristics?

Perhaps the most widely recognized Western ideal is Solomon, with his sharpness of unbiased judgment. When two women claim to be the mother of the same child and Solomon is called upon to decide which woman speaks the truth, his approach to this dilemma is unconventional and ingenious. He suggests to literally cut the child in two, and to give each woman one-half of the body. Apparently one woman immediately gave up her claim in the interest of preserving the child's welfare. The assumption is that this method revealed the genuine mother, and if it actually did, we would call this an act of wisdom. The mind that is required here is alert, with a rich store of human experience, and Solomon appears to be an expert in social living. His judgment is based on the maxim that mother love is stronger than personal interest. At the same time, he has the status of a revered ruler whose judgment is regarded highly by the community. Tacit knowledge would suggest that the *particular* situation by this *particular* person called for this "right" action; someone of lesser social stature or without known "virtue of character" may have been called a lunatic or a maniac if offering this solution.

Another such ideal is Polonius, a Shakespearean character (cf., Assmann, 1991) who, as a dying father, gives advice to his son in the form of maxims. For example, "be considerate, give thy thoughts no tongue," "to thine own self be true," and "don't get involved in quarrels, but be brave in combat." Here we are dealing with a kind of everyday pragmatic wisdom, passed on in terms of guidelines indispensable for a wholesome life, which can only be based on rich life experience.

As those two examples already illustrate, there seem to be different types of situations that call for different instantiations of wisdom. What is interesting is that we seem to be able to recognize and appreciate a kind of special "expertise" involved in them. That kind of recognition is only possible, one could argue, because we have tacit knowledge about wisdom. Even if we ourselves might be incapable of this kind of action, we can recognize it as special when it occurs. A judgment about wisdom seems to be within our competence and, we would claim, this is true for different historical times and different cultures.

Over and above the level of simple recognition, the kind of knowledge involved in wise action seems to require a lot of creativity and unconventionality. Wisdom appears to adhere to the here and now, and to the specifics of the situation. It suggests that good judgment presupposes flexibility which rigoristic personalities cannot possess. It seems to imply all acceptance of the world as it is, in the absence of a zealous fervor of changing it. The mind carrying this knowledge appears to be humble, with an absence of self-serving interests, yet is cunning and sharp. P. B. Baltes and Smith (1990) formalized wise judgment as "expert knowledge in the pragmatics of life," which deals with important, difficult, and uncertain life matters. In their view it is a truly superior level of knowledge, judgment, and advice, and extraordinary in scope and depth. More specifically, wise judgment is indexed by high levels of knowledge about facts and strategies involved in fundamental life matters, as well as high-level knowledge about the temporal and domain-related contexts of a life dilemma. In addition, recognition of relativity and its limits, and of uncertainty and its mastery, involved in difficult life problems are aspects of wise judgment in this view (P. B. Baltes, Staudinger, Sowarka, & Smith, 1990).

## EMPIRICAL STUDIES ON WISDOM

Two empirical approaches to wisdom can presently be delineated. The first focuses on implicit assumptions about "wise persons," culturally shared beliefs, and the layperson's theory on wisdom (Clayton & Birren, 1980; Holliday & Chandler, 1986; Sowarka, 1989; Sternberg, 1985). In a study from the Berlin Wisdom Project, a group of 102 young, middle-aged, and older women were asked to rate 131 descriptive statements on the degree to which they represent a wise person. Here are some of the preliminary findings. First it appears there is a high degree of consensus in our culture about what a wise person is like. Examining the content of items which were rated as highly typical of wise people, it appeared that the kind of expertise which is required is rather different from the ideal of youthful intellectual prowess and a model of intelligence in terms of agility and mental acrobatics, which is often the standard against which cognitive capacity of the elderly is measured. As shown in Table 5.1, the wise person is characterized by a rich store of life experience, by expert knowledge in social and pragmatic aspects of living, and by aspects which may he more common to older people (Maciel, Sowarka, Smith, & P. B. Baltes, 1991).

A second class of studies focuses on wisdom-related performance and a theory-guided study of wisdom and its ontogenesis (e.g., Cantor & Kihlstrom, 1987; Orwoll & Perlmutter, 1990; Ryff, 1982; Smith & P. B. Baltes, 1990; Staudinger, 1989; Staudinger, Smith, & P. B. Baltes, 1992). Based on the notion of wisdom as expert knowledge about the fundamental pragmatics of life, the Berlin wisdom project devised a set of procedures for studying this phenomenon. Subjects are asked to comment and give advice on dilemmas concerning life planning, life review, or life management. The

**Table 5.1 Most Typical Characteristics of Wise Persons**

Comprehends the nature of human existence
Thinks carefully before making decisions
Knows when to give/withold advice
Recognizes the limits of his/her knowledge
Knows that the importance of difficult life domains changes during the life span
Thinks independently and is able to form his/her own opinion
Is capable of empathy in difficult life problems
Is a good listener
Is a person whose advice one would solicit for difficult life problems

Source: Maciel, Sowarka, Smith, & Baltes, (1991).

life management dilemma, for example, goes as follows: "Imagine your friend is about to call you to tell you that she can't go on anymore and has decided to commit suicide. What would you be thinking about, how would you deal with this situation?" (Maercker, 1991). In a think-aloud procedure, a verbal protocol is collected, transcribed, and rated in terms of five wisdom-related criteria (P. B. Baltes & Smith, 1990).

Some of the findings from this line of study are: Overall, as expected in unselected samples, only few wise responses are found; in general old adults perform as well as young adults and older adults are among the top performers; considering task-specific performance, it appears that young and old people seem to know most about situations typically consistent with their own age (Smith & P. B. Baltes, 1990; Staudinger, 1989; Staudinger, Smith, & P. B. Baltes, 1992). From a life-span view of adaptation to developmental tasks, as well as to socio-historical change, we may, as we grow older, transform bodies of knowledge because they are no longer particularly relevant, or less frequently practiced.

Another set of findings concerns first insights into the ontogenesis of wisdom-related knowledge. Which are the factors contributing to a high-level response? Although aspects of the "mechanics" of intelligence, which show decline with age, do play a role, they appear to be of lesser importance than personality characteristics (Maciel, Staudinger, Smith, & P. B. Baltes, 1991). Reasoning aptitude and standard intelligence tasks play a minor role compared to openness to experience, flexibility in thinking and behavior, and an internal self-agency orientation. The latter denote feelings of being in control of one's life rather than subject to external forces. What appears relevant for the development of wise judgment in difficult and uncertain matters of life are those aspects of functioning and selfhood which are less likely to decline with age in general, and in some old people are likely not to decline at all (P. B. Baltes & M. M. Baltes, 1990); Schaie 1983). Furthermore it seems that the kind of life experience an individual is exposed to and the tutoring in life matters he/she receives, play an important role in the accumulation of wisdom-related knowledge (Staudinger, Smith, & P. B. Baltes, 1992).

## CONCLUSIONS

The prophecy of old age has not yet been fully explored from a scientific vantage point. It might be too early to conclude that the picture painted by science is unconvincing. A biological model, and the notion that accumulation of health and wealth is the ideal to strive for, may indeed not prove fruitful, because it does not do justice to the unique gains associated with old age. At the same time, research also indicates that without money and health old people are hardly able to develop their potential.

An area which is perhaps little explored involves studies about mechanisms and external conditions for positive gains in later life. Thomas Cole has warned us that the term "successful aging" may be another form of competitive social Darwinism, and yet one more aspect of a Western capitalist tradition which defines aging again in terms of "good" and "bad" forms. Or, as Paul and Margaret Baltes (1992) anticipate critics' arguments: now ". . . even the last phase of life . . . is about to be captured by the view that success, defined by standards external to the individual, is a necessary part of the good life" (p. 4).

There are at least two answers to these critics. First, it is exactly because of the intuitively antithetical association of success with old age, that novel ways of thinking about aging could be provoked, and that active participation in changing the negative social stereotype could follow. In fact, this process may reveal unique gains associated with growing old, which might be of a different quality than those associated with earlier life phases (P. B. Baltes & M. M. Baltes, 1990). Second, despite factors intrinsic to the individual, the context of the individual needs to provide a certain structure for the person to develop further and to find meaning.

G. Stanley Hall's potential vision of old age, the view of a wisdom prototype (even if that is not what he had in mind exactly), may turn out to be an ideal which is impossible to achieve, even by the few. But then, true prototypes do not exist in reality either. They are idealized versions of reality without material referents (Rosch, 1975; 1978).

When people are asked to name wise persons, most come up with a few nominations: Titian, Solomon, Oliver Wendell Holmes, Winston Churchill, and so on. Some preliminary observations from an ongoing project with people from the public life of Berlin nominated as wise are illustrative (P. B. Baltes, Staudinger, Maercker, & Smith, 1991). When these wise nominees are asked themselves whom they would nominate, they are largely unequivocal about suggesting historical figures, literary imaginary personages, or someone known only from a distance as possible candidates. Yet as soon as nominees are known personally, many nominators hedge. "He was a great diplomat and politician, but he had some difficulty managing his personal life" for example, would be a typical statement.

The real value of a wisdom prototype, then, may be in the aspiration standard it sets in providing a reference point and orientation of an ideal to strive for. In the process of researching issues associated with this ideal, we may learn about aspects of expertise unique to later life phases, which would have otherwise remained undiscovered.

## REFERENCES

Assmann, A. (Ed.) (1991). *Weisheit. Archäologie der Kommunikation.* [Wisdom. Archeology of communication]. Munich: Fink Verlag.

Baltes, P. B. (1987). Theoretical propositions of life-span developmental psychology: On the dynamics between growth and decline. *Developmental Psychology, 23,* 611–626.

Baltes, P. B. (1991). The many faces of human aging: Toward a psychological culture of old age. *Psychological Medicine, 21,* 837–854.

Baltes, P. B., & Baltes, M. M. (1990). Psychological perspectives on successful aging: The model of selective optimization with compensation. In P. B. Baltes & M. M. Baltes (Eds.), *Successful aging: perspectives from the behavioral sciences* (pp. 1–34). New York: Cambridge University Press.

Baltes, P. B., & Baltes, M. M. (1992). Gerontologie: Begriff, Herausforderung und Brennpunkt [Gerontology; Definition, issues, and challenges]. In P. B. Baltes & J. Mittelstrass (Eds.), *Zukunft des Alterns und gesellschaftliche Entwicklung.* [The future of aging and societal development] (pp. 1–34). Berlin: deGruyter.

Baltes, P. B., Dittmann-Kohli, F., & Dixon, R. A. (1984). New perspectives on the development of intelligence in adulthood: Toward a dual-process conception and a model of selective optimization with compensation. In P. B. Baltes & O. G. Brim (Eds.), *Life-span development and behavior* (Vol. 6, pp. 33–76). New York: Academic Press.

Baltes, P. B., & Lindenberger, U. (1988). On the range of cognitive plasticity in old age as a function of experience: 15 years of intervention research. *Behavior Therapy, 19,* 283–330.

Baltes, P. B., & Smith, J. (1990). Toward a psychology of wisdom and its ontogenesis. In R. J. Sternberg (Ed.), *Wisdom: Its nature, origins, and development* (pp. 87–120). New York: Cambridge University Press.

Baltes, P. B., Staudinger, U. M., Sowarka, D., & Smith, J. (1990). Wisdom: One facet of successful aging? In M. Perlmutter (Ed.), *Late life potential* (pp. 63–81). Washington, DC: The Gerontological Society of America.

Baltes, P. B., Staudinger, U. M., Maercker, A., & Smith, J. (1991). A study of wisdom nominees. Manuscript in preparation. Max Planck Institute for Human Development and Education, Berlin, Germany.

Blanchard-Fields, F. (1986). Reasoning on social dilemmas varying in emotional saliency: An adult developmental perspective. *Psychology and Aging, 1,* 325–333.

Botwinick, J. (1967). *Cognitive processes in maturity and old age.* New York: Springer Publishing Co.

Brandstädter, J., & Baltes-Götz, B. (1990). Personal control over development and quality of life perspectives in adulthood. In P. B. Baltes & M. M. Baltes (Eds.), *Successful aging: perspectives from the behavioral sciences* (pp. 197–224). New York: Cambridge University Press.

Brim, O. G. (1988). Losing and winning. *Psychology Today, 9,* 48–52.

Butler, R. N. (1969). Ageism: Another form of bigotry. *Gerontologist, 9,* 243–252.

Cantor, N., & Kihlstrom, J. F. (1987). *Personality and social intelligence.* Englewood Cliffs, NJ: Prentice-Hall.

Clayton, V. P. (1982). Wisdom and intelligence: The nature and function of knowledge in the later years. *International Journal of Aging and Human Development, 15,* 315–323.

Clayton, V. P., & Birren, J. E. (1980). The development of wisdom across the life span: A reexamination of an ancient topic. In P. B. Baltes & O. G. Brim (Eds.), *Life-span development and behavior* (Vol. 3, pp. 103–135). New York: Academic Press.

Cornelius, S. W., & Caspi, A. (1987). Everyday problem solving in adulthood and old age. *Psychology and Aging, 2,* 144–153.

Cowdry, E. V. (Ed.) (1939). *Problems of ageing. Biological and medical aspects.* Baltimore: The Williams & Wilkins Company.

Demming, J. A., & Pressey, S. L. (1957). Tests "indigenous" to the adult and older years. *Journal of Counseling Psychology, 4,* 144–148.

Denney, N. W. (1982). Aging and cognitive changes. In B. B. Wolman & G. Stricker (Eds.), *Handbook of developmental psychology* (pp. 807–827). Englewood Cliffs, NJ: Prentice-Hall.

Erikson, E. H. (1959). Identity and the life cycle. *Psychological Issues Monograph I.* New York: International Universities Press.

Hall, G. S. (1922). *Senescence: The last half of life.* New York: Appleton.

Havighurst, R. (1972). *Developmental tasks and education.* New York: David McKay.

Heckhausen, J., Dixon, R. A., & Baltes, P. B. (1989). Gains and losses in development throughout adulthood as perceived by different adult age groups. *Developmental Psychology, 25,* 109–121.

Holliday, S. G., & Chandler, M. J. (1986). *Wisdom: Explorations in adult competence.* Basel: Karger.

Horn, J. L., & Cattell, R. B. (1967). Age differences in fluid and crystallized intelligence. *Acta Psychologica, 20,* 107–129.

Jeannot, T. M. (1987). Moral leadership and practical wisdom. *International Journal of Social Economics, 16,* 14–38.

Kliegl, R., & Baltes, P. B. (1987). Theory-guided analysis of development and aging mechanisms through testing-the-limits and research on expertise. In C. Schooler & K. W. Schaie (Eds.), *Cognitive functioning and social structure over the life course* (pp. 95–119). Norwood, NJ: Ablex.

Labouvie-Vief, G. (1985). Intelligence and cognition. In J. E. Birren & K. W. Schaie (Eds.), *Handbook of the psychology of aging* (pp. 500–530). New York: Van Nostrand Reinhold.

Labouvie-Vief, G. (1990). Wisdom as integrated thought: Historical and developmental perspectives. In R. J. Sternberg (Ed.), *Wisdom: Its nature, origins, and development* (pp. 52–83). New York: Cambridge University Press.

Lerner, R. M. (1986). *Concepts and theories of human development.* New York: Random House.

Lorge, I. (1936). The influence of the test upon the nature of mental decline as a function of age. *Journal of Educational Psychology, 27,* 100–110.

Maciel, A. G., Sowarka, D., Smith, J., & Baltes, P. B. (1991). *Features of wisdom: Toward a profile of essential attributes of "wise" people.* Manuscript in preparation. Max Planck Institute for Human Development and Education, Berlin, Germany.

Maciel, A. G., Staudinger, U. M., Smith, J., & Baltes, P. B. *What predicts wisdom-related knowledge: Intelligence or personality?* Unpublished manuscript, Max Planck Institut, Berlin.

Maercker, A. (1991, July). *Existential knowledge and wisdom: A new task for investigating adult cognition.* Poster presented at the 11th Biennial Meetings of the International Society for the Study of Behavioral Development, Minneapolis, MN.

Meacham, J. A. (1983). Wisdom and the context of knowledge: Knowing that one doesn't know. In D. Kuhn & A. Meacham (Eds.), *On the development of developmental psychology* (pp. 111–134). Basel: Karger.

Mergler, N. L., & Goldstein, M. D. (1983). Why are there old people? *Human Development, 26,* 72–90.

Orwoll, L., & Perlmutter, M. (1990). The study of wise persons: Integrating a personality perspective. In R. J. Sternberg (Ed.), *Wisdom: Its nature, origins. and development* (pp. 160–177). New York: Cambridge University Press.

Perlmutter, M. (1988). Cognitive potential throughout life. In J. E. Birren & V. L. Bengtson (Eds.), *Emergent theories of aging* (pp. 247–268). New York: Springer Publishing Co.

Perlmutter, M., Kaplan, M., & Nyquist, L. (1990). Development of adaptive competence in adulthood. *Human Development, 33,* 185–197.

Riegel, K. F., & Riegel, R. M. (1972). Development, drop and death. *Developmental Psychology, 6,* 306–319.

Riley, M. W. (1986). The dynamics of life stages: Roles, people, and age. *Human Development, 22,* 150–156.

Rosch, E. (1975). Cognitive reference points. *Cognitive Psychology, 7,* 532–547.

Rosch, E. (1978). Principles of categorization. In E. Rosch & B. B. Lloyd (Eds.), *Cognition and categorization* (pp. 27–48). Hillsdale, NJ: Erlbaum.

Rosel, N. (1988). Clarification and application of Erik Erikson's eighth stage of man. *International Journal of Aging and Human Development, 27,* 11–23.

Ryff, C. D. (1982). Successful aging. A developmental approach. *The Gerontologist, 22,* 209–214.

Salthouse, T. A. (1984). Efforts of age and skill in typing. *Journal of Experimental Psychology: General, 113,* 345–371.

Salthouse, T. A. (1991). *Theoretical perspectives on cognitive aging.* Hillsdale, NJ: Erlbaum.

Schaie, K. W. (1977). Toward a stage theory of adult cognitive development. *Journal of Aging and Human Development, 8,* 129–138.

Schaie, K. W. (1983). The Seattle Longitudinal Study: A 21-year exploration of psychometric intelligence in adulthood. In K. W. Schaie (Ed.), *Longitudinal studies of adult psychological development* (pp. 64–135). New York: Guilford Press.

Schaie, K. W., & Willis, S. L. (1986). Can decline in adult intellectual functioning be reversed? *Developmental Psychology, 22,* 223–232.

Smith, J., & Baltes, P. B. (1990). A study of wisdom-related knowledge: Age/cohort differences in responses to life planning problems. *Developmental Psychology, 26,* 494–505.

Sowarka, D. (1989). Weisheit und weise Personen: Common-sense Konzepte älterer Menschen. [Wisdom and wise persons: common sense concepts of older people]. *Zeitschrift für Entwicklungspsychologie und Pädagogische Psychologie, 21,* 87–109.

Staudinger, U. M. (1989). *The study of life review: An approach to the investigation of intellectual development across the life span.* Berlin: Edition Sigma.

Staudinger, U. M. (1990). Lebensrückblick: Ein Weg zur Weisheit? [Life-review: a way towards wisdom]. *Psychologie Heute, 17*(3), 60–64.

Staudinger, U. M., Cornelius, S. W., & Baltes, P. B. (1989). Aging of intelligence: Potential and limits. *Annals of the American Academy of Political and Social Science, 503,* 43–59.

Staudinger, U. M., & Dittmann-Kohli, F. (1992). Lebenserfahung und Lebenssinn [Life experience and meaning of life]. In P. B. Baltes, & J. Mittelstraß (Eds.), *Zukunft des Alterns und gesellschaftliche Entwicklung* [The future of aging and societal development] (pp. 408–436). Berlin: deGruyter.

Staudinger, U. M., Smith, J., & Baltes, P. B. (1992). Wisdom-related knowledge in a life-review task: Age differences and the role of professional specialization. *Psychology and Aging, 7,* 271–281.

Sternberg, R. J. (1985). Implicit theories of intelligence, creativity and wisdom. *Journal of Personality and Social Psychology, 49,* 607–627.

Sternberg, R. J. (Ed.). (1990). *Wisdom: Its nature, origins and development.* New York: Cambridge University Press.

Taylor, S. E., & Lobel, M. (1989). Social comparison activity under threat: Downward evaluation and upward contacts. *Psychological Review, 96,* 569–575.

Welsch, W. (1989). Weisheit in einer Welt der Pluralität. [Wisdom in a world of plurality]. In W. Oelmüller (Ed.), *Philosophie und Weisheit* [Philosophy and wisdom] (pp. 214–274). Paderborn: Schöning.

# Aging and Prophecy:
# The Uses of
# G. Stanley Hall's *Senescence*

## David G. Troyansky

Thomas Cole's "The Prophecy of *Senescence*: G. Stanley Hall and the reconstruction of old age in twentieth-century America" is part of a larger project in the history of aging linking the classical past, along with the medieval, early modern, and Victorian pasts, to the contemporary United States. It contrasts with the more social scientific approaches that have largely characterized the historical literature on aging (Cole, 1992). However, it is also part of a broader tendency in historical writing, a movement away from the not-so-new social history—whether Marxist, *Annaliste*, or econometric—to the so-called new cultural history (Hunt, 1989). But before we place the chapter in its scholarly context, let us examine its content.

I interpret Cole's title in three ways. Cole is explicit about the first two; the third is implicit, but it strikes me just as forcefully. First, there is the way in which Hall played the prophet in a particular historical juncture in American culture. Second, there is the prophetic role he recommended for old people in general. Third, there is the long context of prophetic literature in Western culture, a context, I would argue, for understanding both Hall and Cole.

"The prophecy of *Senescence*" refers in the first place to Hall himself in the role of prophet, an expected role, as the standard biography of Hall bears the subtitle, "the psychologist as prophet" (Ross, 1972). Indeed, wherever we dip into the vast oeuvre of Hall, we encounter an extraordinary individual, a self-absorbed individual to be sure, but a man who was equally absorbed by the great issues of his day: mediator between Freud and the

New World, founder of Clark University, philosopher, scientist, humanist, and political and social commentator. Cole has captured the resonances between Hall and his era. A figure who comes at just the right time, Hall offers himself as a kind of messianic individual. In the intensity with which he lives, relives, and reinterprets his own life—consider the autobiographical nature of *Senescence* (1922) and the other explicitly autobiographical works, *Confessions of a Psychologist* (1901) and *Life and Confessions of a Psychologist* (1923)—and in the active way in which he meets the world—consider "The Message of the Zeitgeist" (1921)—he is reminiscent of a Romantic poet and even of the subject of his *Jesus, the Christ, in the Light of Psychology* (1917).

Consider how that book begins:

> *Mansoul has two orientations, the one outward the other inward. In our age the former predominates and the latter is restricted as never before in history. Our civilization and all its armentaria are so complex and absorbing that all the powers of the soul have to be focussed with almost a tonic cramp of the attention upon objectivities to the neglect and even depletion of the subjective life. Christianity, on the other hand, was a product of the greatest introvertive movement of history. Hence the age of its rise was the most, as ours is the least, psychological of all periods.*
>
> *Centrifugal evolutive trends have produced literatures, sciences, philosophies, industries, institutions, laws, arts, inventions and so forth, so numerous and intricate that it requires all our psychic energies to know, maintain, defend and advance them, and some even fear that the control of them is now in danger of making too heavy drafts upon our powers, and that man may become the Frankenstein victim of his own creations. (Hall, 1917)*

Such themes reappear in *Senescence*, a work that is both scientific and literary, analytical and Utopian. It is informed by a New England moral tradition loaded with German philosophy. Cole recognizes the difficulties inherent in trying to define what Hall was doing. He calls the text frustrating. What an understatement! Virtually any claim concerning the text would prove to be too constraining. Hall wanted to be all things to all people. That may be the sign of a successful prophet. So Cole may not be terribly surprised if I suggest that focusing on Hall's rejection of religion and his faith in science, albeit tempered with poetry, is to grasp only one part of what is going on in the book. As prophet, Hall rejected everything and embraced everything. The book reviews an impressive literature—it criticizes some writers for being unscientific, others for being too scientific—and it does this by reproducing arguments author by author and blending those arguments, and the authors' life histories, with Hall's own fix on things, his own prophecy.

For all his self-absorption, however, Hall claimed to want to share the role of prophet. Thus, in the second sense of Cole's title, Hall's old age becomes a model for everyone else's. He recommends that old people avoid being alienated, hidden, or infantilized. In short, all old people should become prophets. Throughout the book—and even in the midst of an analysis of mortality rates and pension programs—Hall argues that old people are the most individual or individuated of people. But even as he seems to be writing about the aged in general, he writes specifically about writers, and he concentrates on critical moments in their lives. He gets out of himself when he becomes absorbed in the lives of equally individual thinkers.

Whatever the possibility of creating entire cohorts of prophets, we should pay careful attention to the third meaning of prophecy, the genre in which Hall fits. Cole's quotation from Hall, which serves as the first part of his chapter's epigraph, is yet another rewriting of the maritime metaphor that appears throughout the Western prophetic tradition. Without returning to the Biblical sources, we can find the following (Troyansky, 1989: pp. 81, 84):

> *Let us show that we have arrived in this last season not by way of a storm and in spite of ourselves, but voluntarily and as in a port where we happily conclude our commerce, to see soon the dear country that is heaven. François de La Mothe Le Vayer,* De la vieillesse *(1644)*

Or:

> *Old age is a port where one arrives only after having **run up** against many reefs. Oh! how does one arrive there? The riggings are broken; the sails are torn by the force of fighting against the waves, the crew is exhausted, the vessel leaks water from all parts; only the handling of the pilot has saved it from shipwreck. Abbé Clément,* Réflexions sur la vieillesse *(1757)*

It is instructive to read the passages that tend to follow this metaphor and blunt its impact. The passage itself emphasizes physical damage. One then turns toward more spiritual things. Thus Clément continues: ". . . in old age everything fails us; but God remains for us. We have lost everything; but we are rich if we have ensured our salvation. Let us learn to become old before we are old. . . . In the successive decline that an old man experiences, what will support him, what will console him if he has neither morals nor religion?"

A less biographical and more political context might see the same language applied to the ship of state. Hall himself seems to have been thinking both about his own life and the life of the nation. The ship of his life parallels the American ship of state. He writes of the senility of the United

States in terms of shipwreck, and he evidently sees equal wreckage in his own aging. It is curious that we often think of intellectuals as having no problem adjusting to the more sedentary life. But it's clearly a problem for a man so attracted to the *sturm und drang* of adolescence.

When Cole considers the "reconstruction of old age," we must ask, had it collapsed? Some of the contributors to this volume have addressed the question in one way or another (Achenbaum, 1978; Haber, 1983). According to one recent German account, the American experience of collapse or obsolescence was parallelled by the European experience at the turn of the century (Ehmer, 1990). But what was it that had collapsed? For the social scientific historians it might be the hope of employment for the aged or a certain family structure. For Cole, it is a cultural representation. We then must ask, who read Cole's ministers and popular writers? Did they believe what they read? Was there an erosion of Protestantism's vision of aging? One recent study of aging and death in Scotland finds that vision as strong as ever in at least one part of the world (Williams, 1990).

Even if we accept that there was some form of cultural collapse that had something to do with old age—this is a period in which collapse is seen everywhere, whether we're dealing with the liberal certainties of the nineteenth century or the role of the West in the world—how important was Hall's particular reconstruction? Was his influence on American gerontology as great as Cole implies? Was the American experience different from other national experiences? Should we understand Hall's response as a late echo of the progressive-era discourse on expertise and science?

Cole's critique of the scientific or scientistic approach that he thinks Hall is advocating is standard fare in the historiography of progressivism, but Cole goes beyond just lamenting the alienating, cold social sciences. He recognizes the complexity of the scientific vocabulary of the era when discussing Hall's version of evolution. We tend to forget the variety of ideas concerning evolution, Darwin's model being only one. Hall was attracted to a particular brand of Lamarckian evolution in which people evolve in a certain way because they will it. In *Senescence* (p. 35), he refers to Henry Fairfield Osborn, the leading vertebrate paleontologist of the day and the advocate of a non-Darwinian theory. A new book on Osborn describes the cultural meaning of evolution for a member of the old elite of New York at the American Museum of Natural History, and points to the close tie between evolutionary ideas and fear of decline on the part of the Wasp ascendancy (Rainger, 1991). Hall is finding a new role for some old families in a new and dangerous world characterized by new immigrants from southern and eastern Europe or migrants from the south.

In *Senescence* (p. 432), Hall writes:

> *Class hatred and the antagonisms of capital and labor, national and individual greed, race jealousies and animosities, the ferment of Bolshevism, the ascendancy of the ideals of* Kultur *over those of culture in our institutions of higher education in every land, industrial stagnation and unemployment, the crying lack of leaders and the dominance of mediocrity everywhere, the decay of faith and the dessication of religion, the waning confidence in democracy: these are the prospects we must face if we are not to flee from reality and be cowards to life as it confronts us.*

He mentions three escapes: eugenics, a world state with a unified educational system, and prolongation of life (p. 433). He calls for a "new individuation which is impossible under the domination of egoism." He even borrows from Henri Bergson: "We need not be faith-curers but must be vitalists and believe in some kind of *élan vital* or creative evolution, as opposed to materialistic or mechanistic interpretations of life, to understand the true psychology of the age" (p. 435).

In a piece of utopian/dystopian fiction, "The Fall of Atlantis," one of what he calls "vacation skits" in *Recreations of a Psychologist* (1920), he describes his "profound conviction that certain degenerative changes—industrial, social, hygienic, and religious—are going on in our civilization and especially in our own land which may perhaps be realized by a larger historic perspective, which only imagination can supply. It might have been entitled, 'Strikes of Doctors, Lawyers, Teachers, Clergy, and finally Women, Causing the Downfall and at last the Physical Engulfment of a Superstate.'"

Was the crisis Cole describes felt by any groups other than the traditional elites? Was it perhaps less about old age than it was about power in American culture? Is it one more text in a period of literary obsession with decay and decline, beginning in the late nineteenth century and lasting until after the First World War?

What shall we make of Cole's call to create a "moral economy?" The term brings to mind E. P. Thompson's classic work on English marketplace riots. There it was a matter of understanding popular assumptions that lay beneath crowd behavior, but the term was also employed with an eye toward the development of a modern form of class consciousness. The Thompson "school" wrote history that was politically engaged (Thompson, 1971). Cole's writing is also politically engaged. But in place of class consciousness, Cole offers age consciousness, in the hope of transcending it. In other words, Cole's historical writing shares something with Thompson's, but it signals a shift from a social-science based history to a new cultural one. He is not alone. Many historians, having rejected sociology, and having had their fling with anthropology, have now taken up with literary theory and philosophy.

Cole's approach still has a critical edge, and it may be seen as postmodern in its employment of a phrase like "reconstruction of old age." Within the broader political landscape, it parallels the search by the American left for values. Criticizing social analysis and social engineering, evoking ideas of community, it sounds like the Democratic Party rediscovering "family values."

Cole's article brings to historical gerontology the kind of serious questioning so evident in historical writing today. If we look again at Cole's first page and the second part of his epigraph, the remark by Lawton referring to "real lives," we see the problem. Are there *any* real lives? How are they determined? If Cole refuses to be forced back to the social scientific model with its emphasis on the workplace or economic cycles, and if he insists on finding "meaning" and a new "moral economy" in historical gerontology, is Cole, in essence, rewriting Hall in his own book for his own time?

## REFERENCES

Achenbaum, A. (1978). *Old age in the new land: The American experience since 1790.* Baltimore: Johns Hopkins University Press.

Cole, T. R. (1992). *The journey of life: A cultural history of aging in America.* New York: Cambridge University Press.

Ehmer, J. (1990). *Sozialgeschichte des Alters.* Frankfurt am Main: Suhrkamp.

Haber, C. (1983). *Beyond sixty-five: Old age in nineteenth-century America.* New York: Cambridge University Press.

Hall, G. S. (1917). *Jesus, the Christ, in the light of psychology.* New York: D. Appleton & Co.

Hall, G. S. (1920). *Recreations of a psychologist.* New York: D. Appleton & Co.

Hall, G. S. (1922). *Senescence: The last half of life.* New York: D. Appleton & Co.

Hunt, L. (Ed.) (1989). *The new cultural history.* Berkeley: University of California Press.

Rainger, R. (1991). *An agenda for antiquity.* Tuscaloosa: University of Alabama Press.

Ross, D. (1972). *G. Stanley Hall: The psychologist as prophet.* Chicago: University of Chicago Press.

Thompson, E. P. (1971). The moral economy of the English crowd in the eigthteen century. *Past and Present, 50,* 76–136.

Troyansky, D. G. (1989). *Old age in the old regime: Image and experience in eighteenth-century France.* Ithaca: Cornell University Press.

Williams, R. (1990). *A Protestant legacy: Attitudes to illness and death among older Aberdonians.* Oxford: Clarendon Press.

# CHAPTER 6

# (When) Did the Papacy Become a Gerontocracy?

## W. Andrew Achenbaum

Gerontologists have paid curiously little attention to *institutions* that link individuals' behavioral patterns and attitudes in old age with structures and processes associated with societal aging. For instance, most of the work in political gerontology, to take one subfield, falls into one of two categories. At the micro-level, attention is generally focused on the political attitudes and behavior of older persons. Investigators analyze individuals' voting patterns and political interests; the range and stability of the elderly's ideological orientations, including beliefs about specific issues; and the relationship among aging, leadership, and incumbency (for reviews, see Hudson & Binstock, 1976; Jacobs, 1990; Tibbitts, 1962). Studies at the macro-level, in contrast, deal with issues surrounding the politics and structure of age-based lobbying organization. In addition, inquiries into the development of social policies and programs for the aging have resulted in first-rate studies of the old-age welfare state (Pratt, 1977; Quadagno, 1990).

Lately scholars have embarked on comparative studies to learn how different types of political systems affect the elderly in advanced-industrial and industrializing countries (Minkler & Estes, 1991; Schulz & Myles, 1990). Paradoxically although this work might appropriately emphasize institutional linkages, there is little sense of the "cultural" and "structural" lags between individuals and processes stressed in the work of Matilda White Riley,

Bernice Neugarten, and James Birren. Nor is much said about how the cohort dynamics that inhere in generational succession may alter amid rapid societal aging. To address such issues researchers must pay greater attention to institutions—"structures that shape our society at the individual and collective levels and that reciprocally connect individuals and society" (Jackson, 1990, p. 7).

There are models for doing the sort of gerontologic institutional case studies I propose, such as William Graebner's history of the meanings and functions of "retirement" (1980) and Howard Eglit's analysis of age discrimination in constitutional and statutory law (1985). Both works seek to connect micro- and macro-levels of analysis by distinguishing between institutional rules that govern interpersonal behavior and those organizational/ individual strategies that people employ in specific situations. But we need more studies of how institutional arrangements and dynamics evolve over time in order to understand continuities and shifts in who has the power to effect incremental and long-term changes in ideas and processes, including those that affect what it means to grow older.

Ideally, this collection of essays will contribute to a greater integration of historical analysis and organizational theory in aging research by highlighting the centrality of institutional dynamics. The essay by Richard Sutch, Roger Ransom, and Samuel Williamson is a fitting opening chapter. They emphasize a key institution—tontine insurance. They place great emphasis on strategies. They recognize that seemingly minor institutional developments sometimes catalyze cross-cutting changes that have a great impact on ordinary people's lives as well as the evolution of society at large. Their essay reflects the continuing debt of at least two of the authors to their mentor, Douglas North. Institutions, North argues, are "the underlying determinant of the long-run performance of the economies. If we are ever to construct a dynamic theory of change . . . it must be built on a model of institutional change" (1990, p. 107).

My essay complements the institutional focus that runs through this volume, although my topic and data diverge from the preponderance of U.S. materials. I explore some institutional aspects of a gerontocracy, "a society in which the political system is in the hands of the oldest community members" (Harris, 1988, p. 79). Being especially interested in the social and cultural transformation of age relations in western societies during the past two centuries, I looked for a gerontocratic case study that had institutional features which, for a long sweep of time, enabled older people to exercise power (Van Tassel, 1986). The best work on gerontocracies, a word coined by Jean-Jacques Fazy to describe Parisian politics after Napoleon, has been done by anthropologists investigating pre-industrial, non-western communities (Baxter & Almagar, 1978; Hamer, 1972; Kertzer, 1978; Werner, 1981). Judeo-Christian institutions merit consideration, given the important roles that older people have played in maintaining religious customs and ceremonies (Achenbaum, 1992). In his landmark survey, *Senescence* (1922), G. Stanley Hall emphasized the important role that aging clerics historically played in conserving and organizing religious traditions:

> *Both youth and age seek truth and thrill when they feel a deep sentiment of inner conviction. But age lays more stress upon the pragmatic sanction of working well and can better understand even Loyola and Machiavelli. Thus it came that while men in their prime conceived of the great religions, the old made them prevail. Thus, too, instituted and dogmatic religion owes its existence chiefly to men past the meridian of life. The old did not invent belief in supernatural powers or persons but needed and used it to sustain their position when physical inferiority would have compelled them to step aside and so they made themselves mediators between gods and men. They directed and presided over rites and ceremonies and took possession of the keys of the next world, enforced orthodoxies for the sake of order, and established and equipped the young to aid them in this work. (pp. 420–421)*

Although Hall offered little evidence to substantiate his thesis, Harvey Lehman presented some data to support Hall's claims. Based on biographical details of about 51 popes, 148 Protestant bishops, 101 presidents of 13 religious organizations, and 54 deceased founders of religious movements, Lehman (1953) concluded that most new religious groups are started by individuals still in their thirties, whereas established organizations are led by "somewhat elderly" men. Lehman's findings, in turn, have been corroborated by Dean Keith Simonton's bold forays (1988) into the historical literature to determine relationships among age, achievement, and leadership.

Some U.S. historians have investigated in the rise and retirement of aging ministers as a measure of broader attitudes and experiences associated with growing older. David Hackett Fischer (1977), for instance, argued that the long-term incumbency enjoyed by Puritan divines attested to colonial New England's gerontocratic ethos. John Demos (1978) and Carole Haber (1983) demurred. Maris Vinovskis has engaged in the most extensive analysis thus far. In a 1982 essay, he noted striking shifts: Second-generation ministers were disadvantaged compared to their predecessors; adverse economic and political conditions worsened the situation of eighteenth-century clergy. In a study of 1,143 Congregational ministers from the 1630s to 1875, Vinovskis (1990) reported an overall shift from permanency in the pulpit to transiency, which began as early as the eighteenth century. Young as well as old ministers were affected by new institutional rules that still affect ministerial mobility patterns today (White, 1970).

These excursions into U.S. gerontologic history are helpful, but they do not permit us to limit focus to *institutional* dynamics. As John Jackson notes, "a single organization is an institution only to the extent that its structure, rules, or dominant norms are not replicated elsewhere" (1990, p. 7). Because the Papacy is a unique institution, reconstructing papal history seems a useful way to analyze certain institutional dynamics relevant to gerontocracies. The elegant quotation from Hall, in particular, raises three sets of questions:

- First, we need to investigate biographical details. What was the average age when men were elected to be popes? Did the average age at election rise over time? Were aged popes generally infirm? Did they tend to be conservative? Were pontiffs presumed to grow wiser with age? Did reigns lengthen with increasing life expectancy?
- Second, we should determine the place of the Papacy in the Roman Catholic episcopal hierarchy. Was the bishop of Rome always considered the chief priest? If so, why? If not, when did the bishops of Rome come to wield the greatest authority in the Christian church?
- Third, we must deal specifically with matters of institutional rules and strategies. Were the *papabili* always expected to have held certain posts before assuming St. Peter's seat? Did the institution itself become more gerontocratic over the centuries? That is, did the Papacy increasingly come under the control of older men, who endorsed the reigning orthodoxies of the day? Or have elderly popes proven as likely as younger ones to be instigators of institutional change?

Note that this triology of questions assumes that even institutions like the Papacy are not divinely inspired. What "St. Peter's chair" means to faithful Roman Catholics has been shaped by developments in the papal institution and the character of the men elected to sit in that throne. Analyzing the Papacy's institutional story requires us to look at the lives of popes, European history, and their connections.

## "AGE LAYS MORE STRESS UPON THE PRAGMATIC SANCTION OF WORKING WELL." (HALL, 1922)

The development of papal institutions is sometimes traced back to Peter's confession of faith at Caesarea Philippi. After Peter acknowledged Christ to be the Messiah, Jesus responded: "You are Peter, the Rock; and on this rock I will build my church, and the powers of death shall never conquer it. I will give you the keys of the kingdom of Heaven; what you forbid on earth shall be forbidden in heaven, and what you allow on earth shall be allowed in heaven" (Matthew 16:18–19). Acts 2 shows Peter's prominence: he was the one who preached the sermon on the first Pentecost. Other books in the New Testament portray Peter as a dominant figure, particularly in the early Church in Jerusalem. Tradition says Peter was the first bishop of Rome, where he apparently was martyred ca. 64. Roman Catholic doctrine states that Peter's right to forbid evil-doing and to forgive sins was transferred to his successors. Accordingly, popes are entitled to wield considerable spiritual, though not necessarily temporal, power.

Can a case for papal supremacy be based on a verse describing Peter as the "Rock?" The evidence is not incontrovertible on hermeneutic or social grounds. Some scholars argue that Matthew 16:18 was not introduced into the Gospel until the third century (Cheetham, 1982; Tillard, 1983), which casts doubts on whether Jesus really made the statement. Furthermore, other biblical sources imply that no single human was to be head. Paul asserts that Christ is the Church's only foundation (1 Corinthians 3:11). Rights assigned to Peter in Matthew 16:19 subsequently were accorded to all the disciples in Matthew 18:18. In several passages Jesus bestows privileges on the 12 apostles (Matthew 19:28, Luke 22:24; the apocalyptic themes resonate in Revelations 21:14), but they are empowered to act like servants, not princes. Since Jesus's contemporaries found it hard to grasp the radical sense of authoritative power set forth in the Gospel, it is not surprising that the New Testament is full of struggles over hierarchy. Furthermore, it is significant that no popes appear in the Bible. The apostles are never called "bishops." That title was reserved for charismatics, not organizers or fundraisers (Argyle, 1963; McKenzie, 1966; Burn-Murdoch, 1954; Holmberg, 1978).

Bishops became increasingly important in the decades after the apostles died. Institutionally, they ensured that local churches mutually could defend themselves against heresy. The principle of *shared* power in the early Christian notion of episcopal collegiality means that the bishop of Rome had not yet been designated as *primus inter pares*. Although "the hierarchy of the bishops . . . was formed in close correspondence with the gradations of civil power," the nineteenth-century historian Leopold von Ranke observed, "it is, indeed, a vain pretense to assert that [Rome's] supremacy was universally acknowledged by East and West" (1966, Vol. I: 9). Ignatius of Antioch (110–117), a leading Church Father, called for unity consolidated around the bishopric, but he did not base it on Petrine doctrine. Nor did he indicate that anyone was the **chief** presiding officer. St. Cyprian, bishop of Carthage from 248–258, wrote that St. Peter's chair was shared equally by all bishops. Revealingly, the clergy in Rome referred to him as "Pope

Cyprian," addressing him as the "most blessed and glorious pope" (Burn-Murdoch, 1954, p. 74). At the time, the Roman emperor, not the bishop of Rome, was called "pontifex maximus."

Signs of special authority being ascribed to the Papacy first appeared in the fourth century. An inscription (304 AD) commemorating the late St. Marcellinus referred to "my papa Mercellus," but this just may have been a term of affection. The Council of Arles (314) was the first to "salute" a bishop of Rome, Silvester I (314–335), "with due reverence, most glorious Pope" (in Petry, 1962, p. 185). Canon 6 of the Council of Nicaea (325) affirmed that four sees (Alexandria, Antioch, Constantinople, and Rome) enjoyed certain prerogatives. (Significantly, the bishop of Rome did not participate in the proceedings.) Damasus I (366–384) persistently promoted Roman primacy—he referred to it as the "apostolic see"—but he did not object when Jerusalem was designated as a patriarchy at the 1st Council of Constantinople (381). Indeed, it was not until 445, when Valentinian decreed that ecclesiastical peace would be better served if the churches recognized Rome's authority, that the institution of the Papacy was accorded official recognition. The emperor took this step at the request of Leo the Great (440–461).

Consistent with New Testament language, Leo the Great called himself "the servant of the communion." Contemporaries wrote that he humbly admitted countless failings. Despite such an avowed sense of unworthiness, however, Leo felt confident enough about what it meant to sit in Peter's chair to recast conventional wisdom about the Papacy into a novel theory of papal monarchy. He invoked Matthew and other Church Fathers to justify rights that he asserted had been exercised by St. Peter himself. Leo I made subtle distinctions. Although the pope portrayed himself modestly as "the vicar of Peter," he was not shy about stating the institutional ramifications of such a statement: Hence he declared that "the blessed apostle Peter does not cease from presiding over his see" (Tillard, 1983, p. 60). Successors to Leo the Great were presumed to be "'the primate of all the bishops,' the Apostle's mystical embodiment" (Kelly, 1988, p. 43). And to keep the record accurate, Leo the Great rewrote the historical record: For instance, he directed that the Nicaean Canon 6 be altered to read "the primacy has always belonged to the Church of Rome" (Grant, 1965, p. 40)—a revisionist interpretation action endorsed at the Council of Chalcedon (451).

Leo the Great was, in Weberian terms, a "charismatic" pope. He described his pastoral office as "the servant of the servants of God," a phrase still used in ceremonies and official documents to characterize popes. He maximized the advantages available to a powerful prelate by changing the institutional boundaries of the office: Leo intended that his characterization of the

Papacy would facilitate the transfer of authority and disarm challenges to a new pontiff's legitimacy, thus anticipating problems which typically beset a new leader (Grusky & Miller, 1970, p. 423). From the perspective of 15 centuries later, it is tempting to assume that Leo enabled his successors steadily to accrue more and more power.

Yet the Papacy remained a fragile institution. Its prestige and authority rose and fell over time. With varying degrees of success, popes had to struggle to preserve their independence from heretics, schismatics, antipopes, Eastern patriarchs, and temporal rivals. Extending the Papacy's doctrinal and canonical authority over a scattered Church was a daunting task. Some, like Gelasius I (492–496), appreciated the importance of "bureaucratic persistence in the pursuit of power" (Johnson, 1976, p. 131). To consolidate institutional powers, he seized on symbolic politics: Gelasius was the first pope to be proclaimed as the "vicar of Christ." Yet gains in power secured by one pontiff sometimes were lost by the next. Gelasius' successor, Anastasius II (496–498), was an inept diplomat who infuriated secular and spiritual leaders alike. "His critics were quick to claim that his death was the result of divine judgment" (Kelly, 1988, p. 50).

Most accretions in papal institutional power were incremental in nature, which took shape in response to prevailing circumstances. During his papacy, for instance, Honorius I (625–638) assumed temporal responsibilities that civil officials could no longer handle. Similarly, Paul I (757–767) became a residual legatee of imperial authority in Italy after the eclipse of Byzantine power—a position the bishop of Rome was to occupy for more than 1100 years. Leo III (795–816) resolved a power struggle between Latins and Greeks when, by crowning Charlemagne, he tied the papacy's future to feudal fortunes in the West. He paid a price for such involvement with secular powers, however: Leo III became the first and last pope to pay obeisance to an emperor. Still, his efficient administration of papal patrimonies enabled him to initiate several social-welfare programs and to rebuild Christian Rome. Nicholas II (1058-1061) used his power to exercise internal reform: He changed the procedures for papal elections to ensure that the proceedings were "right and lawful" (Petry, 1962; Johnson, 1976; Kelly, 1988; Morris, 1991).

Daring innovations, such as those taken by Gregory VII (1073–1085), suggest that powerful prelates could effect institutional developments that went far beyond incremental accretions of power. Gregory VII increased papal rights by redefining their limits. He decreed that the title of "Pope" was reserved exclusively for the bishop of Rome. The first pope to call himself "bishop of bishops," he accentuated the outward marks of his sovereignty by wearing a tiara. Gregory's *Dictatus papae* (1075) set forth 27 propositions—

such as "No one may condemn a decision of the Holy See," "He may depose emperors," and "His name is unique in the world" (Tillard, 1983, p. 54)— that greatly expanded papal judicial and legislative prerogatives. He sought to augment the wealth at his disposal by investing part of his personal patrimony in monastic orders. Gregory VII forged feudal ties with Scandanavian, Spanish, and Hungarian rulers. But for all his manifest concern to broaden his institutional authority, Gregory declined the title of "Universal Bishop." In refusing to insist that Roman rites be observed in every congregation, this pope recognized the legitimacy of other patriarchs to settle liturgical matters. Similarly, he insisted that missionaries respect the indigenous Christian cultures that had gained recent converts for the Church. Gregory's vision of the papacy as an institution was genuinely imperialistic in manner without being blatantly hegemonic in politics.

Those who succeeded Gregory VII from 1085 to 1870, not surprisingly, were a diverse group who exercised their papal authority in strikingly different ways. Some enhanced the office's prestige. Innocent III (1198–1216) succeeded in his triple-crown efforts to launch a crusade, reform priestly behavior, and fight heresy. Paul II (1464–1471) decreed that only popes could be called *pontifex maximus*. Still others left mixed legacies. For instance, Alexander VII (1655–1667) is usually remembered for commissioning Bernini to enclose the piazza of St. Peter's with a colonnade. But it is worth recalling that Alexander also used papal funds to buy family members estates and high posts so that they could live in the profligate manner to which he was becoming accustomed.

Many pontiffs had to deal with internal and international crises. During the schisms that occurred between 1378 and 1418, papal families vied for hereditary sovereignty. Insults were traded between temporal and spiritual leaders. Some popes simply failed to rule wisely. Urban VIII (1623–1644) was an authoritarian, reckless nepotist, criticized for spending so lavishly. Despite his grasp of diplomatic affairs, Urban showed a penchant for picking the losing side during the Thirty Years War. More than a few prelates took advantage of the power at their disposal. Paul III (1534–1549) made a mid-life career out of getting himself chosen (without bothering to get ordained) for bishoprics with sizable revenues; as pope, he helped family members to do likewise. Leo X (1513–1521) was such an inveterate nepotist and free-spender that his actions led Martin Luther to protest: "The principle, for which Gregory VII had moved the whole world, was resigned with little difficulty by Leo X" (von Ranke, 1966, I:28).

This review of contemporary judgments and scholarly assessments of the performances and personalities of the popes should not divert attention from larger trends. Analyses of the Papacy as an institution must illuminate how the office changed as well as how the various incumbents performed. Accordingly, we should note three institutional developments that transformed the Papacy between 1085 and 1870.

First, the bishop of Rome and other high-ranking officials literally became "princes" of the Church. Four men chose to call themselves Pius between 1458 and 1572, but *pietas* counted for less than politics in their exercise of power. Sometimes popes asserted new ecclesiastical rights: Canonization of saints became an exclusive papal privilege during the 12th century (Burn-Murdoch, 1954); Clement IV (1265–1269) declared that only the pontiff could appoint officials to episcopal posts. Some, like Nicholas V (1447–1455), who brilliantly placated rivalries among papal families, proved adept conciliators. Many of the Renaissance men who served as popes, however, were worldly in the most literal sense of the term: They gave their illegitimate children lucrative appointments; they indulged their love of the arts; they felt that they were entitled to live like secular lords. As Paolo Paruta reported from Rome in 1595, "this authority of the popes has been increasing for some years already and becoming merely a monarchy" (in Prodi, 1987, p. 37).

To the extent that Machiavelli's *The Prince* serves as a better guide to the medieval papacy than might the *Acts of the Apostles*, a second institutional pattern becomes evident. Papal monarchs were among Europe's most powerful nation-builders during the early modern period. At the beginning of the 14th century, Dante sharply distinguished between the sacred and profane realms: Popes were to lead flocks to eternal life; emperors were to direct subjects toward temporal happiness. Writing in 1349, the Franciscan William of Ockham warned that papal bounty did not include temporal domination (Petry, 1962, pp. 508, 513). But the boundaries between temporal and spiritual realms were becoming fuzzy. The way that Alexander VI demarcated the Spanish and Portugese zones of exploration in 1493, for example, influenced politics in Iberia and Latin America for centuries.

Papal abuses of power and popes' efforts to reconcile competing interests and ideas are an integral part of the story of the Reformation and Counter Reformation, which themselves inextricably transformed European maps. From the various sessions of the Council of Trent (1545–1563) onwards, Roman Catholic church leaders reiterated the primacy of papal authority (Todd, 1962). Even fleeting diplomatic victories, such as the Concordat of 1801 reached between Pius VII and Napoleon, affirmed the papacy's status as a supranational authority. Perhaps more significant, however, was the perdurance of papal institutions, which according to writers at the time demonstrated the value of relying on centralized authority. The range of powers gradually acquired by popes—to institute uniform procedures, levy taxes, engage in diplomacy, reward talent, sanction corruption—became a model for policymaking that secular leaders would emulate.

The third major institutional development in this history is the elaboration of papal bureaucracies. Although the word *curia* has political connotations that date back to the Classical era, the term *Curia* was not used to refer to the central administration of the Roman Catholic church until the 11th century. Before then, popes generally asked priests and deacons in the Roman diocese to assist them with legal and financial matters. Thereafter, papal appointments to the Curia were coveted by Italian bishops and young clerics from other places. Service in Rome was a good way to get recognized by power brokers. Curial experience often enabled an ambitious man to gain membership in the Sacred College of Cardinals, which (after 1179) had the exclusive right to elect popes. Typically, but not always, Cardinals chose pontiffs from within their ranks.

Curial powers augmented so much that, in retrospect, it seems that the Curia might have become an ecclesiastical Roman Senate. The body periodically made demands for greater collegiality in exercising papal authority with the pontiff. Had the balance of power shifted slightly more to the cardinals, then it would not have been enough for this study of the Papacy as an institution to delve into the lives of the popes. The case study also would have had to canvass the views and deeds of ranking princes of the Roman Catholic Church.

But until very recently, the Curia has played a subordinant role. Popes in various ways resisted demands by senior cardinals to share power. Beginning with Paul III (1534–1549) and lasting into the late seventeenth century (Kelly, 1988), many pontiffs appointed younger family members to be trusted assistants. (According to the *Oxford English Dictionary*, the term "cardinal nephew" entered the language in the 1600s.) This, of course, increased the nepotism occurring during the period. Second, popes took steps to foment tensions within the cardinalate. Sixtus V, for instance, sought to unsettle alliances in the Curia's power blocs in 1586 by increasing the number of cardinals from 26 to 70. (Given the importance of family connections in papal elections at the time, this move increased opportunities for factionalism, making it as likely that popes would be succeeded by their foes as by their proteges.) Finally, during the 16th century, various Roman Congregations were established to perform specific tasks. Enjoying considerable autonomy, heads of these Congregations quickly set into motion a new layer of curial politics, which provided greater opportunities for jockeying for power that might ultimately effect papal outcomes (*Encyclopaedia Brittanica* 26: 946, 1985). Amid converging chains of command the institutional rules of the game changed: Henceforth, legal studies and curial service counted for more than blood relations in choosing popes. The "right" resume, well-placed patrons, success in bureaucratic infighting, broker politics—all hallmarks of power politics in "modern" times—mattered in the Vatican.

Institutional patterns of papal rule, by happenstance and by design, did not change greatly until the reign of Pius IX (1846–1878). Pius proved a master politician, if not necessarily a noble leader. Pius IX declared that when the pontiff spoke *ex cathedra*, his words were "divinely endowed with the infallibility promised by the Divine Redeemer." A pope's views on doctrine, Pius declared in 1870, were "irreformable of themselves and not by consent of the Church. If any one contradict this, let him be anathema" (in Burn-Murdoch, 1954, p. 30).

The doctrine of papal infallibility reveals much about Pius's ability to capitalize on the comparative advantages afforded by an efficient, centralized administration—particularly when coupled with minimal resistance from docile bishops. That the pope chose this historical moment to assert such authority suggests a certain blindness to the need to accommodate diversity at a time in which Europe and most of the rest of the world were in the throes of political modernization. After all, the U.S. delegation of bishops, seeking to demonstrate that it truly subscribed to America's democratic credo, opposed the decision (Fogarty, 1989). But Pius's successor, Leo XIII (1878–1913) saw nothing new in the principle of infallibility. With no legerdemain intended, the Pope stressed the doctrine's deep institutional roots, claiming that it was "the venerable and constant belief of every age." Carrying such logic to a remarkable conclusion, Pius XII (1939-1958) blamed the outbreak of World War II (in his opinion, itself a curse of modernism) on the failure of Christians to accept Truth as expounded by the Papacy (Johnson, 1976, p. 406).

Popes are not the only leaders who have tried to mould institutional changes by downplaying the novelty of innovations. Political, business, and social leaders often clothe fresh ideas in "conservative" garb. Radical departures from the status quo are sometimes said to have venerable roots. "Inventing tradition," as Hobsbawm and Ranger (1983) remind us, has gone on for centuries. And it would overstate the case to argue that recent pontiffs have been able to cope with "modern" times *primarily* by ignoring some of its realities or by playing tricks with the historical record. On the contrary, some of the institutional innovations popes have made since World War II suggest that popes have rightly appreciated the value of tradition and custom in dealing with events that neither they nor any single organization can control. Accommodating to the forces of modernization sometimes has required them to search for a usable institutional past.

In convening Vatican II, for example, John XXIII encouraged a frank reexamination of the nature of episcopal authority and papal power. He deliberately viewed himself as a constitutional sovereign; real power was unmistakably transferred to bishops who were invited to debate an extraordinary range of issues on parliamentary grounds. Documents from Vatican II attested to a new respect for Muslims, Buddhists, and agnostics. By eschewing a papal coronation and accepting only a woolen *pallium*, an ancient symbol of episcopal rank, John Paul I did much to eliminate the monarchial trappings of papal office. Even people who have difficulty accepting John Paul II's views on human sexuality and liberation theology tend to respect his efforts to reach out to believers around the world. In an age of pluralism, such symbolic gestures, ones that give legitimacy to "modern" practices by building on tradition, enhance the institutional prestige of the papacy among Catholics as they give non-believers a sense of the office's eminence.

Sometimes, however, popes seem to yield to conventional thinking in ways that repudiate the Church's own history. Paul VI (1963–1978) fixed a mandatory retirement age of 75 for priests and bishops. Cardinals over 80 henceforth could no longer serve in the Curia or vote in papal elections. Presumably Paul was seeking to promote collegiality and institutional flexibility by bringing in new blood. How ironic that Paul VI should have adopted a mandatory retirement policy at the very time it was being reevaluated in secular organizations. Cynics interpreting Paul's papacy, who are willing to invoke ageist stereotypes, might suggest that it is too bad that popes do not retire. Paul was a vigorous 73 when he instituted the retirement rule. Arthritis, however, noticeably diminished his activities 8 years later; he withdrew from most public functions during the last 3 years of his pontificate.

Described as a liberal at his coronation, Paul VI seemed increasingly conservative with advancing age. *Humanae vitae* (1968) and *Matrimonia mixta* (1978) disappointed many followers; his troubles with priests who wanted to marry and with Archbishop Marcel Lefebvre prompted rumors of his imminent resignation. Have the solitary demands of the Papacy simply been too great for old men? Is it possible, as Robert Michels suggested in his classic treatise *Political Powers* (1914), that in modern times age *per se* counts for less than it once did in hierarchies like the Roman Catholic episcopacy, even in the highest echelons? Do aging religious leaders typically respond to the burdensome institutional responsibilities of their office in a cautiously conservative manner?

The historical development of the Papacy as an institution just presented suggests otherwise. Most of the popes highlighted in this section were old men, many of whom happened to be in poor health. Leo the Great was over 50, a relatively mature age, when he was elected in 440; Gregory VII died in 1085 of natural causes at the age of 65. Alexander VI and VII, Clement IV, Damasus I, John Paul I and II, Paul III and VI, Pius VII and XII, Silvester I, Sixtus V, and Urban VIII also served past the age of 65. Pius IX was 78 when he enunciated the doctrine of papal infallibility. Angelo Roncalli, age 76, was expected to be a caretaker; as John XXIII, he accomplished enough to be revered as the greatest pope in the twentieth century. Are such pontiffs exceptional figures? Or, have there been enough old men elected to St. Peter's throne to suggest that that institution's continuing success has long depended on the contributions of older men? Such a pattern has been reported in other organizations. "Age-set systems arise and function in those societies in which the basic allocation of roles is not overwhelmingly determined by membership in kinship groups," S. N. Eisenstadt observes, "and where some important integrative functions remain to be filled beyond these groups" (1965, p. 112). What evidence is there that the Papacy operates as an age-set system? When, if ever, did the Papacy become a gerontocracy?

## "MEN IN THEIR PRIME CONCEIVED OF THE GREAT RELIGIONS, THE OLD MADE THEM PREVAIL."

John Paul II, according to *Annuario Pontifico* (1984), is the 263rd bishop of Rome. This figure does not include the 38 anti-popes. Nor does it count Pope Joan, who, according to legend, served as a Vicar of Christ sometime between the 9th and 11th centuries. Official documents record the birthdates of only 113 men who became popes These data occupy this section of the essay.

It is commonplace to note that life expectancy at birth has risen sharply over time. Samuel Preston (1976) estimates that two-thirds of the improvement in human longevity since the prehistoric era has occurred since 1900. Historical gains in adult life expectancy at age 40, in contrast, are less dramatic. Historians have yet to posit a generally accepted, much less transhistorical, set of baselines that mark the onset of middle age or the entry into old age in the past. David Fischer (1977) and Howard Chudacoff (1990) stress that people in earlier times did not always know their exact birthdates. Age-consciousness, they assert, is historically conditioned. In addition, chronological age has never been a reliable predictor of aging (Bookstein & Achenbaum, 1992). Because of dietary changes and fewer physical hardships to endure, most of our parents "act" younger in their 60s and 70s than did their parents who survived to the same age. (It must be quickly added that for a subset of the aged population, good genes, reduced caloric intake, and vigorous activity seem to make some older people hale at ages long after persons with a profile similar in class, habits, and background have died.)

That said, it is highly unlikely that men and women once upon a time considered people "old" at 20 and "decrepit" at 40. A fair number of people have always survived to higher ages. For at least a millennium, the mean life expectancy was no less than 25 or 30, except in times of plagues, epidemics, wars, and famine. Those who reached 30 might well on average live another 30 years (Laslett, 1985; D.W.E. Smith, 1991, personal communication). Art and writings from the classical and medieval periods refer to the elderly being at least 55; their images usually appear strikingly "modern" (Burrow, 1986; Falkner & deLuce, 1989). What has changed over time is the increasing proportion of babies and youth who nowadays make it to age 40, and then, with increasing probability, survive for several more decades.

This digression into historical demography is a necessary prelude to exploring *when* the Papacy became a gerontocracy, a powerful institution dominated by men past their prime. Because gains in average life expectancy have been less remarkable for the middle-aged than for the very young over time, especially in this century, it seems reasonable to predict that the age at which men were elected to the papacy has risen over time. There have been more cardinals over 60 in absolute numbers alive in the twentieth century than there were in the Middle Ages, which means that the pool of older *papabili* should have increased commensurately. As a corollary to Eisenstadt's institutional/generational thesis, one might hypothesize that a peculiar "age-set" of surrogate-networks have characterized papal patron/client relations. When family politics dominated the conclave, aging prelates tried to prepare cardinal-nephews or other younger household retainers to succeed them on the throne. Later on, when a succession of curial, diplomatic, and episcopal posts came to be perceived as enhancing one's papal candidacy, then seniority became an advantage.

The evidence presented in Figures 6.1 and 6.2, based on evidence drawn largely since 1066, reveals no dramatic or sudden upward trend in the age at which pontiffs were elected. Figure 6.1 shows that the age range of men selected for office has narrowed over time. Figure 6.2 reveals no important shifts over time. Both the oldest (Celestine V, elected at age 85 in 1294) and the youngest (John XI, elected at 21 in 931) known popes predate the "modern" era. John XXIII is the only very old person chosen in the last 20 elections. There seems to be no propensity over time to elect men at 60 or 65; even so, successful candidates have tended to be relatively older men.

Arithmetic confirms the impression. On average popes were 59.5 years

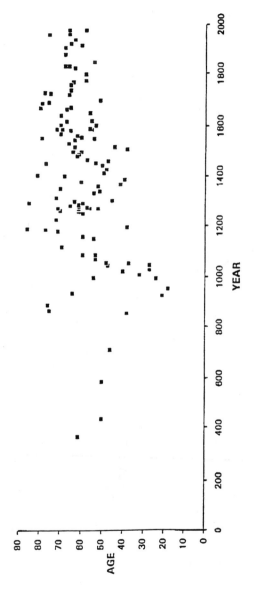

Figure 6.1 Age of Pope by year elected

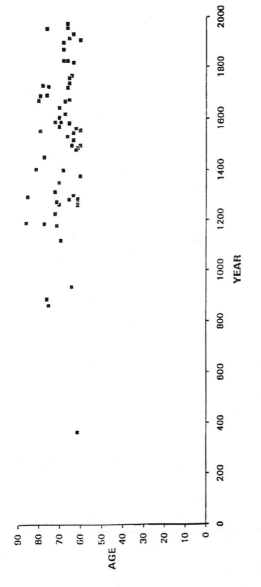

**Figure 6.2 Age of Pope (60+) by year elected**

of age when elected, and then served for 8.7 years. Those elected before they reached age 60 ($N = 50$) serve on average only 3 years longer (10.5 years) than those elected after age 60 ($N = 63$).

Like many other whites of European origin, recent popes have been living a little longer than their predecessors. Consider the papal records by periods, taking the election of major figures (Gregory VII, Leo X, and Pius IX) as turning points in the institution's development. We know the ages of 19 popes who served between 336 and 1073; these men on average were 45.3 years old upon election and served 9 years. After the reign of Gregory VII, the average age at election increased very gradually, though the average length of pontificates has increased, noticeably in the last century. From Victor III to Leo X (1086–1513), 47 men with a mean known age of 60 at election reigned on average 7 years. From Hadrian VI to Pius IX, 38 men with a mean age of 64.5 at election reigned on average 9 years. Since 1878, nine men (including John Paul II) have been elected at a mean age of 65.5 years; they served on average at least 13 years.

What cannot be adduced from the popes' biographical data, however, is whether the three major figures whose reigns serve as turning points in the history of the papacy were themselves the product or the producer of an innovative set of intellectual currents that transformed papal institutional dynamics. How likely is it, for instance, that the fact that Gregory VII (Pope number 156) served as chaplain to Gregory VI (Pope number 148, who reigned from 1045 to 1046) was a formative event? The latter prelate was known as a reformer—but he also was guilty of simony. Gregory VII's successors were two competitors, one an anti-pope, and the other Victor III, who was not one of his three top choices. Three years after Gregory's death, one of his proteges, Urban III (Pope number 158) managed to advance Gregory's views. But Urban was succeeded in turn by Pascal II, who set back the agenda; the next three popes had no intellectual or social ties to Gregory.

Similarly, the secular politics surrounding the Reformation precluded much institutional continuity after Leo X's death. His successor, Hadrian VI, was a man of good intentions, but he only served 20 months. It took the conclave more than 50 days to decide upon Clement VII; caught in the struggle between French and Spanish monarchs, he wavered and procrastinated through his reign. Paul III was the dean of the cardinals when elected. A protege of Alexander VI, who actually had been Leo's predecessor, Paul III followed his own agenda, not his mentors'.

In the case of Pius IX (Pope number 254), there seem to be more similarities among his predecessors than among his successors. Pius VII (Pope number 250, who reigned from 1800–1823) was keen to restore the papacy's supranational authority. His successors, Leo XII and Pius VIII, preferred to attend to more parochial matters. Pius IX's immediate predecessor, Gregory XVI (1831–46), was considered uncompromising and narrow in ways that fit the increasingly conservative pattern of papal decision-making. Although his successors endorsed many of the principles enunciated by Pius IX, this was not necessarily the intention of the conclaves convened. Cardinals expected Leo XIII to be a stopgap pope; during his 9-year reign he blended conservative piety with a flair for modernizing operations. Pius X was expected to break the mould. Benedict XV was also presumed to be a "new" man—having received his cardinal's hat only 3 months before his papal election. At age 60, Benedict was younger than Leo or Pius when elected. He was destined to reign for fewer years.

Age at election actually reveals little about the probable length of a person's tenure. Older popes might be expected to die sooner in their reign than men in their prime. As it happens, three men over 70 served less than a year—but so did two who were elected under the age of 60. Excluding outliers, the spread in length of service (0–25 years) rendered by men over the age of 65 is actually wider than that (2.5 to 17 years) compiled by those elected at the age of 50 or younger.

In sum, the Papacy has never been the exclusive preserve of old men. Nonetheless, since the election of Gregory VII, and possibly before, it has been, in terms of Harris's definition, "in the hands of the oldest community members." But does that make it a gerontocratic institution? Were men elected to be popes because they were old? Might not seniority and experience have counted for more than chronological age in selecting successors to St. Peter? Could it be that most popes were old simply because most *papabili* did not possess the right credentials until late adulthood? For proof that age *per se* counted in this gerontocracy, there must be evidence that the institution demanded or produced a distinctive style of old-age leadership.

## "THE OLD DID NOT INVENT THE BELIEF IN SUPERNATURAL POWERS OR PERSONS BUT THEY USED IT TO SUSTAIN THEIR POSITION WHEN PHYSICAL INFERIORITY WOULD HAVE COMPELLED THEM TO STEP ASIDE"[1]

Titian's portrait of Paul III (1534–1549) captures the ideal of a vigorous, clear-minded, experienced, shrewd pontiff in his 75th year. "Good" popes seem remarkably alike in old age. Callistus II was 72 when he negotiated the Concordat of Worms (1122), ending a long struggle between the church and emperor over investiture. Gregory IX (1227–1241), a friend of Francis

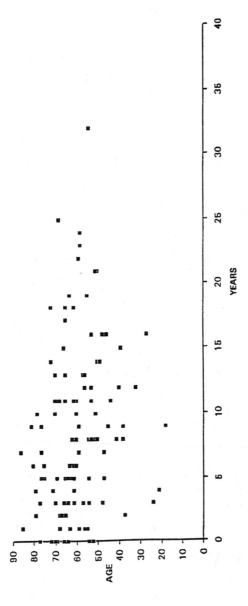

Figure 6.3 Length of reign of Pope by age at election

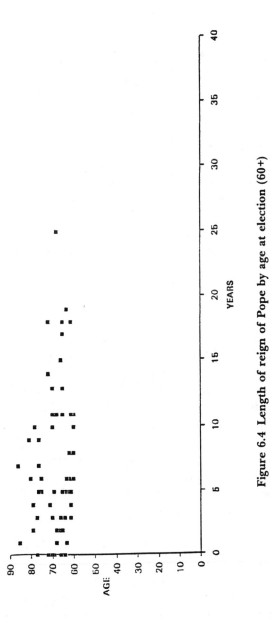

Figure 6.4 Length of reign of Pope by age at election (60+)

of Assisi, is glowingly described by chroniclers as masterful, unyielding, and intensely religious. Alexander III (1159-1162) showed his political savvy by successfully fending off assaults by four anti-popes. At 79, Gregory XIII (1572-1585) developed the calendar for which he is remembered. Accomplishments during 65-year-old Innocent XI's 13-year reign cause him to be remembered as the seventeenth century's outstanding pope. Septuagenarian Innocent XII (1691-1700) instituted judicial, administrative, and welfare reforms. Benedict XV (1914-1922) was chosen to be pope for his diplomatic experiences and "transparent goodness"; he did not disappoint his peers.

Perhaps the prototypical "good" elderly pope was Benedict XIV (1740-1758). A doctor of theology at 19, he began curial service at 45, earning his cardinal's hat 8 years later. Elected pope at age 65, he strengthened ties with both Spain and Portugal, and improved the finances of the papal states. A connoisseur of church history, Benedict was renowned for his wit and political realism. Voltaire dedicated *Mahomet* to him. Walpole praised Benedict as "a priest without insolence or interest, a prince without favorites, a pope without nephews" (Kelly, 1988, p. 298). Walpole's allusion to nepotism reminds us that "goodness" is a relative term, not one to be confused with "saintliness." Julius II (1503-1513) fathered three daughters and was feared for his ruthless violent temper; being Michelangelo's patron, however, ensured him lasting (if only vicarious) fame. Gregory XVI (1831-1846) was praised for denouncing slavery and appointing 200 missionary bishops, but he was hardly forward-looking: His ban of railroads set the stage for papal expressions of anti-modernism for the rest of the nineteenth century.

Some old popes were resolutely "bad." John VIII (872-882) apparently deserved to be assassinated by a member of his own entourage—and he was. Alexander IV (1254-1261) was indecisive and weak, lacking the insight to nominate any cardinals: there were only eight when he died. The pope ironically named Innocent VIII (1484-1492) treated his cardinals as if they were *grand seigneurs* and left the papal states bankrupt and in anarchy. Paul IV (1555-1559) hated Protestants, confined Jews to ghettos, and supported the Inquisition. Upon his death at 83, the populace rioted, and his statue was mutilated.

So inherent goodness or evil, not surprisingly, is not the hallmark of late-life papacies. Do health factors determine how the reigns of old men turn out? Once again, the evidence is mixed. The frail health of Boniface I (418-422) did not prevent him from engaging in shrewd diplomacy or supporting Augustine of Hippo. Gregory the Great ruined his health in his 30s, fasting in a monastery. But arthritis and lameness in old age did not foreclose an eventful papacy (590-604). Illness did wear others down. Stephen

II (752), Celestine IV (1241), Hadnan V (1276), and Urban VII (1590) were so frail upon their election that they did not live long enough to be crowned. Leo XI (1605) and John Paul I (1978) died suddenly after less than a month in office—though only the former's demise is attributed to old age. Sisinnius (708) was so crippled with gout that he could not feed himself. Some of the indecisiveness of Innocent VI (1352–1362) is said to be due to his being prematurely old, even before his election at age 70. Constant debilities over time diminished the capacity of Honorius III (1216–1227), Gregory XV (1621–1623), Innocent XIII (1721–1724), Clement XII (1730–1740), Pius VIII (1829–1830), and Pius XII (1939–1958) to serve efficiently toward the end of their pontificates.

Occasionally, however, the fact that a man was old and (better yet) frail enhanced his chances of being elected to serve as a caretaker pope. This was the logic that impelled cardinals to crown Hadrian II (867–872) after he had twice before turned down the papacy. They were right: Infirmity and vacillation kept the 75-year-old out of mischief. Sometimes the strategy backfired. John XXII was wisp-like and in feeble health when elected at age 72. He managed to last another 18 years, dispensing legal and financial expertise while showering the Church's resources on his relatives. Did this story inspire another custodian-turned-reformer to call himself John XXIII? He expanded the College of Cardinals from 70 to 87 before convening Vatican II, which broadened representation and assured the new pope more allies in the inner circle. A seasoned negotiator, John made the best of his grandfatherly corpulence, seeming indifference to the trappings of his office, and ability to reach others.

Aged prelates often emerge as compromise candidates whose supporters are desperate. This appears to have been the scenario that led to the elections of Callistus III (1455–1458), Pius III (1503), Paul V (1605–1621), and Pius XI (1922–1939) who won on the 14th ballot. Age was not the only critical factor in electoral contests, of course. Cardinals chose Benedict XIII (1724–1730) not so much on account of his age (75) but because they felt his political inexperience would keep him neutral. Pius X (1903–1914) was chosen because he apparently made it clear that he would be a religious rather than a political pope.

Were the personalities of the *papabili* sufficiently fixed in later years that cardinals could gauge a colleague's capacity for leadership? Possibly, but there are a lot of confounding issues at stake. No single personality type emerges. Attributes that would be taken as complimentary if ascribed to presidents and premiers are not always flattering descriptions of popes: Alexander VI (1492–1503) was judged too "ambitious" to be great; Boniface

VII (1294–1303), arrogant and cruel; Urban VI (1378–1389), harsh and obstinant; Pius VI (1775–1799), worldly. Not that meekness in a pope is always a virtue: Clement XIII (1758–1769) and Clement XIV (1769–1774) get low marks for being too indecisive. Old popes—Eugene I (654–657), Gregory VIII (1187), and Clement X (1670–1676)—seem to have fared well in chronicles of the papacy, not because they did much but because they are remembered as devout, saintly, and kind. In old age, it would seem, popes should do all things in moderation: yet Leo XII (1823–1829) was so mild, so lacking in leadership skills, that the papal states became one of the most backward in Europe during his reign.

Nor does an examination of the personality traits attributed to men elected to the papacy after the age of 75 sharpen our understanding of what might be distinctive about late-life papal leadership. Celestine III (1191–1198) was elected more than 50 years after he entered curial service. A sharp-sighted jurist and financier, he commissioned the *Liber censuum*, a survey of all properties in the see. Through connivance he outwitted and then outlived his main rival, Henry VI, who died at the age of 32. Gregory XII (1406–1415) excommunicated two antipopes before abdicating in favor of a third. Celestine V (1294) accepted the tiara at age 85 only because the throne of St. Peter's had been vacant for 27 months. Hailed as the "angel pope" who would usher in the 13th century, he abdicated 5 months later to devote himself to solitary prayer. His successor would not permit him to make a retreat to a monastery, fearing it would prompt a schism. Celestine died under house arrest. Dante made him a character at the "Gate of Hell." Clement V, under prompting from Philip IV of France, canonized Celestine in 1313.

For one ancient pope, events after his death were even stranger than fiction. Formosus was elected in his 76th year, after serving more than 25 years as a bishop, missionary, and legate. Throughout his career he displayed exceptional intelligence—though for coveting the papacy, he had been exiled at age 61 in 876. The same pattern—competence marred by a bit too much ambition—characterized his 5-year papacy (891–896). A year after his death his successor arranged a mock trial. Formosus's body was exhumed, dressed in pontifical vestments, and placed on a throne. Found guilty of perjury and covetousness, Formosus's acts were nullified, the three fingers he used to bless people were cut off, and he was buried in a common grave—only to be dug up again, further mutilated, and thrown into the Tiber. A hermit retrieved the corpse and reinterred the body. Would a younger man's corpse have been treated so bizarrely? Are restrained echoes of Formosus' funeral rites to be found in twentieth-century funeral preparations for burying a Supreme Pontiff? Is this a story of excessive mob action? Or, is this drama an instance of treating the old ritualistically like "a stranger" (Gutmann, 1987), in part out of fear, in part out of respect? If the latter, then we may be getting in a roundabout way, to the religious aura surrounding late-life spiritual leaders.

## "SO THEY MADE THEMSELVES MEDIATORS BETWEEN GODS AND MEN."

"Institutions provide the basic structure by which human beings throughout history have created order and attempted to reduce uncertainty," North (1990, p. 118) observes. "They connect the past with the present and the future so that history is a largely incremental story of institutional evolution." The Papacy fits North's definition of an institution. For more than 19 centuries, bishops of Rome have been vested with enough authority to enable them to provide leadership that empowers their followers to raise their level of interpersonal conduct and ethical leadership. Many successors to St. Peter ably fulfilled the Church's expectations. Some, however, preferred to satisfy their private desires and ambitions rather than to act in accordance with the Church's institutional rules.

Papal biographies indicate that for many centuries the Papacy has been a gerontocracy. Unlike hereditary monarchies or constitutional democracies, older men tend to be prime candidates to sit on St. Peter's throne. This demographic reality has governed some of the office's institutional rules and arrangements at various points in historical time. In a deadlocked conclave, older frail candidates who do not threaten any faction seem to be good choices to serve as caretaker popes, until a younger man gains in maturity or secures enough votes. The authority of cardinal-nephews, who carried out the wishes of feeble relatives (and/or were cunningly controlled by aging men), tells us something about generational reciprocity in ecclesiastical office. The lives of the popes, moreover, dispel certain myths of aging. Crippled men seem to have been blessed with enough other strengths to engage actively and successfully in church affairs. Quite a few were innovators who (unlike leaders of many organizations) did not require a crisis to prompt their actions (Wilson, 1973).

Different types of evidence than cited here are needed to gauge the extent to which individual popes succeeded in institutionalizing changes in the papacy. Has the certainty of lifetime tenure affected popes' performances in office any more than, say, the ways that Supreme Court justices age(d) on the bench? Have pontiffs been any more successful than other leaders in persuading their likely successors to hew to their principles once they are gone? To what extent has a succession of mainly old men affected rules governing papal protocols and modes of behavior over time?

Nor does this paper address one of the most interesting questions to be asked about papal institutions as a case study of "religious" institutions: do older men, on account of their age, perform the spiritual, sacramental, and pastoral dimensions of that office better than younger men? Pursuing that issue might advance gerontologic research in three ways:

1. First, recent work on wisdom (Baltes, 1987; Sternberg, 1990; Achenbaum & Orwoll, 1991) emphasizes the capacity of older people to think in universal terms, including the ability to reflect profoundly on transcendent matters. By these criteria, one might expect older pontiffs to grow wiser: Popes are called to mediate between the Divine and the moral, meditating on this world and the next. Given their cumulative experiences, not to mention their proximity to death, have pontiffs at advanced ages been thought to be ideally suited to communicate the transcendent message of the Christian Gospel? Or is serving as a high-ranking prelate, on theological and sociological grounds, considered an age-irrelevant vocation?

2. Analysts who characterize aging as a spiritual journey (Cole, 1991) often speak in metaphorical terms. With a few obvious exceptions, most pontiffs are said to have been devout believers. Are aged popes more inclined to delve into issues of spirituality than younger ones? Might the desire of some older popes to return to a monastery, to be alone, reflect their religiosity more than possible signs of frailty or cowardice?

3. It is not known when popes first were called "Holy Father," but the papal office has indisputable patriarchial overtones. Artists' portrayals of men from humble backgrounds who attain the papacy are no less majestic than those from noble families. At a time in which the gender-specific dimensions rightly command attention, would it not be helpful to explore the histories of how aging men wield power?

Reconstructing the history of the Papacy, in short, permits an integration of micro- and macro-level inquiries. It is a case study in how well men shape a major institution. It raises fresh possibilities for grappling with the psychological, religious, and social dimensions of growing older.

## ACKNOWLEDGMENTS

I wish to thank Patricia Blackman for all her help and Joan Bennett for generating the figures in this essay. I also thank Fred L. Bookstein, Mgsr. Charles Fahey, Sr. Mary Honora Kroger, Roger Ransom, David W.E. Smith,

David D. Van Tassel, and Maris Vinovskis for their constructive criticisms of an earlier draft of this paper.

## NOTE

[1]The prosopographic evidence in this section comes from the entries on 95 popes who were elected or served as popes past the age of 60 in Kelly (1988) and the *Encyclopaedia Britannica* (1985) or were cited by **both** sources as "elderly."

## REFERENCES

Achenbaum, W. A. (1992). Lost traditions/horizons reclaimed: Religious institutions and productive aging. In S. Bass, F. Caro, & Y-P Chen, *Achieving a productive aging society.* New York: Springer Publishing Company.

Achenbaum, W. A., & Orwoll, L. (1991). Becoming wise. *Intergenerational Journal of Aging and Human Development, 32,* 21–39.

Argyle, A. W. (1963). *The Gospel according to Matthew.* Cambridge: Cambridge University Press.

Baltes, P. B. (1987). Theoretical propositions on life-span developmental psychology. *Developmental Psychology, 23,* 611–623.

Baxter, P. T. W., & Almagar, U. (1978). *Age, generation and time.* New York: St. Martin's Press.

Bookstein, F. L., & Achenbaum, W.A. (1992). Aging as explanation. In T. R. Cole, W. A. Achenbaum, & R. Kastenbaum (Eds.), *Critical voices in gerontology.* New York: Springer Publishing Co.

Burn-Murdoch, H. (1954). *The development of the papacy.* London: Faber & Faber.

Burrow, J. A. (1986). *The ages of man.* Oxford: Oxford University Press.

Cheetham, N. (1982). *The keepers of the key.* London: Macdonald & Co.

Chudacoff, H. (1990). *How old are you?* Princeton, NJ: Princeton University Press.

Cole, T. R. (1991). Voyage *of life.* New York: Cambnsige University Press.

Demos, J. (1978). Old age in colonial New England. In J. Demos & S. S. Boocock (Eds.), *Turning points.* Chicago: University of Chicago Press.

Eglit, H. (1985). Age and the law. In R. H. Binstock & E. Shanas (Eds.), *Handbook of aging and the social sciences,* 2d ed., (pp. 528–553). New York: Van Nostrand Reinhold.

Eisenstadt, S. N. (1965). *Essays on comparative institutions.* New York: John Wiley.

*Encyclopaedia Brittanica.* (1985). 15th ed. ser.

Falkner, T. M., & deLuce, J. (Eds.) (1989). *Old age in Greek and Latin literature.* Albany: State University of New York Press.

Fischer, D. H. (1977). *Growing old in America.* New York: Oxford University Press.

Fogarty, G. P. (1989). *Patterns of Episcopal leadership.* New York: Macmillan.

Graebner, W. (1980). *A history of retirement.* New Haven: Yale University Press.

Grant, F. C. (1965). *Rome and reunion.* New York: Oxford University Press.

Grusky, O., & Miller, G. A. (Eds.) (1970). *The sociology of organizations.* New York: The Free Press.

Gutmann, D. (1987). *Powers reclaimed.* New York: Basic Books.

Haber, C. (1983). *Beyond sixty-five.* New York: Cambridge University Press.

Hall, G. S. (1922). *Senescence.* New York: D. Appleton and Company.

Hamer, J. H. (1972). Aging in a gerontocratic society. In D. O. Cowgill & L. D. Holmes (Eds.), *Aging and modernization*. New York: Appleton-Century-Crofts.

Harris, D. K. (1988). *Dictionary of gerontology*. Westport, CT: Greenwood Publishing.

Hobsbawm, E., & Ranger, T. (1983). *Inventing tradition*. Cambridge: Cambridge University Press.

Holmberg, B. (1978). *Paul and power*. Amsterdam: CWK Gleerup.

Hudson, R. B., & Binstock, R. H. (1976). Political systems and aging. In R.H. Binstock & E. Shanas (Eds.), *Handbook of aging and the social sciences* (pp. 369–402). New York: Van Nostrand Reinhold.

Jackson, J. E. (Ed.) (1990). *Institutions in American society*. Ann Arbor: University of Michigan Press.

Jacobs, B. (1990). Aging and politics. In R. H. Binstock & L. George (Eds.), *Handbook of aging and the social sciences*, 3rd ed., (pp. 350–361). New York: Academic Press.

Johnson P. (1976). *A History of Christianity*. London: Weidenfield and Nicolson.

Kelly, J. N. D. (1988). *The Oxford dictionary of the popes*. New York: Oxford Press.

Kertzer, D. I. (1978). Theoretical developments in the study of age group systems. *American Ethnologist, 5*, 368–374.

Laslett, P. (1985). Societal development and aging. In R. H. Binstock & E. Shanas (Eds.), *Handbook of aging and the social sciences*, 2nd ed., (pp. 199–230). New York: Van Nostrand Reinhold.

Lehman, H. C. (1953). *Age and achievement*. Princeton, NJ: American Philosophical Society.

McKenzie, J. L. (1966). *Authority in the church*. New York: Sheed and Ward.

Michels, Robert (1966; 1914). *Political parties*. New York: The Free Press.

Minkler, M., & Estes, C. (Eds.) (1991). *Critical perspectives on aging: The political and moral economy of growing old*. Amityville, NY: Baywood Press.

Morris, C. R. (1991, July). The three ages of the Catholic Church. *The Atlantic Monthly, 268*, 105–112.

North, D. C. (1990). *Institutions, institutional change and economic performance*. New York: Cambridge University Press.

Petry, R. C. (1962). *A history of Christianity*. Englewood Cliffs, NJ: Prentice-Hall.

Pratt, H J. (1977). *The gray lobby*. Chicago: University of Chicago Press.

Preston, S. (1976). *Mortality patterns in natural populations*. New York: Academic Press.

Prodi, P. (1987). *The papal prince*. Cambridge: Cambridge University Press.

Quadagno, J. (1990). *The transformation of the old-age welfare state*. Chicago: University of Chicago Press.

Schulz, J. & Myles, J. (1990). Old age pensions. In R.H. Binstock & L.K. George (Eds.), *Handbook of aging and the social sciences*, 3rd ed. New York: Academic Press.

Simonton, D. K. (1988). Age and outstanding achievement. *Psychological Bulletin, 104*, 251–267.

Sternberg, R. J. (1990). *Wisdom*. New York: Cambridge University Press.

Tibbitts, C. (1962). Politics of aging: Pressure for change. In W. Donahue & C. Tibbitts (Eds.), *Politics of age*, (pp. 16–25). Ann Arbor: University of Michigan Press.

Tillard, J M. R. (1983). *The Bishop of Rome*. London: SPCK.

Todd, J. M. (1962). *Problems of authority*. Baltimore: Helicon Press.

Van Tassel, D. D. (1986). *Stepping stones: Old age, leadership, and gerontocratic institutions*. Paper presented at Gerontological Society annual meeting.

Vinovskis, M. A. (1990). Aging and the transition from permancy to transiency among New Hampshire Congregational and Presbyterian ministers. (Unpub. mss.)

von Ranke, L (1966). *History of the popes.* 3 vols. (1901 ed.) New York: Frederick Unger Publishing Company.

Werner, D. (1981). Gerontocracy among the Mekranoti of Central Brazil. *Anthropological Quarterly, 54,* 15–27.

White, H. C. (1970). *Chains of opportunity.* Cambridge, MA: Harvard University Press.

Wilson, J. Q. (1973). Innovations in organizations. In J. D Thompson (Ed.), *Approaches to organization design.* Pittsburgh: University of Pittsburgh Press.

# Institutional Gerontocracies, Structural or Demographic: The Case of the Papacy

## David D. Van Tassel

Andrew Achenbaum always studies important issues, always in an interesting way, and always with a great deal of insight and knowledge. He has in the past usually chosen to deal with the issues of old age only in the context of the United States. This time he has not only taken on a huge topic, but has also taken a breathtaking leap across the Atlantic, and perhaps an even greater leap for most modern American historians, into the *terra incognita* of church history. In taking this assignment, I have learned more in the past few weeks than I ever thought I would know about the Papacy. It is an important and generally neglected subject area for American historians. The general topic of gerontocracy, however, is one that I have been wrestling with for some years now, and it will be from this perspective that my comments are directed.

At the outset Achenbaum states that little attention has been paid to those institutions that link individual behavior patterns and attitudes in old age with structures and processes associated with societal aging. He cites Graebner's *History of Retirement* and Howard Eglit's *Analysis of Age Discrimination in Constitutional and Statutory Law*; both connect different levels of analysis by distinguishing between institutional rules that govern interpersonal behavior and those organizational and individual strategies that people employ in specific situations. I certainly would agree that more such studies are needed. This essay is a beginning. Achenbaum has chosen the papacy as a case study of an institution that covers a long period of time and which enables older people to exercise power. (At this stage he has already decided

232

that the Papacy is a gerontocracy; now the question is when?) He also aims to test a thesis found in G. Stanley Hall's *Senescence* (1922) in which he argues that "the young created the great religions of the world, but the old made them prevail" (p. 240).

He then sets out to reconstruct a history of the Papacy as a way to analyze "certain institutional dynamics relevant to gerontocracies." This raises a number of questions, summed up by the question of whether the papacy actually increasingly came under the control of older men who endorsed the reigning orthodoxies of the day. He raises as a question his preferred answer, "or have the elderly popes proven as likely as younger ones to be instigators of institutional change?" He asserts that the issue transcends the history of the Papacy. (In this I am in agreement.) The question of aging leadership, both individual and collective, is important now and will be in the future. In fact it is already a rising issue as members of Congress attempt to reintroduce mandatory retirement, and as the mandatory retirement cap on university professors is about to be removed in 1993.

I am leery of numbers, for they answer few questions, although they do have the effect of raising questions. So I will not comment on the adequacy or inadequacy of the statistical sample. I believe, with one of my younger colleagues, that the only important numbers are the ones that appear at the bottom of the page. Mind you, I am not averse to numbers—they do answer the question of how many, how frequently, what are the numerical dimensions of a situation. Questions of cause and effect, of meaning, are usually found in traditional literary sources. Andrew Achenbaum, being the good historian that he is, does note that there are a variety of reasons explaining the election of one pope over another. He does suggest that the development of the Curia and bureaucracy in Rome placed additional rungs on the ladder to the papacy, thus requiring an increased amount of time to attain that exalted position. In addition, the choice of one above all others who were qualified was usually determined by politics. Sometimes two factions, deadlocking, compromised by selecting an elderly candidate as a caretaker. He also demonstrates the way, in which age and cunning win out over youth and virtue, as when some popes thwarted the Curia's demands for a share in papal power by appointing "cardinal nephews," or as John Paul XXIII did by enlarging the College of Cardinals with 17 new positions in addition to the 23 created two months after his election, before calling Vatican II to ensure that his views might prevail.

He asks if the demands of the Papacy have become too great for old men. Do the responsibilities prompt religious leaders to respond to situations in a cautiously conservative manner? His answer from the record suggests otherwise. He then recites a litany of Roman-numeraled popes, culminating in Pius IX who was 78 when, in 1870, he enunciated the doctrine of papal infallibility (the ultimate measure in securing power to old men) and when John XXIII at age 76 called Vatican II. The question, however, should not be whether the older popes were active or inactive or conservative, or even whether they represented new departures and reforms in the church, but rather, how old were the ideas that they espoused? How long did the people who backed them have to wait before someone moved up the hierarchical/political ladder to furnish leadership that would give voice to their concerns? To answer these questions one would have to look more deeply into the history of the Roman Catholic church. For example, more than half of 52 cardinals created by John XXIII were elderly, conservative, and members of the Curia. These were the leaders of the Second Vatican Council. Who were they, and how did they stand? Many Catholics have said that Vatican II was long overdue. The liturgical and Catholic Action movements were well underway before World War I. These movements had spread throughout western Catholicism by 1951. Pius XII was conscious, if suspicious, of the increasing significance of the laity in the life of the church. In fact, although he was known as a church reformer in the early years of his reign, he attempted to stem the tide with the encyclical Humanae Generis in 1950, which "revokes some of the concessions made in the field of biblical studies, marked the return to a more intransigent approach, which was made even worse by the overenthusiastic, intemperate way in which this encyclical was sometimes applied on the local level." It was, according to one historian, "one of the strongest condemnations of theological error since the condemnation of modernism" (Holmes, 1981, p. 188). As far back as 1870 there were signs of modern challenges to the church, when the 36-year-old American bishop, James Gibbons, later to be cardinal, attended the ecumenical council of 1870, where he was one of two who voted against the issuing of the papal declaration of infallibility. He was later reprimanded as one of the leaders of the movement to nationalize the church. Certainly many of the reforms represented by Vatican II were urged by elements of the church in the late nineteenth and early twentieth centuries.

In assessing the relative ages of the popes at election over a period of 400 years, Achenbaum concludes that it has never been the exclusive preserve of old men and therefore does not strictly fit the definition of gerontocracy. He then seeks other evidence of gerontocracy—a common denominator in the style characteristics of older popes. Starting with a quotation from Hall, "The old did not invent the belief in supernatural powers or persons, but they used it to sustain their position when physical inferiority would have compelled them to step aside." Then he goes into a disquisition on good and bad popes. By the way, I would certainly characterize the declaration of papal infallibility as the act of an old pope, as the preeminent example of maintaining one's position in authority. In the end Achenbaum finds no common characteristic of late life papacies. I think the example of Formosus' corpse in 896 is intriguing, but one can hardly generalize about the perception of old versus young bodies, or even perception of age, as a result of this particular case, even with the support of Guttman. A more recent and equally interesting case is that of Pius XII who, at the end of his life, reinforced his authoritarian rule by claims of supernatural experiences and reports of papal visions. But within hours after his death stories were reported of scandals involving his nephews and the influence of one of his sisters. The pope's doctor tried a new method of preserving his body which failed. Decomposition set in even before lying in state was over and members of the noble guard were said to have fainted at their posts. The Pope's physician sold his diaries of the pope's last days to a newspaper. Questions of Pius XII's psychological and physical health during the years immediately prior to his death have surfaced. Is this kind of treatment due to society's perception and attitude toward the very old, or the result of and release from authoritarian rule?

The chapter finally concludes that the Papacy is and has been a gerontocratic institution for at least 200 years, but that the individual popes varied widely in their activities, characteristics, and effectiveness. Finally, there are additional questions I am not certain an historian as social scientist is equipped to answer in any objective or fair way. How would you answer the question as to whether older men, on account of their age, perform the spiritual, sacramental, and pastoral dimensions "better" than younger men, or the subquestion, which is less related to chronological age than to a capacity to absorb and grow with experience. In any case, this essay is examining popes and in so doing so is looking at individual leaders and not, I would argue, at the Papacy—an institution. When we study an institution, we need to look at the development of the structure—the whole organism and not simply the head.

Nevertheless, this is a very useful study, for it demonstrates the limited fruitfulness of this particular direction of inquiry. The question, it seems to me, should not be whether the old can do this or that. There is plenty of evidence that some can and many can't. But the real question is one that Acherbaum raises (chapter 6) when he asks, "were men elected to be popes because they were old? Might not seniority and experience have counted for more than chronological age in electing successors to St. Peter?" But of course, age never has been the sole consideration for the attainment of status except that of being the oldest person on earth. Age is an issue only when it is used to bar an age group from participating in some activity. Even in these cases, the age qualification is always based upon some other cultural, social, political or economic reason. The Constitution bars people under 25 from serving in the House of Representatives, under 30 from serving in the Senate, and under 35 from serving as President. It assures all citizens 18 and over of the franchise. No reason is given in the Constitution, but it was clear that the authors agreed that by raising such bars they would avoid the danger of inexperienced youth, prone to rash judgments and sudden reactions, from holding important positions of power. Mandatory retirement, now outlawed, was adopted by corporations and other institutions to clear out deadwood, to make room in the work force for younger men and women. Gerontocracy was coined as a pejorative word, to characterize the rigid conservative old parliament in Paris of the 1820s.

Most institutions go through gerontocratic phases during the course of their history. The Supreme Court is a good example, having gone through several such phases. In 1937 it was characterized by Franklin Roosevelt as "Nine Old Men practicing horse and buggy law." (We now may be witnessing eight young men and a woman practicing 'horse and buggy law.') The American Red Cross went through a wrenching experience during the changing of the guard early in the twentieth century, when the elderly Clara Barton and her supporters were removed from control. The implication of this essay is that a gerontocratic institution, the Papacy, is no different from the others; it has its good and bad, its periods of change and periods of stasis, but I submit that more evidence is needed before we can safely assert that there is nothing inherently wrong with gerontocracy as represented by the Papacy. I would suggest that the question we are faced with today is how to make openings for new leadership, new ideas, new generations within our institutions, without creating arbitrary age barriers.

## REFERENCES

Hall, G. S. (1922). *Senescence.* New York: D. Appleton and Company.
Holmes, J. D. (1981). *The papacy in the modern world.* New York: Crossroads.

# Comment on (When) Did the Papacy Become a Gerontocracy?

## Roger L. Ransom

Andrew Achenbaum's discussion of when the Papacy became a *gerontocracy* looks at the question of how that institution, which was founded by relatively young men, evolved into a church that "for a long sweep of time enabled older people to exercise power" (Achenbaum, this volume, p. 205). He begins with the observation that the Papacy was not always exclusively the domain of older leaders; prior to the modern age the age distribution of popes ranged from the youngest to the oldest. "Nonetheless," he concludes, "since the election of Gregory Vll [in 1073], and possibly before, [the Papacy] has been . . . 'in the hands of the oldest community members.'" (Achenbaum, this volume, p. 221). To support his claim that the Papacy was a gerontocracy, Achenbaum presents data on the ages of popes from Roman times to the present. On the face of it, the statistical evidence does seem convincing. Despite a smattering of younger men before 1500, popes from Gregory Vll on were relatively elderly (i.e., at least 60 years old) when they were elected, and the average age after 1500 increased to the point where, by the nineteenth century, all popes were in their mid-sixties upon election. Achenbaum wants to know how this came about.

At this point I must hasten to echo Achenbaum's disclaimer that I am neither a religious historian nor a practicing Catholic. Consequently, much of the historical detail in his paper is well outside my areas of expertise. I do not even have the advantage of his background in gerontology. Nonetheless, I did find one familiar face in Achenbaum's discussion of institutional change. "Institutions," writes Douglass North (1990), "provide the

237

basic structure by which human beings have created order and attempted to reduce uncertainty. They connect the past with the present and the future so that history is a largely incremental story of institutional evolution."[1] The Papacy, according to Achenbaum, is just such a case of institutional evolution. It evolved into a gerontocracy because of three incremental changes that emerged from the structure of the papacy: (1 ) once elected to office, popes served for life; (2) elections came under the control of a body of older men (the college of cardinals) who almost invariably chose a new pope from their own ranks; and (3) demographic factors led to longer lives of popes, thus increasing the average age of popes.

Now all this seems plausible enough. But is this outcome a result of "control" by the elderly in the Church? Or are the attributes of elder statesmen held in high esteem by all church members in selecting their spiritual leaders? Because I know relatively little about the details of the Church, my way of shedding light on this question would be to look at the age distributions produced by *other* systems of selecting leaders in a comparison to Achenbaum's analysis of the ages of popes. In what I concede is a very cursory analysis, I will offer two alternative cases: the British monarchy and the United States presidency.

## THE KINGS AND QUEENS OF ENGLAND
## AND GREAT BRITAIN

The British monarchy has two traits that make it an interesting comparison to the Papacy. First, the monarchy is one of the more enduring systems of leadership in the western world. Reasonably complete data are available on the ages of British monarchs from 934 to the present—a total of 55 reigns. Second, monarchs, like popes, have lifetime tenure upon ascension to office. There is one important difference, of course; unlike popes, monarchs assume the throne by right of birth upon the death of the reigning king or queen.[2]

Figure 6.1 presents the age of British monarchs at the time they ascended to the throne. At first glance, this picture looks surprisingly like Achenbaum's data on the age of popes upon election. Granted, the age at ascension to the British throne is substantially less than that of the popes over a comparable period. But there is a distinct upward drift in the distribution of ages that is confirmed upon closer statistical inspection. Prior to 1500 the average age of a new monarch was 25; from that time to 1760 (the year George III became king) it was 36; after 1760 it was 42. Obviously, British monarchs were beginning their reign at an older age as we enter the modern era. (We might note that this period is the point at which Achenbaum observes that the Papacy fell under the most complete control of the *curia*.).

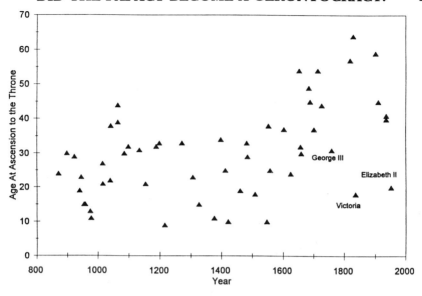

**Figure 6.1 Monarchs of Great Britain by age of ascension to the throne.**

But did this aging of newly crowned monarchs signal the onset of a monarchical gerontocracy? Upon closer inspection, the answer is "probably not." Although the appearance of older monarchs after 1760 is pronounced, one should note that the three *youngest* monarchs over that period—George III, Victoria, and Elizabeth II—reigned for a total of 152 years. For only 65 of those years were these monarchs over the age of 60. Consequently, for much of the period in question, the British monarchy was headed by a relatively young king or queen.

The dominance of these three long reigns raises the question of increasing life expectancy, which Achenbaum cites adding to the average age of popes. But this did not happen for the monarchy. As Figure 6.2, which presents the average length of reign of British monarchs, shows, the average length of reign for British monarchs does not seem to have changed markedly over the past 800 years. One reason for this is that when monarchs ascend the throne at an early age and remain in power for long periods of time, they are often succeeded by a relatively old heir, who will have a short reign. (Note that the reigns of George and Victoria were both followed by a series of short reigns by monarchs who were in their fifties when they took the throne). But there is no inherent tendency for a gerontocracy to emerge over the longer term, since at any time the line of succession may fall to a young

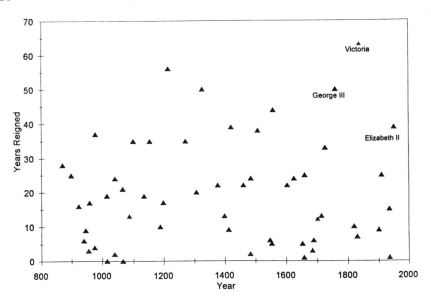

**Figure 6.2 Monarchs of Great Britain by number of years reigned.**

heir and begin a new demographic cycle. By contrast, when popes live to a very old age, they are always succeeded by another relatively old person. Not surprisingly, the kings and queens of Britain are younger than popes.

## THE UNITED STATES PRESIDENCY

If the periodic infusion of youth through extremely young heirs is what prevents a gerontocracy from emerging in monarchies, the presidency of the United States is an institution that offers a marked contrast. The Constitution stipulates that presidents must be at least 35 years of age. In fact, only seven presidents have been under the age of 50. American presidents, like popes, have been drawn from a pool of older men. There is further similarity: Presidents are elected by a "college" of electors. Presidents are not, however, elected for life. With the exception of Franklin Roosevelt, no president served more than 8 years in office. Still, the indirect election and a constitutional age bar could have produced a tendency for the executive office to be controlled by older men. Indeed, one might argue that this was the intent of the founding fathers, who sought to insulate democratic institutions from excesses of youthful control.

Figure 6.3 presents the age at inauguration of 39 men elected president from 1788 to the present.[3] The results are dramatically different from either popes or monarchs. Initially it does appear that the presidency was held by men who might be considered to be "senior statesmen." Beginning with Washington (57) in 1789 through the inauguration of Henry Harrison (68) in 1841, Martin Van Buren (54) was the youngest man elected to office. But for the next century there appears to be a distinct preference for younger leaders. From 1841 through 1944 only two presidents (James Polk and James Buchanan) were 60 years old, whereas six men were under the age of 50. The average age over this span was 52.5 years. Since the election of Harry Truman (60) in 1948, the tendency has once more been to choose elder statesmen—only John F. Kennedy (43) and Bill Clinton (47) break the pattern, with four men assuming office over the age of 60.

There seems little in all this to suggest that a gerontocracy has evolved in the U.S. presidency. Yet the possibility for domination by elder statesmen clearly existed. Before 1952 there was no formal limit on the number of terms a president could serve; only the custom established by Washington acted as a constraint limiting the tenure of an incumbent. The age of elected presidents must therefore reflect whatever underlying "desires" there may have been for elder leaders in the electorate. In that case, the U-shaped pattern in Figure 6.3 offers very little support for the proposition that age

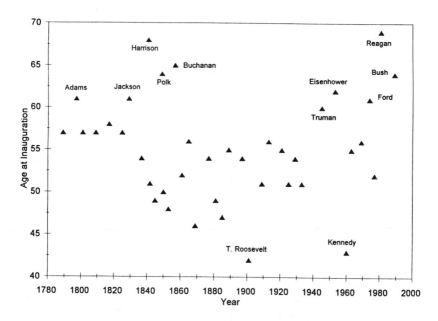

**Figure 6.3 Presidents of the United States of America by age at inauguration.**

is a positive attribute in presidents. In the early years (before 1840) an appreciation for age may have been a factor in the election of men in their late fifties and early sixties. Thereafter a sentiment favoring younger men seems to emerge, as the age of presidents falls. Although it is risky to push this point too far, the relative youth of mid-nineteenth century presidents may have been a reflection of Americans' views of the elderly over this period. Some—including Achenbaum (1978) and David Hackett Fischer (1978) have argued that perceptions of elderly people became more negative in the nineteenth-century. Were these feelings reflected in our choice of presidents? Perhaps so.

## WHAT CREATES A GERONTOCRACY

What does one make of this? It would appear that all three conditions for a gerontocracy noted in our introduction—age restrictions, long tenure of office, and lengthy life expectancy—are needed to ensure the stability of a gerontocracy. The need for an age restriction is clearly demonstrated by the demographic behavior of the British monarchy. The ascension of young monarchs—particularly when combined with longevity of life—ensured prolonged periods where a relatively youthful monarch was on the throne. However, putting a minimum age does not, by itself, ensure leadership by the elderly if the term of office is not guaranteed for a long period. American Presidents tended to be 50 years or older when they were inaugurated. But after a relatively brief tenure of office, they were typically replaced by a younger man. Only six presidents have been at least 2 years older than their predecessor. The result was a compression of the age distribution of presidents such that only two (Teddy Roosevelt and JFK) were younger than 45 when they took office, and only two (Dwight Eisenhower and Ronald Reagan) were 70 or over when they left office.[4]

My rather cursory investigation has touched upon some features of institutions that might have a tendency for domination by older leaders as a basis of comparison to the papacy. Neither the British monarchy nor the U.S. presidents exhibited such a tendency, because each lacked a crucial element that was present in the case of the papacy. Of course, this hardly exhausts the institutional arrangements for leadership that might be candidates for gerontological tendencies. Two that come to mind in the United States are the Senate, which, like the presidency has an age bar, but does not have any limit on tenure, and the Supreme Court, which, like the papacy, is an office held for life upon appointment. These institutions, like those we have looked at, must in Achenbaum's phrase, grapple with "psychological, religious, and social dimensions of growing older" (this volume, p. 228).

## NOTES

[1]North (1990), quoted by Achenbaum, (1992, p. 26).

[2]One other major difference should be pointed out: Monarchs included female rulers whereas popes were all males. While this would not seem to bear directly on the issue at hand, it is interesting to note that in the period after 1500 three of the four longest reigns on the British throne have been women.

[3]Figure 6.3 presents the age of each president at the time of his first inauguration. One President—Grover Cleveland—served two terms not in succession. Cleveland's age is included only for his first inauguration.

[4]Andrew Jackson was 2 weeks short of his 70th birthday when he left office.

## REFERENCES

Achenbaum, W. A. (1978). *Old age in the new land: The Amerlcan experience since 1790.* Baltimore: Johns Hopkins University Press.

Achenbaum, W. A. (1993). (When) Did the papacy become a gerontocracy. In K. W. Schaie & W. A. Achenbaum (Eds.), *Societal impact on aging: Historical perspectives.* New York: Springer Publishing Co.

Fischer, D. H. (1978). *Growing old in America: The Bland-Lee lectures delivered at Clark University.* New York: Oxford University Press, Expanded Edition. (Original Edition 1977.)

North, D. C. (1990). *Institutions, institutional change and economic performance.* New York: Cambridge University Press.

# Afterword

## W. Andrew Achenbaum

Historians' individual reputations are made and broken by the books they write. Some contemporary historians—such as John Higham, David Hollinger, and Carroll Smith-Rosenberg—are best known for their essays, but in this discipline it is generally the status of book manuscripts and quality of reviews that matter in making tenure, promotion, and salary decisions. The current status of a given historical subfield, in contrast, can be adequately gauged by examining the contents and evaluating the contributors to successive collections of essays that purport to represent "the state of the art." Do questions that engaged scholars in one volume appear in the next? Do the "problems" under scrutiny complement (or diverge in important ways from) issues being discussed in other communities of historical discourse? Is the subfield considered "hot"? Are distinguished historians migrating to this area because they find it challenging? Can neophytes make their mark by concentrating in this specialty? Or, is the subfield deemed marginal, attracting only second-rate minds?

David D. Van Tassel was not the initial American-born professionally trained scholar to delve into the history of old age—those kudos rightfully go to two physician-historians, the late Joseph T. Freeman and Gerald Gruman, or to Bessie Richardson and G. Stanley Hall, authors who published earlier in the century[1]—but he was the first with the requisite savvy and skills to engage historians' curiosity about the meanings and experiences of being old in past times. With support from the National Endowment for the Humanities, Van Tassel invited luminaries ranging from Leon Edel and

Erik Erikson to Juanita Kreps and Peter Laslett to share insights on old age with more than three dozen research associates and graduate students.[2] After the 1975 symposium adjourned and the first halves of their honoraria were cashed, several promising scholars (including historians Thomas Ganschow, Walter G. Moss, Daniel Scott Smith, Steven R. Smith, David E. Stannard, and Maris Vinovskis) prepared essays that explored themes of aging and questions about the elderly which then were presented the following year.[3] Van Tassel hoped that this project would lay the foundations for bridging the humanities and gerontology. "The fundamental assumption on which I based the project was that there does indeed exist an important body of materials and that humanists should be studying this vast and untapped source of human experience recorded in history, literature, folklore, artifact, and art, created by past generations and cultures," he declared. "Such an effort would not only give new perspectives to the field of gerontology and widen the horizons of each of the disciplines of the humanities, but above all would enhance the appreciation and understanding of the late stages of life."[4]

David Van Tassel did not intentionally assign the inside track to members of his disciplinary clan. In retrospect, however, historians have proven more successful than other scholars in the humanities in creating a niche for themselves among researchers in aging. Their achievement was facilitated in part by the network created through Van Tassel's project. In his acknowledgments to *Growing Old in America*, David Hackett Fischer referred to the "seminal conference on 'human values and aging'" and thanked Van Tassel for permitting him to use unpublished materials. I, too, appreciated the intellectual stimulation I had received in the course of writing a dissertation that eventually became *Old Age in the New Land*.[5] Equally important were the wider affinities established between historians and anthropologists, sociologists, and psychologists as the theories and methods of the so-called "new social history" captured scholarly imaginations during the 1970s. If women and minorities had pasts worth investigating, then so too must the elderly. Historians who wrote essays on aging found receptive audiences among social scientists.[6]

Given the sudden outpouring of books and articles on aging by historians after 1976, Van Tassel soon saw the need to take stock of prevailing interpretations and disagreements. So with support from the Rockefeller Foundation, he convened a follow-up meeting in 1983. The proceedings differed from the earlier project in two ways. First, most of the participants had done graduate training in history; even the sociologists and political scientists in attendance "passed" as heirs of Clio. Second, rather than promote humanistic inquiry wherever it might go, participants were committed to "the continuing historical analysis of old age." As if to correct social historians' then prevailing penchant for studying menarche and ignoring monarchy, Van Tassel and his co-editor, Peter Stearns, urged their colleagues to "focus new research efforts on the problems of bureaucracy and social policy, and to bring the power of historical knowledge and analysis together in addressing the challenges posed today by the crisis of the welfare state."[7] It was no mere coincidence that Van Tassel and his colleagues at Case Western Reserve University at the time were launching a graduate program in the social history of policymaking, nor that one of Stearns's students at Carnegie Mellon University was earning the first Ph.D. in Applied History and Social Science. Far from being an exotic specialty, the study of old age now seemed to be at the cutting edge of historical research and curricular innovation.

The resulting volume, *Old Age in a Bureaucratic Society,* conveys the sense of excitement, self-consciousness, and unevenness usually to be found in the formative stages of the development of any subfield. Part One assessed the state of the field. That Brian Gratton's footnotes filled nine pages of text suggests how much scholarship had been generated in a short period of time. That Gratton found fault with much that I and others had written underlined the opportunities for revisionist historians of aging to make their mark. The middle sections of the book dealt with attitudes toward the elderly and with issues in family/demographic history. There were five essays in the section entitled "policies toward the elderly," to which two sociologists, John Myles and Jill Quadagno, contributed. Charles Rosenberg's concluding essay suggested that the ways that historians understood medical structures and studied their systemic economic, bureaucratic, and ideological components in past times might provide strategies for doing historical research on aging. "We cannot remove the aged from the web of social realities and relationships in which they must inevitably function as patients; similarly, we cannot remove the worker or the primary school student or the dependent mother from their particular social situation," Rosenberg stressed. "Our problem is to be precise in specifying the relationship between such individuals and the institutions that at once constrain and support them."[8]

Against this backdrop, how does this volume compare with its predecessors? For openers, many of the same names recur. Maris Vinovskis, David Van Tassel, and I participated in all three of the conferences that resulted in historical volumes. Michel Dahlin was active at the first and third conferences. In addition to their work here, Thomas Cole, Brian Gratton, Carole Haber, and Jill Quadagno contributed papers to *Old Age in a Bureaucratic Society.* Those of us who were still in graduate school in the 1970s have now

earned tenure at good places on the basis of our work in historical gerontology. Scholars with more seniority, such as Tamara Hareven and Daniel
Scott Smith, enhance the visibility of the subfield with their continuing
output. So there now exists a "critical mass" of historians with a primary,
or at least strong secondary, interest in aging research. Although we have
developed distinctive modes of analysis, each of us has flourished by pursuing dual-track careers. We hew to historians' professional canons as we
interact with scholars from other disciplines who happen to share our interest in the demographic, cultural, economic, social, and political dimensions of senescence in past times.

Note, moreover, that the "institutional" theme enunciated by Charles
Rosenberg in *Old Age in a Bureaucratic Society* became the underlying motif
that links together the very disparate essays in this volume. The emphasis
on institutional structures and dynamics was intended to broaden, in the
words of the conference brochure, "an examination of how the relationship between social structures and the aging processes has changed over
time." Work in historical gerontology can build on the collaboration of social
historians and political scientists in efforts to "bring the State back in."[9]
Analogous bridges can be made with researchers who study the ideological
commitments and structural contexts of various segments of the population. And as gerontologists wrestle with (dis)continuities in behavioral and
organizational processes of human aging at the macro- and micro-levels,[10]
it is clear that probing institutional nubs and networks serves as a useful
research focus. Institutional analyses thus deserve a high priority on current historical and gerontological research agendas.

This convergence of interests, in fact, enabled Warner Schaie and me to
reach out to a different type of audience than Van Tassel had targeted. It
is significant that this gathering of historians, the sixth in a series of conferences at Penn State, was supported in part by the National Institute on
Aging. Schaie felt that the subfield of historical gerontology was mature
enough to yield a volume worthy of consideration by bench scientists. I,
too, felt that it was important for historians to address directly issues that
mattered to social scientists in the gerontological community. Accordingly,
the first session was aimed primarily to economists; the second, to sociologists and political scientists; and the third to psychologists. Efforts were made
to bring scholars with historical sensitivities from these four disciplines into
the historians' conclave. (Unfortunately, the three political sociologists we
had invited declined due to prior commitments.) So, without discounting
our hope that historians will find much that is "new" here, a major aim of
*Social Structure and Aging: Historical Perspectives* is to stimulate first-rate work

in gerontology by enticing behavioral and social scientists to see the value of incorporating studies of the past in their research.

What lies ahead? We can anticipate spin-offs from each session. Even familiar-sounding topics will be handled in novel, cross-disciplinary ways. For instance, Richard Sutch, Roger Ransom, and Samuel Williamson have raised, in a provocative way, fundamental questions about the timing of transformations in public and private retirement vehicles. Brian Gratton seems persuaded by the main lines of the trio's thesis, but the critiques by Emily Andrews and Jon Moen suggest that economists have some reservations about the assumptions on which their argument rests. Ideally, early twentieth-century historical trends in this U.S. work will shortly be linked, theoretically and substantively, with the historical analyses of contemporaneous patterns being done in other advanced-industrial countries.[11] Similarly, cross-cultural analyses, which link the papers by Carole Haber and by Debra Street and Jill Quadagno with other U.S. case studies by Ann Orloff, Theda Skocpol, Paul Starr, and Margaret Weir and with such Commonwealth scholars as Paul Johnson, Chris Phillipson, David Thomson, and Alan Walker, should enrich the empirical and analytic qualities of emerging theories of the political economy of aging.[12] Finally, as reactions to Tom Cole's analysis of G. Stanley Hall and my papal prosopography intimate, historians of aging might turn more earnestly to biography as a way of forging links with psychologists and those interested in the attitudes of aging and life experiences of members of various racial, ethnic, class, religious, and regional groupings.

That there is so much to be done demonstrates the intellectual promise and payoffs that inhere in working in historical gerontology. One nettlesome issue must be mentioned. Are there better ways of recruiting graduate students and professors of history to the subfield, and of empowering scholars from other disciplines to join forces with historians in studying the past? Ideally, at the beginning of the 21st century, some familiar figures will appear among the contributors when the fourth wave of collected essays is being designed. But there must be a greater percentage of "new" names on the list if the subfield is to remain vibrant. *Social Structure and Aging: Historical Perspectives,* hopefully, will serve to advance the field of gerontological history by stimulating interest in using history among non-historians.

## NOTES

[1]Joseph T. Freeman became a prominent Philadelphia physician because his banker-father refused to permit him to pursue a Ph.D. in history. As an "amateur" in the best

sense of the term, however, Freeman amassed one of the finest collections of first editions of classics in aging-related works. He also was the author of several valuable essays on the history of gerontology and wrote biographical sketches about some of the field's founders. As a past president of the Gerontological Society, moreover, he facilitated the entrance of historians into the tribe of researchers on aging. See his *Aging: Its History and Literature* (New York: Human Sciences Press, 1979).

Gerald Gruman earned a Ph.D. in the history of science at Harvard in addition to receiving his M.D. at Pennsylvania. His monograph, *A History of Ideas about the Prolongation of Life* (Philadelphia: American Philosophical Association, 1966), remains a classic. G. Stanley Hall's *Senescence* (New York: D. Appleton & Son, 1922) is a cross-disciplinary *tour de force*, invoking ethnographic data, psychological results, social-science evidence, and historical insights to underscore the potential to be capitalized in the second half of life. Bessie E. Richardson's monograph, *Old Age among the Greeks* (Baltimore: Johns Hopkins Press, 1933), remains a valuable case study.

[2]Most of the essays by senior scholars appeared in *Aging, Death, and the Completion of Being*, ed. David D. Van Tassel (Philadelphia: University of Pennsylvania Press, 1979). There were three essays by historians—Peter Laslett's "The Traditional English Family and the Aged in Our Society," John Demos's "Old Age in Early New England," and Tamara K. Hareven's "The Last Stage." Hareven's piece also appeared in a special issue of *Daedalus*, reprinted as *Adulthood*, ed. Erik H. Erikson (New York: W. W. Norton, 1978).

[3]These essays, complete with an introduction by Erik and Joan Erikson with an afterword by NIA director Robert N. Butler, were published as *Aging and the Elderly: Humanistic Perspectives in Gerontology*, ed. Stuart F. Spicker, Kathleen M. Woodward, and David D. Van Tassel (Atlantic Highlands, NJ: Humanities Press, 1978). Significantly, a third of the essays were written by historians.

[4]David D. Van Tassel, "Preface," in *Aging and the Elderly*, p. v.

[5]David Hackett Fischer, *Growing Old in America*, expanded edition (New York: Oxford University Press, 1977), p. 281; W. Andrew Achenbaum, *Old Age in the New Land* (Baltimore: Johns Hopkins University Press, 1978), p. xi.

[6]For example, John Demos's essay, "Old Age in Early New England," appeared in the *American Journal of Sociology*, volume 84, supplement (1978): S248–287. Peter Laslett prepared an article entitled "Societal Development and Aging" for the *Handbook of Aging and the Social Sciences*, ed. Robert H. Binstock and Ethel Shanas (New York: Van Nostrand Reinhold, 1976), pp. 87–116. See also Howard P. Chudacoff and Tamara K. Hareven, "From the Empty Nest to Family Dissolution: Life Course Transitions into Old Age," *Journal of Family History*, vol. 4 (1979): 69–83; and Michel Dahlin, "Perspectives on the Family Life of the Elderly in 1900," *The Gerontologist*, vol. 20 (1980): 99–107.

[7]Peter N. Stearns and David D. Van Tassel, "Introduction," in *Old Age in a Bureaucratic Society* (Westport, CT: Greenwood Press, 1986), p. xi.

[8]Charles E. Rosenberg, "The Aged in a Structured Social Context," in *Old Age in a Bureaucratic Society*, pp. 242–243.

[9]Theda Skocpol, *Bringing the State Back In* (New York: Cambridge University Press, 1985).

[10]See, for instance, the dimensions of the theoretical problem as evidenced in essays in *The New Generational Contract,* ed. Vern L. Bengtson and W. Andrew Achenbaum (New York: Aldine Gruyere, forthcoming). See also Gordon F. Streib and Robert H. Binstock, "Aging and the Social Sciences: Changes in the Field," in Robert H. Binstock and Linda K. George, ed., *Handbook of Aging and the Social Sciences,* 3rd ed. (New York: Academic Press, 1990), pp. 1–16.

[11]See, for instance, Martin Kohli, Martin Rein, Anne-Marie Guillemard, and Herman van Gunsteren, eds., *Time for Retirement* (New York: Cambridge University Press, 1991).

[12]Useful entries into this literature include *The Politics of Social Policy in the United States,* ed. Margaret Weir, Ann Shola Orloff, and Theda Skocpol (Princeton: Princeton University Press, 1988); *Workers versus Pensioners,* ed. Paul Johnson, Christoph Conrad, and David Thomson (Manchester: Manchester University Press, 1989); and *Aging in Society,* ed. John Bond and Peter Coleman (Beverly Hills, CA: Sage Publications, 1990).

# Indices

# Name Index

# Subject Index

# Springer Publishing Company

# HANDBOOK OF THE HUMANITIES AND AGING

**Thomas R. Cole,** PhD, **David Van Tassel,** PhD, and **Robert Kastenbaum,** PhD, Editors

Serves as a major resource for research into the contributions of the humanities to our understanding of aging and the aged. Offers an authoritative examination of humanistic perspectives on aging spanning history, the arts, religious/spiritual studies, and philosophy. The text is notably free of jargon, and thus equally useful to researchers from the broad range of fields it encompasses.

### Contents:

A View from Antiquity: Greece, Rome and Elders, *T.M. Falkner & J. de Luce* • The Older Person in the Western World: From the Middle Ages to the Industrial Revolution, *D.G. Troyansky* • Old Age in the Modern and Postmodern Western World, *C. Conrad* • Aging in Eastern Cultures, *C.W. Keifer* • Aging and Meaning: The Christian Tradition, *S.G. Post* • Aging in Judaism: "Crown of Glory" and "Days of Sorrow," *S. Isenberg* • Islamic, Hindu, and Buddhist Conceptions of Aging, *G.R. Thursby* • Fairy Tales and Spiritual Development in Later Life: The Story of the Shining Fish, *A.B. Chinen* • Images of Aging in American Poetry, 1925–1985, *C.H. Smith* • Old Age in Contemporary Fiction: A New Paradigm of Hope, *C. Rooke* • Walking to the Stars, *M.G. Winkler* • The Creative Process: A Life-Span Approach, *R. Kastenbaum* • Story of the Shoe Box: The Meaning and Practice of Transmitting Stories, *M. Kaminsky* • Literary Gerontology Comes of Age, *A.M. Wyatt-Brown* • Aging in America: The Perspective of History, *C. Haber & B. Gratton* • Elders in World History, *P.N. Stearns* • Bioethics and Aging, *H.T. Moody* • Wisdom and Method: Philosophical Contributions to Gerontology, *R.J. Manheimer* • The Older Student of Humanities: The Seeker and the Source, *D. Shuldiner* • Afterword: Integrating the Humanities into Gerontologic Research, Training, and Practice, *W.A. Achenbaum*

512pp     0-8261-6240-1     *hardcover*

536 Broadway, New York, NY 10012-3955 • (212) 431-4370 • Fax (212) 941-7842

 **Springer Publishing Company**

# VOICES AND VISIONS IN AGING
## Toward a Critical Gerontology

**Thomas R. Cole,** PhD, **W. Andrew Achenbaum,** PhD,
**Patricia Jakobi,** PhD, and
**Robert Kastenbaum,** PhD, Editors

A critical gerontology requires more than a simple elaboration of existing humanistic scholarship on aging. This exceptional new work introduces a basis for genuine dialogue and collaboration across humanistic, scientific, and professional disciplines.

*Contents:*

368pp    0-8261-8020-5    *hardcover*

536 Broadway, New York, NY 10012-3955 • (212) 431-4370 • Fax (212) 941-7842